A CHRISTIAN GUIDE TO THE QUR'AN

BUILDING BRIDGES IN MUSLIM EVANGELISM

RAOUF GHATTAS
CAROL B. GHATTAS

Kregel
Academic & Professional

A Christian Guide to the Qur'an

© 2009 by Raouf Ghattas and Carol B. Ghattas

Published by Kregel Publications, a division of Kregel, Inc., P.O. Box 2607, Grand Rapids, MI 49501.

Library of Congress Cataloging-in-Publication Data
Ghattas, R. G.
   A Christian guide to the Qur'an : building bridges in Muslim evangelism / by Raouf and Carol Ghattas.
      p. cm.
   Includes bibliographical references and index.
1. Koran—Christian interpretations. 2. Apologetics.
3. Christianity and other religions—Islam. 4. Islam—
Relations—Christianity. I. Ghattas, Carol. II. Title.
BT1170.G43   2009
297.1'22702427—dc22   2008042647

ISBN 978-0-8254-2688-9

Printed in the United States of America

09 10 11 12 13 / 5 4 3 2 1

To all our sons and daughters in Christ
who have taught us so much along the way
and loved us even more.

But you are a chosen people, a royal priesthood, a
holy nation, a people belonging to God, that you
may declare the praises of him who called you out
of darkness into his wonderful light. Once you were
not a people, but now you are the people of God;
once you had not received mercy, but now you have
received mercy. (1 Peter 2:9–10)

And also to our sons, David and Nathan.
May you grow to become mighty men of God.

Contents

Contents

Contents

Introduction

As witnesses for Christ, the only source of salvation for all mankind, we have several tools available that help us convey the message of the gospel. Our personal testimony and the Word of God are the most powerful resources we have in sharing. However, in reaching Muslims with the good news of Jesus Christ, many Christian workers and lay believers find that there are many barriers to overcome before the essence of the gospel can be grasped and understood by the recipient.

When the apostle Paul spoke to the people of Athens, he began his message of salvation by commenting on their own beliefs and religious practices.[1] He talked to the people about what they understood and then built a bridge to the gospel. The main intention of this volume is to help Christians build bridges in order to reach Muslims for Christ. The Qur'an is the most treasured book for Muslims. The Jesus of the Qur'an, however, cannot bring salvation to the lost, since his deity is denied. Though we begin with the Qur'an, because it is familiar to the Muslim, our goal in building bridges is always to lead Muslims to the Jesus of the Bible as the only way to God. We have to *cross* the bridge and therefore do not remain long-term in their book, but move them as quickly as the Holy Spirit allows to ours.

---

1. Acts 17:16–34.

The bridge itself is not the salvation message—we know we have crossed the bridge when we have shared the truth of the gospel.

By gaining a deeper understanding of the Qur'an, the Christian worker also can overcome his own fear in sharing. We do not intend that the material presented in this book be used to "get back at" or ridicule Muslims. When we do that, our effectiveness is totally lost. We want merely to bring awareness to the reader of various issues as presented in the Qur'an and how they can affect our witness.

This commentary will deal with each sura, or chapter, of the Qur'an to provide a Christian and Muslim understanding of the text, as well as practical application of the material to be used in witness. Islamic, secular, and Christian resources in Arabic and English have been used for this study. The main text of this work is the Qur'an in the Arabic language, explained and commented on directly in English. We would recommend the use of a good Arabic-English dictionary, which can provide the literal translation of words found in the Qur'an, if you find any discrepancies between this work and other sources in English. While many of the resources listed in the bibliography focus on a strictly academic view of the Qur'an, this book seeks to balance academic and practical applications.

All written works come from an author's perspective, and this work is no exception. Because of our backgrounds, education, and experience, we not only understand our subject but also know well the people to whom it is directed, as we have lived among them and loved them for many years and will continue to do so as long as the Lord gives us life.

Many efforts have been made in various countries around the world to use the Qur'an as a bridge to reach Muslims. This work is one of the first efforts to help Christian workers gain an overall understanding of the Qur'an, including its main themes and *tawhid* (oneness). By examining the background of the material, we will connect ideas and thoughts behind each sura in order to understand a Muslim's worldview and the Prophet Muhammad's mind.

Muhammad never claimed to be deity or anything more than a man, yet his religion is the second largest religion in the world. He was very smart, very patient, and very ruthless. Muhammad, who is viewed as the living example of the perfect Muslim, was born around AD 570 into the Quraish tribe of Mecca. Muhammad's parents died while he was young, and he was raised first by his uncle, Abu Talib, but then later adopted by his grandparents. At the age of twelve Muhammad traveled with his uncle on his first caravan trip to Syria, where he probably made contact with people from the two great monotheistic religious groups in the region: Christians and Jews. Most likely he contrasted his own pagan society and that of these two groups.[2]

Muhammad became a caravan leader himself. The owner of the camels, a woman named Khadija, asked Muhammad (then age twenty-five) to marry her; he agreed. Khadija was fifteen years his elder. Eventually, the caravan business slowed down, and Muhammad started spending more time in meditation. At the age of forty, while in a cave, he saw something that terrified him. He went to Khadija and shared the vision with her. Khadija in turn consulted her cousin, Waraqa, a Christian. He told Muhammad that this had to be Gabriel, bringing him good tidings from God. As the Jews were waiting for a Messiah, so were the Arabs. Though there was a significant period of time between this first revelation and subsequent ones, they continued for the next twenty-three years.

Khadija was the first believer. Muhammad remained faithful to Khadija until the day of her death, when he was fifty-one. However, after Khadija's death, he took many wives. While Khadija was fifteen years older than Muhammad when they married, his later wives were younger. Aisha, one of his favorites, was six years old when he married her during his first year in Medina, though some believe he did not consummate the marriage until she was nine.[3] She grew to become one of the smartest and most beautiful of his wives.

The Qur'an consists of 114 suras. Muslims believe that the angel Gabriel recited it to Muhammad. Because Muhammad was considered either functionally illiterate or religiously illiterate (i.e., he had no deep understanding of Jewish or Christian religion), the receipt of the Qur'an is viewed as Muhammad's greatest miracle.[4]

The revelation of the Qur'an is quite different from that of the Bible. The writers of the Bible were inspired by the Holy Spirit, but God allowed their circumstances and personalities to come through in the text in a way that spoke to the people of their given time. Gabriel told Muhammad, "Read" (recite), but Muhammad replied three times that he was not able. Then Gabriel said, "Read in the name of your God," so Muhammad started reciting

---

2. Elass, *Understanding the Koran*, 22.

3. Gabriel, *Jesus and Muhammad*, 58.

4. Elass, *Understanding the Koran*, 39.

letter by letter and word by word what Gabriel said. The words that Gabriel spoke, Muhammad repeated without any interference of his character on the text. This is known as the "dictation theory" of revelation.[5]

All the words written in the Qur'an are considered as uttered by God, who is said to have dictated it to heavenly scribes.[6] It is not like the Bible, in which we are given the background of the story, and then what God said or did in a certain circumstance. Instead, we will find certain statements followed by others, sometimes without any connection. In order to know the background, we have to go to the *Hadith* (sayings) or commentaries. For Muslims, the Qur'an is the highest authority, the nonchangeable word of God, though the majority of Muslims also consider the *Hadith* as scripture.[7] Interpretation of the Qur'an can be different from one sect to another or from one country to another. For this reason, it is important for a Christian to know something of the Qur'an as he or she seeks to reach out to Muslims.

The Qur'an was given at various times and in two different cities. Of the 114 suras, 86 were revealed in Mecca, while the remaining 28 came during the later years of Muhammad's life in Medina.[8] The revelations came to him in relation to various issues, but at times they addressed certain issues that arose in his personal life or in the lives of the people around him. Many verses in the Qur'an came to Muhammad to give permission for a certain marriage or to give him the right in a specific relationship.[9]

The suras of the Qur'an are not chronologically ordered but are organized from longest to shortest, with the exception of the opening sura (*Fatiha*). Many have tried to connect the sequence of Muhammad's life to the suras of the Qur'an, but there is no solid proof to confirm the chronological order of the suras. Neither is subject matter organized within the Qur'an, so any serious student will need a thorough index or concordance of the Qur'an to find all the verses relating to a specific subject. In this work, we are including in the overview of each sura the approximate time frame as found in Yusuf Ali's translation of the Qur'an, and we do so merely to help the reader have a better grasp of the time and thus the attitude reflected in the sura itself.

For example, those suras that fall in the Meccan Period (611–622) reveal

---

5. Ibid., 95.
6. Ibid., 27.
7. Esposito, *What Everyone Needs to Know About Islam*, 14.
8. Geisler and Saleeb, *Answering Islam*, 94.
9. For example, sura 33:37, which allows Muhammad to marry the wife of his adopted son, Zaid.

Muhammad as a warner and speak primarily of the end day and what awaits the believers and blasphemers. Muhammad faced growing opposition in these years and thus referred to the stories of the Old and New Testament prophets to support his claim to be an apostle of God. The suras of the Medinan Period (622–632, or AH 1–11 [AH stands for "year (*anno*) of the immigration (*hijra*)" in the Muslim calendar]) take a different approach as Islam gains a following and demands organization. It is important to note that it is in these suras that Muhammad takes his strongest stand against Jews and Christians, since they have not been supportive of his message. Because dating the Qur'an is a matter of dispute, we do not necessarily endorse Ali's dates but see them only as a possible reference point and help.

Throughout those years (611–632), Muhammad continued to receive revelations. There was never a sense that God had finished speaking, but with the Prophet's unexpected death came the end of God's word to the people.[10] There is no evidence in the traditions that Muhammad ever purposefully set out to have the Qur'an collected into written form. By and large, it was maintained in the memories of those closest to the Prophet, though others wrote parts of it on parchments, skins, bones, and clay and even tattooed it on men's chests. However, after the death of Muhammad, several of these loyal followers were killed in the battle of Yamama.[11] Abu Bakr, Muhammad's successor, commissioned Zaid Ibn Thabit to collect all the fragments of the Qur'an and put them together in one collection. Many opposed the idea of writing down the Qur'an, but Abu Bakr insisted. Abu Bakr took what Ibn Thabit collected and kept it for safekeeping. In the meantime, other collections had been made, therefore leading to different readings of the Qur'an. It was not until Uthman was caliph that this problem was solved. He had four followers write out the Qur'an basically based on Ibn Thabit's work. These four identical copies became the sole source of the Qur'an, as all other fragments and copies were ordered burned.[12] However, other versions are known, some of which are discussed in the *Hadith*, such as Ibn Masud's.[13]

---

10. Elass, *Understanding the Koran*, 26.
11. Ibid., 41.
12. For further study of the collecting of the Qur'an, read the chapter titled "And the Word Became . . . Paper?" in *Understanding the Koran* by Mateen Elass.
13. Elass, *Understanding the Koran*, 179; referencing the work by Arthur Jeffrey, *Materials for the History of the Text of the Qur'an* (1937; reprint, New York: AMS Press, 1975).

Muslims hold the Qur'an with extreme high regard, both spiritually and physically. For many Muslims, the Qur'an is the standard of the perfect human personality.[14] Even if they do not apply it or read it, it will take the most honored place in the house. They will write verses from their holy book on the most lavish material they own. They will keep it on the highest shelf in the house, never to be topped by anything. It is important for a Christian to respect the Qur'an, not because of what is in it, but because of what it means to his or her Muslim friend.

Recitation of the Qur'an is a must in the life of a Muslim, as it is seen as a source of enormous power. In sura 17:82, the Qur'an is described as a source of healing and mercy for people of faith. Recitation is considered one of a Muslim's good works, and he gains merits even if he does not understand the meaning of the words. The Prophet is reported as saying that in reading the Qur'an "you will be rewarded at the rate of ten good deeds for reading every *letter* of the Qur'an."[15] Children from the age of ten are encouraged to memorize the whole Qur'an.

Because Muslims believe the Qur'an is the most important book in their lives, exactly as Christians view the Bible, using the Qur'an as a bridge is very effective. Once we share with a Muslim that we have read the Qur'an, he will be excited and more interested in talking to us, due to the common ground we now have between us. Whatever his motive is, he will be more willing to talk to us than to someone who has not read his book. As Christians, we have to overcome our own shortcomings of not wanting anything to do with the Qur'an or of being afraid to read it, because the time reading and preparing will enable us to be much more effective for the sake of the gospel.

In closing, we want to give a word of caution. If you believe the Lord is leading you to reach Muslims by gaining insight into their book, we do not want you to be naive about what you will face. For every hour you spend in the Qur'an, spend another two or more in the Bible and in prayer in order to remain strong against the attacks of the Evil One. For this reason, we have worked hard to include as many Scripture references as possible so that you may always be drawn back to God's Word as you seek to grow in your understanding of the Qur'an. All Scripture references are from the New International Version unless otherwise noted. It is our hope and prayer that many will come into the kingdom as a result of what you learn and apply from this material.

---

14. Esack, *The Qur'an: A User's Guide*, 17.
15. Ibid., 19, italics added.

We see many Muslims today taking jihad (holy war) into the intellectual realm, and they are equipping themselves with different Bible translations. Some go back to the Hebrew and Greek, read commentaries, and even attend our seminaries to be prepared for the war. Therefore, as Christians, we need to be prepared, not for a holy war, but for the battle in which the love of Christ can prevail in hearts.

Al-Fatiha

The Opening

Overview

The first sura of the Qur'an, though only seven verses, is very important for a Muslim. It is widely used in the Muslim life. It is recited during prayers, and has been referred to as the perfect prayer.[1] It is interesting to note that the *Fatiha* is a prayer directed to God, while the rest of the Qur'an claims to be God's address to Muhammad and the world.[2]

When two Muslims agree together on any deal or contract, they will say, "Let's read the *Fatiha* together." This gives the impression of remembering God in that situation. The *Fatiha* also is recited at funerals, memorial services, births, and during illness, earning it the title of *Um al-Qur'an* (Mother of the Qur'an).[3] Muhammad is said to have called this sura the "exalted reading."[4] The Prophet said that those who fail to recite the *Fatiha* cannot "be credited with having observed prayer."[5]

---

1. Ali, *The Holy Qur'an*, 13.
2. Elass, *Understanding the Koran*, 74.
3. Ibid.
4. Ibid.
5. Ibid.

Even though the sura has no direct antagonistic view toward Christians and Jews, we need to be aware that most commentators will interpret the last verse as meaning that the Muslim is not only asking God to give him the straight path, but also separating himself from the ones God is angry with, the Jews, and the ones who have gone astray, the *Nassara* or Christians.[6] Most Muslims, however, will not refer to the Christians and Jews when we share with them from this sura.

Because it is the first sura we will look at, as well as the most important in Islam, we print it in its entirety:

> In the name of God, the Merciful, the one who gives mercy.
> Praise be to God,
> The Lord of two worlds;
> The Merciful, the one who gives mercy;
> Owner of the Day of Judgment.
> To you we are enslaved (worship),
> And to you we ask help.
> Show us the straight way,
> The way of those on whom
> You have given grace,
> Those who have no wrath on them,
> And who go not astray.[7]

The words of the *Fatiha* give adoration to God and recognize his omnipotence over all creatures. In this sura also, a Muslim confesses to God that he worships him and asks for his help. He seeks guidance from God.

Comments and Possible Bridges

Day of Judgment: Verse 4

In verse 4, the Qur'an refers to God as the Master of the Day of Judgment. We can share with our Muslim friend that we agree with this attribute of God, because a Muslim understands from this verse that God is in control

---

6.   Mahali, *Tafseer al-Galileen*, 1.

7.   Translation by Dr. Raouf Ghattas from the original Arabic manuscript. (Note: Yusuf Ali in many places makes his translation read like the King James Version of the Bible to the extent that sometimes he compromises the meaning. We are looking for the literal meaning of the words.)

of the end day and that it is God alone who knows when that day will be. He is the owner of that day. This means he is in total control of the end. We can encourage our friend to reflect on this fact, while adding that as only God knows how a person's soul will be as it stands before him on that day, it is important for each individual to know that he or she is ready to meet God at any moment. If we examine ourselves, can we say that our souls are ready or acceptable to God? If a person discovers his destiny only on that day, it will be too late for him to make a correction.

Straight Path: Verse 6

In verse 6, a Muslim is asking God to guide him to the straight path. What a wonderful thing to ask God. The straight path for a Muslim in this verse is to know God. It is different from the straight path on the Day of Judgment. From this verse a Muslim is seeking God to show him or her his way in everyday life. It would be a great opportunity to share with our Muslim friend the one who said, "I am the straight Path and the Truth and the Life."

Praying the *Fatiha*

We should take no offense when a Muslim asks us to pray the *Fatiha* with him. Of course we should share that even though we are Christian, we would love to pray the *Fatiha* with him, but we will share our Lord's Prayer as well. As a Muslim highly regards the *Fatiha*, he will willingly accept our sharing of the Lord's Prayer with him too, knowing that it is very important to us as Christians. Out of courtesy, hospitality, and curiosity, he will be willing for us to share the Lord's Prayer after we recite the *Fatiha* with him. It would be important to have both the *Fatiha* and the Lord's Prayer memorized in order to touch his heart.

Al-Baqara

The Heifer

EARLY MEDINAN

Overview

Sura *al-Baqara* is the longest sura in the Qur'an, and in it the Qur'an testifies for itself that it is the true message from God. We find in *al-Baqara* that people are classified into three categories: believers, blasphemers, and hypocrites. Half of the sura speaks to the sons of Israel (the Jews of Muhammad's time) in order to call them into Islam—reminding them of their history with stories of Moses, Abraham, and Ishmael, and then revealing how Abraham and Ishmael built the Ka'ba, the unifying center of the Islamic faith.

The remainder of this sura handles a variety of issues: idolatry, fasting, inheritance, warfare, pilgrimage, drinking wine, cards, marriage, divorce, and breastfeeding. It also deals with other important subjects such as unity and the afterlife, as well as general doctrines like spending, charging interest, and doing business. *Al-Baqara* is basically a summary of the entire teaching of the Qur'an.

Some of the fundamental thoughts of Islam are exposed in this sura. It teaches that following God's way and being a Muslim are the main sources of happiness in this life and the hereafter. Muslims should elevate good over evil. Justification is by both faith and works. The foundation of the faith is for a Muslim to be wholehearted and to agree totally, without any reservation, to what the Prophet Muhammad said.

God warns Muslims through Muhammad that the Christians and Jews will never accept Muslims unless they become like them (that is, convert to either Christianity or Judaism). We can see through this statement that Muhammad's message was not being accepted by the Jews and Christians of the day, and he was preparing his followers to face opposition.

It is clear in this sura that Muhammad believed that the law of the land (the official government) should be for Muslims, not for the blasphemers. This means that non-Muslims cannot be put in charge of Muslims, as is evident in many Muslim lands today.

Al-Baqara reveals that only God has the power to allow and forbid certain things, but if a person is under great stress, he can break this rule (necessity allows the forbidden) and God will forgive him. In general, God gives all things for people to eat, but he forbids a few detestable things according to the Qur'an: meat from an animal that has died a natural death, blood, swine meat, and food sacrificed to an idol or other god. Suicide is also forbidden, and fighting is allowed only for defense, the spreading of Islam, and the securing of Islam in a given culture.[1]

The sura starts with the three letters *aleph*, *lam*, and *meem*, and there is a great variety of interpretation among Islamic scholars as to their meaning. Some commentators say they compose one of God's names. Other writers believe that each letter can be found in God's names. Some have taken all of the mysterious letters in the Qur'an (*aleph*, *lam*, *meem*, *seen*, *rey*, *kaf*, *hey*, *rey*, *ain*, *tah*, *seen*, *qaf*, and *noon*) and created a sentence out of them that means, "Precise, wise text with a secret." Followers of folk Islam have used the belief that each letter is a symbol equal to a certain number to apply the letters to practices of magic. Still other commentators say that these letters are the key for the suras they begin. In general, there is no agreement as to the precise meaning of these letters, yet most writers do agree that God began particular suras with them to show that the Qur'an is unique and is therefore above human ability.

The first verses of the sura declare that the Qur'an was given by God and that any person with a sound mind will understand that it is from God and has been given to Muhammad. They also will believe in the previous books that were given, meaning the *Tawrat* (Torah) and *Injil* (Gospels). Those who do not believe are only deceiving themselves.

---

1. Committee of the Qur'an and Sunna (Traditions), *Al-Muntakhab*, 2–3.

Comments and Possible Bridges

Superiority of the Qur'an: Verse 23

In the Qur'an praise is given to the believers, while unbelievers are seen as disgraced. In verse 23, God challenges the nonbelievers to write a sura as unique as those he has given to the Prophet, if they are in doubt of what they hear from him. There are many Arabic writers who have challenged this verse by saying they could write even better quality material.[2] Also, we know there are two versions of the Qur'an (*Shi'ite* and *Sunni*), which hold different texts.[3] There is no linguistic difference in the extra sura of the *Shi'ite* Qur'an, which raises a question about the authority of this verse. Also, if we examine the Arabic literature of the pre-qur'anic period, we will discover that it was at its highest standard. The best poetry of the time was selected and hung in public places. Of these "hangings," seven are considered very important.[4] Much of the text in the Qur'an is similar to the material given in these "hangings." Understanding these matters will help us not to take an argument of our Muslim friend at face value and give us wisdom in how to respond to a possible challenge.

Parables: Verse 26

The Qur'an says that God does not mind using examples or parables as illustrations of truth. This can work very well when speaking to a Muslim. We can say to our friend, "Let me tell you some more parables God spoke through *'Isa* the Messiah that we find in the Bible." Jesus' parables of the kingdom are especially good to use with Muslims.[5]

Creation of Man and Origin of Sin: Verses 30–37

We find in these verses a dialogue between God and the angels about the creation of man. The angels question God's desire to create man by saying that the man will shed blood. The disagreement we would have here is that God does not need to confer with anyone before he creates something. Also, these

---

2. "Is the Qur'an Miraculous?" http://www.answering-islam.org/Quran/Miracle/mirac1.html (accessed May 29, 2008).
3. The *Sunni* version is 114 suras in length, while the other has 115 suras.
4. "Mu'allaqat," http://inthenameofallah.org/Mu'allaqat.html (accessed May 29, 2008); and Irwin, *Night and Horses and the Desert*, 1–6.
5. See the following references: Matt. 20:1–16; 22:1–14; 25:1–30; and Mark 4:26–34.

verses seem to imply that the angels know the future, whereas God is the only one who knows the future. However, we can use this concept as a bridge—God, knowing that man would sin, still created him. We know that he also had a plan of redemption in mind, and we can share it with our friend.

In verse 32, we see that Adam is above angels in knowledge. The Qur'an does not say that Adam was created in God's image, but if Adam is above the angels, and God asked all the angels to bow before him (v. 34), then we can share with our Muslim friend that Adam is created in God's moral image. This means that we have the God-given ability to love, know justice, be imaginative, understand truth, and so on. A Muslim will be quick to turn this into a physical comparison between Adam and God. We need to stress the concept here of the moral image instead of the physical image he may have in his mind. One illustration that could be used, for example, is that when a person steals even the smallest item, in his conscience he realizes that he is a thief. This demonstrates the ultimate justice of God within each one of us.

When God asked the angels to bow before Adam (v. 34), they all did except Satan (*Iblis*), and this is the origin of sin in the Qur'an. We can use this as a bridge to explain the origin of sin in Christianity. From our understanding of two Old Testament passages,[6] we see that God created the morning star as an angelic being, perfect in all ways. Then the morning star at an unknown time decided to take God's throne. He was cast from heaven and took the name Satan, among others.

Verse 36 reads as if Satan forced Adam and Eve (her name is not mentioned in the Qur'an; she is referred to simply as his wife) to fall. Here we need to share with our friend that when God created man, he gave him free will. Therefore, Satan could not force the man and woman to sin but merely tempted them with the goodness of the fruit and the opportunity to become like God by eating it. They each ate out of their own free will.

Forgiveness: Verse 37

According to the Qur'an, when Adam ate from the tree, he was inspired to ask forgiveness from God, and God guaranteed forgiveness. According to Islamic teaching, as long as man is repentant, God is merciful and will forgive. We can use this as a great bridge to explain to Muslims that repentance is not enough for forgiveness, because God is not only merciful, but also wholly just.

---

6. Isa. 14:12–15 and Ezek. 28:11–19.

Justice and mercy cannot meet; they contradict each other. If you give mercy, you are not giving justice, and vice versa. However, God himself provided the solution to this dilemma for mankind. The Word became flesh and paid the price for our sin in order to provide for us the mercy we did not deserve as sinful human beings.

Moses and the Consequences of Sin: Verses 47–54

The story in the Qur'an then skips forward thousands of years and talks to the Israelites. In verse 49, the sons of Israel are reminded that God saved them from Pharaoh, who used to kill the boys and keep the girls, and that God drowned Pharaoh's people within their sight. The Qur'an condenses a lot of details from the end of Genesis through Exodus in these few verses. The lack of details provides an opportunity to build a bridge. We can share with our Muslim friend here how God dealt with the Israelites and how he sent Moses to lead them out of Egypt.

In relation to verse 51, which discusses the calf Aaron made for the Israelites to worship in the Sinai, again not many details are given. Actually, in order to understand the story well, a Muslim would need to go to the *Hadith* and other sources. This would be a great place to share God's work through Moses and the punishment the sons of Israel received for worshiping the calf. Verse 54 says God just forgave them, and he is the merciful Forgiver. We need to explain here the punishment he actually gave when they worshiped the calf.[7] It is important to talk about the consequences of what they did. God did not just forgive them; he also applied a punishment. Moses took the golden calf, smashed it, scattered it in the water, and made the people drink it. Thousands of Israelites died because of their sin, either by the swords of the Levites or by the plague with which they were struck. God cannot deal lightly with sin and just forgive it.[8]

God's Provision in the Wilderness: Verse 57

This verse declares that God provided the sons of Israel with manna and quail and covered them with clouds. The clouds were not a covering but a guide to them. Here would be a good time to talk in more detail about God's food for them in the wilderness and the forty years they lived off of it.[9]

---

7.   Exod. 32.
8.   See also verse 93.
9.   Exod. 16.

Moses' Sin: Verse 60

Here the Qur'an briefly touches on the incident in the wilderness, when Moses hit the rock in order to provide water for the sons of Israel. However, the Qur'an does not mention that Moses sinned during this act. This provides a good opportunity to share with our Muslim friend the biblical account and talk about how Moses did wrong and thus was not allowed to enter the Promised Land. Again, it is an example of sin having consequences, which is not taken into account as much in Islam as in Christianity.

Entry into Heaven: Verse 62

In this verse, the Qur'an very clearly says that the Jews, Christians, Sabians (those who worshiped the stars and angels), and Muslims go to heaven, along with anyone who believes in God and the last day and has good deeds. The Qur'an does not reveal directly that these must believe in Muhammad; however, most commentators will say that these people make it to heaven after they believe in Muhammad. Within the wider Muslim body, an individual will choose the interpretation depending on the person's opinion of Christians.

If we consider the Muslim belief of the corruption of all the holy writings (*Tawrat* and *Injil*) before the Qur'an, this will help us to draw the conclusion that the sons of Israel were favored until Christ came (i.e., they could go to heaven), but when Christ came, they had to believe in Christ in order to merit salvation. Likewise, Christians could make it to heaven until Muhammad came, but if they refused him, heaven was refused to them. In order to be able to build a bridge with this verse, we can share with our friend that this verse clearly states that Christians can get to heaven, and they will not fear or be sad. However, do not go deeply into this, because it can get complicated. If we take it at face value, and if our friend accepts us as believers, it can be used as a good step for that Muslim to continue dialogue with us.

Created in the Image of God: Verse 65

In this verse, God curses people for breaking the Sabbath and turns them into apes. This is acceptable in Islam, basically because the concept of man being created in God's image does not exist. There is no correlation to this in the Old Testament. The closest story in the Bible is when King Nebuchadnezzar's heart became full of pride over the greatness of his kingdom, and he lost his mind, was driven away from people, and ate grass like cattle.[10] Then when he lifted his eyes to the heavens, his sanity was restored, he acknowledged God, and became a great king again. The idea of God cursing people and making them monkeys is refuted in Christian theology, because of the understanding that we are created in his image. We can share with our Muslim friend that in many places in the Old Testament God condemns any sexual approaches between man and animal, because his image is not to be reduced by such intimate contact with animals. This discussion is not for the average Muslim but for the scholar who is ready to read more of the Bible and compare.

Hardened Hearts: Verses 67–74

These verses reveal the background for the name of this sura. According to the Qur'an, there was a murder among the sons of Israel, but no one knew who committed the crime. Moses told the people that God was requiring them to bring a certain cow, about which he gave the qualifications. They were to slay the cow, take a part of it, and strike the corpse with it. The dead person then would come back to life, tell them who had killed him, and then die again. This is one of the great miracles of Moses in Islam.

The sons of Israel kept delaying in choosing the cow and asked for more signs to know exactly what cow. Moses condemned the hardness of their hearts but said that even from the hardest rocks God could bring forth water. This can be used very effectively as a bridge, by sharing that when we soften our hearts in obedience to God, accepting 'Isa as Savior, out of our (innermost) hearts can flow rivers of water.[11]

Using Religion for Financial Gain: Verses 78–79

In these verses some of the sons of Israel are condemned for seeking to use God's Word for personal gain. This ties nicely with the passage that talks about those who spread false doctrine and use godliness as a means to financial gain.[12]

Faith, Then Works: Verse 82

This verse reads that those who have faith and works of righteousness will be in paradise. We can bridge this concept to that found in James,[13] which

---

10.   Dan. 4.
11.   Heb. 3; John 7:37–39.
12.   1 Tim. 6:3–10.
13.   James 2:14–26.

talks about faith made complete by good works, while also tying it to the verse that says that any righteousness we have comes from God when we put our faith in Jesus.[14]

Failure to Keep the Law: Verses 83–86

In this passage the sons of Israel are condemned for not following the covenant of God, which told them to respect their parents and neighbors, to care for the orphans and the poor, and to pray and give tithes. They did not live according to God's law.

We can tie this to Jesus' condemnation of the scribes and Pharisees for knowing the Law but burdening people with even more laws without mercy.[15] Along with this, two other passages in Matthew can be used to emphasize the need to be even "better" than the Law, knowing that God will judge people based on what is on the inside.[16] We can explain to our Muslim friend here that, yes, many Jews did fail to live by the laws of God but that it is not just obeying the Law that pleases God; it is the spirit in which we do it that makes a difference.

Murder of Prophets: Verse 87

Here Jesus is referred to as being strengthened and supported by the Holy Spirit and given the clear signs by God. However, the sons of Israel did not believe him. The verse continues, accusing the sons of Israel with rejecting many prophets (apostles) God sent and even killing some of them. This is a good verse to reinforce the idea that people can kill a prophet, and this will help when we try to convince our friend that God allowed Jesus to die.

Circumcision of the Heart: Verse 88

We find an amazing sentence in this verse: "Our hearts are uncircumcised." It is important to note here that Yusuf Ali does not translate this properly. *Ghulifan* is not a covering for a book but the covering of the penis, which is removed in circumcision. It is the same word used in the Arabic Bible for circumcision. Because this is actually biblical terminology, we can use it to build a bridge on the subject of circumcision of the heart. There is a beautiful verse in the Bible that reads: "The LORD your God will circumcise

---

14. Rom. 3:21–26.
15. Matt. 23.
16. Matt. 5:17–20; 15:1–20.

your hearts and the hearts of your descendants, so that you may love him with all your heart and with all your soul, and live."[17] Also, Romans talks about the importance, not of outward circumcision, but of that of the heart, which is what matters to God: "Circumcision is circumcision of the heart, by the Spirit, not by the written code. Such a man's praise is not from man, but from God."[18]

Veracity of the Bible: Verse 89

Here we read that God gave Muhammad the Qur'an, which agrees with the books in their hands, but they (the sons of Israel) refused it. The "books in their hands" refers to the Old and New Testaments as a proof text for the Qur'an. We can use this verse to begin a discussion with our Muslim friend that if the Bible was true during Muhammad's time, their argument about the corruption of the Bible does not work, because we have biblical manuscripts from even before Muhammad's time. Some manuscripts date back to around AD 300, which is about three hundred years before Muhammad's time.[19]

Consequences of Sin: Verse 93

Once again we see a reference to the story of the golden calf. However, Muslim commentators do not go into detail to explain the actual story of the golden calf but rather interpret it allegorically. The key in this verse is: "They drank the calf in their hearts," which is understood to mean that the poison of their disobedience was taken to heart. Here we need to bring their attention to the biblical account, noting that it is to be interpreted literally and not allegorically. Again we can discuss the issue of consequences of sin.[20]

Evil Spirits: Verse 102

The Qur'an in this verse says that devils blasphemed Solomon. Solomon himself was not a magician, but these devils taught the sons of Israel magic and witchcraft. We can build a bridge by sharing about the biblical concept of evil spirits and how they can possess individuals and lead them to commit evil acts. This is in contrast to the Islamic concept of devils teaching people witchcraft.

---

17.   Deut. 30:6.
18.   Rom. 2:29.
19.   See also sura 2:97 on the same subject.
20.   Exod. 32. See also verses 47–54.

Abrogation: Verse 106

This is a very important verse in the *tawhid* of Islam. It says that when a verse is abrogated, meaning that the context of the verse is no longer applicable or needs to be contradicted, then God will bring another text better than the first one. The main idea here is that the Qur'an has some verses given to Muhammad, but then God revised these verses and made a second revelation for Muhammad.

We need to share that God's Word should be unchangeable because of his unchanging nature. As an example we can use the Ten Commandments (or the Law) of the Old Testament in relation to Christ. In the New Testament we find that Jesus says, "Do not think that I have come to abolish the Law or the Prophets; I have not come to abolish them but to fulfill them." He continues to say that not one iota of the Law would change until the end of time.[21]

Jesus gave more spiritual depth to the Law. For example, he said that not only are we not to commit physical adultery but we are to keep our hearts pure as well.[22] In a loving way we can bring our friend's attention to the fact that there is no abrogation in the Bible. Earlier revelation is not revised by later revelation. Unlike the Qur'an there is no need for such revision because the Bible was and is factually consistent from beginning to end. The geographical and historical facts recorded in the Bible have stood up against all challenges.

Role of Judaism in Christianity: Verse 113

We find in this verse an impression the Qur'an gives as to the relationship between Christians and Jews (today this applies to Israel, in the eyes of Muslims): that they are accusing one another of not telling the truth. Here we need to bring our friend into the light of knowing that Christianity completes Judaism; it does not contradict it. The Jews before Jesus' time were looking forward to the Messiah, who came in Jesus, though a modern-day Jew would not agree that Jesus was the Messiah for whom they continue to wait. A Muslim will be happy to realize that the Christian position is that the Jew of today also needs Christ to make it into God's kingdom.

---

21. Matt. 5:17–18.
22. See the Sermon on the Mount in Matthew 5 and 6 for more examples.

Omniscience and Omnipotence of God: Verse 115

This verse says that God is all-pervading, all-knowing. This is a point of agreement with which we can build a bridge with our Muslim friend, including verses from the Bible that share this same concept.

Rejection of Jews and Christians: Verse 120

The Qur'an reads in this verse that Christians and Jews completely refuse Islam and that they will never agree with a Muslim until he changes to their own religion. Reverse psychology is applied by this statement in order to convince the people of the total truth of the Qur'an. This leads to the position that a Muslim will never accept Jews or Christians until they become Muslims, and this is the heart of the Muslim nation (*umma*).

Ka'ba: Verse 125

Abraham is viewed in Islam as the first Muslim, along with his son Ishmael. Together they cleansed God's house (Ka'ba) for the pilgrimages. Muslims also believe that Abraham and Ishmael actually built the Ka'ba.[23] Tradition says that angels brought heavenly stones to build the Ka'ba. In general, Muslims agree that this is the first holy place to be built on earth.

Within the Ka'ba is a black stone, which has been recognized scientifically as a meteorite. It is true that it came from the sky, but not from heaven (or from God). This makes it a physical phenomenon, not a miraculous one. It is important for us to know that there were many sites prior to that time where meteorites were worshiped because the local population saw them fall from the sky. The ancient Greeks were one such people group who held meteorites as objects of veneration. Also meteorites have been found at various Roman temples as well. Native tribes in Greenland, Tibet, India, Mongolia, and Australia have been found to follow the worship of meteorites.[24]

Surrendering to God: Verse 131

This verse reads: "Behold, his Lord told him (Abraham): Submit (to me or surrender to me)." Abraham answered him, "I have become a Muslim, I surrender." This verse could be taken politically, claiming that Abraham was a Muslim, with all that the word means today. However, we can bring any

---

23.   See verse 127.
24.   "Meteorites in History and Religion," at http://www.meteorite.ch/en/basics/history
      .htm (accessed June 25, 2006).

Muslim into the full knowledge of the meaning of the word as "surrender." When Abraham said, "I surrender to the Lord of the two worlds," it does not mean that he became a Muslim in the modern sense of the word; it simply means that he fully surrendered to God. We as Christians can agree with the fact that Abraham was fully surrendered to God, and we can share stories from the Bible to support his devotion. The same argument goes for verses 132–133 in relation to Abraham's offspring.

Equality of Prophets: Verse 136

This verse makes a very powerful statement in saying that the revelation given to all the prophets is the same. Basically, Muslims believe in all the Old Testament prophets, as well as Jesus. This makes Jesus like all the other prophets. As we share about the prophets from the Bible, we can discuss with our Muslim friend the various purposes of their messages to the people and how the Old Testament prophets pointed the way to the Messiah (Jesus). While the prophets spoke about things to come, Jesus said, "The kingdom of heaven is near."[25]

God Tests the Believers: Verse 143

The Qur'an gives an explanation for why the direction of prayers was changed from the Qibla in Jerusalem to the Ka'ba in Mecca. This verse provides the proof that Muhammad did change the direction of prayers. The explanation given for God changing his mind was in order to test the genuine quality of the believers and to see who would be obedient to him regardless of what directions he gave. Here we can share that God does not need to test people, because he is omniscient and knows how people will behave under different circumstances. However, God does allow people to go through temptations in order that they may know him more through the experience.

We also can discuss the issue that God is everywhere. There is no need to focus our prayers in a certain direction. Jesus told the woman at the well that "true worshipers will worship the Father in spirit and truth."[26] While the Old Testament does have an account of Daniel facing toward Jerusalem for prayers, there are many other examples in the Bible of prayers offered where

---

25. Matt. 4:17.
26. John 4:23.

a direction is not required.[27] We can also move here into a discussion about prayer in general.

Death in the Way of God: Verse 154

The Qur'an states clearly that whosoever dies in a holy war is not dead but alive with God. Many places in the Qur'an, as we will indicate later on, even encourage people to die in the holy war. It does not explain exactly in what way they need to sacrifice their life for God; therefore, the issue of martyrdom has been taken to the extreme by radical Muslims, believing they have the right not only to die for God but also in the process to kill many. The more infidels they kill, the better off they will be in paradise.

Good and Evil Come from God: Verses 156–157

We can see here that the Qur'an emphasizes fatalistic thinking. Those who accept evil or good without questioning are praised. Most Muslim commentators explain this verse by saying that a good Muslim will accept good or evil as coming from God. Here is a great opportunity to share that God is not the author of evil. When we have evil in our life, it is not from God, but comes from our own temptations, our fallen nature, or from mistakes we have made. God thus allows Satan to put this evil in our path. God is in ultimate control, but he is not the author of evil.

Hajj: Verse 158

God tells the Muslims in this verse that the pilgrimage to the house (Ka'ba) is a good deed. He encourages them not to be afraid of what the people will say about them (i.e., that they are continuing pre-Islamic rituals). God himself will thank them for visiting his house.

Food Restrictions: Verse 172

The Qur'an puts restrictions on certain foods. Muslims cannot eat animals that have died a natural death, the blood of animals, pork, or food offered to idols. However, if someone is really in hunger, he can eat these things and he will be forgiven, because God is merciful and forgiving. Here we can see a parallel to the restrictions given to Christians in the book of Acts: "Abstain from food polluted by idols, . . . from the meat of strangled animals and from blood."[28] While finding this area of agreement with our Muslim

---

27.   1 Kings 19:4; Jonah 2:1; Matt. 26:36–44.

28.   Acts 15:20.

friends, we can also share with them the words of Jesus: "What goes into a man's mouth does not make him 'unclean,' but what comes out of his mouth, that is what makes him 'unclean.'"[29] It is the condition of the heart that is really important to God.[30]

Corruption of the Bible: Verses 174–176

In these verses the Qur'an talks about undefined people who have the book (*Tawrat*) but do not share with others all that is in it. The reason given for their withholding the truth is financial gain. It also claims that the people of the Book are divided over this issue. If we look at an accurate English translation of these verses, we find this basic understanding in the reading. However, most commentators explain these verses by saying the Jews hid a lot of material in the *Tawrat* that talked about Muhammad. Verses like this, which never refer directly to the issue, have been twisted and misinterpreted by Islamic scholars all through Muslim history. These verses have been the source of big issues like the corruption of the Bible. We need to be boldly stating that there is not one clear, direct verse in the Qur'an that proves their claim.

Righteousness: Verse 177

The description of a righteous person begins with faith in God, the last day, angels, the book, and the prophets. Interestingly, nothing is mentioned specifically about Muhammad as the Prophet or accepting him, or about Islam as a religion. It is merely a description of righteousness. However, the righteousness in the Qur'an is very works-oriented, as seen in the list that follows the required beliefs. We can wisely use part of this verse to build an effective bridge with our Muslim friend as we delve deeper into the subject of true righteousness. Several New Testament passages are very helpful. One reads: "For in the gospel a righteousness from God is revealed, a righteousness that is by faith from first to last, just as it is written: 'The righteous will live by faith.'"[31]

In looking at the following passage, we can share with our friend the role of the Law in God's plan for mankind and how through Christ, we now have a righteousness through faith:

---

29.   Matt. 15:11.
30.   See also sura 16:115.
31.   Rom. 1:17.

Now we know that whatever the law says, it says to those who are under the law, so that every mouth may be silenced and the whole world held accountable to God. Therefore no one will be declared righteous in his sight by observing the law; rather, through the law we become conscious of sin. But now a righteousness from God, apart from law, has been made known, to which the Law and the Prophets testify. This righteousness from God comes through faith in Jesus Christ to all who believe. There is no difference, for all have sinned and fall short of the glory of God, and are justified freely by his grace through the redemption that came by Christ Jesus.[32]

Of course the story of Abraham as given in the Bible is a great source for understanding the righteousness that God truly seeks. The following passage from Romans gives an easy-to-understand explanation for righteousness:

Is this blessedness only for the circumcised, or also for the uncircumcised? We have been saying that Abraham's faith was credited to him as righteousness. Under what circumstances was it credited? Was it after he was circumcised, or before? It was not after, but before! And he received the sign of circumcision, a seal of the righteousness that he had by faith while he was still uncircumcised. So then, he is the father of all who believe but have not been circumcised, in order that righteousness might be credited to them. And he is also the father of the circumcised who not only are circumcised but who also walk in the footsteps of the faith that our father Abraham had before he was circumcised. It was not through law that Abraham and his offspring received the promise that he would be heir of the world, but through the righteousness that comes by faith. For if those who live by law are heirs, faith has no value and the promise is worthless, because law brings wrath. And where there is no law there is no transgression.[33]

---

32.   Rom. 3:19–24.
33.   Rom. 4:9–15.

Does God's Word Regress? Verse 178

Even though the Qur'an comes more than five centuries after the completion of the Bible, in this verse we see a return to the Mosaic law, which allowed for punishment to be an eye for an eye and a tooth for a tooth. If God's Word is true, as the Qur'an claims it to be, then why would God change the words of Jesus when he said, "Love your enemies and pray for those who persecute you."[34] Islam goes backward, not forward.

Relativity of the Law/Rights of Others: Verse 182

If the will of a deceased person is found unfair, his heirs may change it to better distribute the wealth. God will forgive them for not respecting the will of the dead and not hold them accountable for any wrongdoing. It is clear in this verse that laws and rights are held as relative in Islam, which should make us aware of the Muslim mind-set in respect to such issues when we deal with them in business and other matters.

Fasting: Verses 183–185

According to Islam, fasting is a duty God bestows on a Muslim. Each person should fast during the month of Ramadan. This is the month they believe God gave them the Qur'an. A person who is sick or traveling can fast some other days to make it up. A Muslim who is fasting cannot eat until the last light of the sun. He or she then breaks fast and can continue to eat until the first light of the sunrise. A Muslim man can sleep with his wife once he breaks fast. Ramadan provides a good opportunity to discuss fasting from the biblical view, using passages such as Isaiah 58:1–7 and Matthew 6:16–18.

Women as Garments: Verse 187

This verse continues the issues surrounding the month of Ramadan, by saying that it is permissible for a man to approach his wife on the nights of the fasts. An interesting phrase is used as husbands and wives are described as "garments" (covers/coats) for one another.

Many Muslims use this part of the verse to misuse some Christian principles, by saying that a woman can protect her husband by keeping him safe around other women (i.e., if the wife is around, she will protect him from the lust of other women). We do not need to be deceived by such an approach, but we can use this topic as a bridge, while recognizing that Islam is a male-dominated religion. We need to use this bridge wisely.

---

34. Matt. 5:44.

Kill in the Name of God: Verses 190–193

These verses are very serious in their implications for non-Muslims today. Here the Qur'an states, "Kill in the name of God those who kill you."[35] If anyone starts to attack Muslims in any way, a Muslim has the right to kill that person, as long as the circumstances allow. We can compare this with the words of Jesus, when he says, "Love your enemies."[36]

The verses that follow offer many comments about killing. Basically Muslims can kill their enemies anywhere, even in the most holy place, the sacred mosque.

Way (Cause) of God: Verse 195

This is a very important verse, because we can see in it a religion that encourages people to participate in the holy war. Here the holy war can be supported by giving money or by being involved directly. Islam encourages people to give money to build up a war machine in God's name. While the United States (seen as a Christian country by Muslims) has the biggest war machine in the world, we need to make clear that the Bible does not encourage this, and that the West's war machine is secular, not religious, in nature. The West does not build armies or start wars based on religion but on principles of freedom and human rights. While we want to stay out of politics with our Muslim friend in order to share Christ, we must be aware of these differences in order to offer a clear response to their perceptions of the West in general and the United States in particular.

Hajj: Verse 196

This and succeeding verses provide a good description of the hajj, or pilgrimage. At least once in his or her lifetime, a Muslim is to visit the Ka'ba in Mecca at a specified time of the year. Verse 200 illustrates clearly that the rites of the pilgrimage were in fact pre-Islamic but spiritualized under Muhammad, for it reads that one should "celebrate the praises of God, as ye used to celebrate the praises of your fathers." Another interesting note about the hajj is that trading is allowed during the pilgrimage. This would be a good point to share the story of when Jesus cleared the temple.[37]

---

35.   Though Yusuf Ali translates *kill* as "fight," the Arabic word is *kill*.
36.   Matt. 5:44.
37.   Matt. 21.

Assurance of Salvation: Verse 209

In general, Islam has no assurance of salvation. This verse also could be understood as meaning that a Muslim believer can lose his or her salvation by committing a sin after becoming a Muslim.

Jihad: Verses 214–217

In this passage we find a few verses that parallel the Sermon on the Mount of Matthew 5, as the verses read like a type of dialogue between Muhammad and God, giving directions concerning certain issues. As the Prophet is supposed to answer his people about fighting, God tells him to tell the people they are demanded to kill (fight) even though they hate it. They must do it for their own good, because God knows what is best for them. A Muslim should not seek war during four months of the year,[38] but if somebody is fighting, they should fight back. Yusuf Ali notes on this topic, "To fight in the cause of Truth is one of the highest forms of charity."[39]

Wine and Gambling: Verse 219

This verse indicates that drinking wine and gambling are great sins for a Muslim, even though there could be some benefit in both. This could be used as an area of agreement from which we can build a bridge. It will help our Muslim friends to understand the difference between what they perceive as "Christian" behavior and what the Bible truly teaches.

Marriage Issues: Verses 221–223

A Muslim man cannot marry an unbeliever until she believes. It is better to marry a believing slave than an unbeliever. Men also are instructed not to sleep with a woman during her menstrual period.

Verse 223 is a much-discussed verse concerning sexual relations between married couples. Referring to wives as a tilled piece of property that can be approached when and however the husband desires, some commentators view this as giving total freedom for a man to enjoy his wife any way he wants. Other writers take a more moderate approach, relating it simply to the issue of her ability to bear children.

We can use these verses to build bridges with Muslims. We can begin by asking them their opinion of these controversial issues, in the hope that they

---

38. Zukkaga, Zuhegga, Muhara, and Ragab. See Ali, *Qur'an*, 77; and Committee of the Qur'an and Sunna, *Al-Muntakhab*, 58, sura *al-Tauba* 9:25.

39. Ali, *The Holy Qur'an*, 84n. 236.

will then allow us to express the biblical view of marriage, which includes marriage between believers only and mutual respect in relation to the sexual relationship.[40]

Divorce: Verses 227–235

There are several notes in these verses concerning divorce. A woman cannot be married immediately after divorce but must wait three menstrual cycles to make sure she is not pregnant. In verse 230, we see a most illogical solution for multiple divorces between the same couple. If a man divorces his wife and remarries her three times, he cannot remarry her for the fourth time. She must marry another man and divorce again, and then her first husband can remarry her. From these verses we see that Islam applies a mixture of Old Testament laws and heathen practices in its rules regarding marriage and divorce.

This is a good opportunity to refer to the Law of Moses and the teachings of Jesus concerning divorce. The Old Testament is clear that a man cannot remarry his ex-wife once she has married another man. This would be detestable in the sight of God.[41] We can then find the ideal God intended, as proclaimed by Jesus.[42] While the world may demonstrate other practices, the teachings of our Lord are clear in this matter.

Ark of the Covenant: Verse 248

While this verse refers to the ark of the covenant, it does not describe the articles within the chest or give a clear understanding of its purpose. This is a good opportunity to share in more detail about the ark of testimony as we know it in the Bible, using it as a bridge to discuss God's covenant with the Israelites.[43]

Saul, David, and Goliath: Verses 246–51

We can share with our Muslim friend a lot of spiritual truth as we tell these stories and relate the time difference between Moses, Saul and David, and Jesus. Within a few verses the Qur'an jumps over about 1,500 years without much explanation. Very little detail is given to the stories of Saul, David, and the prophets. It is helpful to know that in the Qur'an Saul is referred to as

---

40.   1 Cor. 7:1–5; 2 Cor. 6:14; Eph. 5:25–33.
41.   Deut. 24:1–4.
42.   Matt. 5:31–32.
43.   Exod. 16:31–35; 25:10–22; Num. 10; Deut. 10:3–5.

Talut. We can share the story of how the Israelites sinned in asking for a king.[44] We also can relate the story of how David slew Goliath (*Galut* in the Qur'an).[45] A Muslim will be very interested to hear the details of these stories.

Jesus: Verse 253

This is the first time Jesus ('Isa) is mentioned in the Qur'an. God spoke to Moses, but to Jesus God gave clear signs and the Holy Spirit. (Most commentators confuse the Holy Spirit and Gabriel.) It is a great opportunity to explain to the true seeker about the Holy Spirit.

Throne Verse: Verse 255

This is viewed as the most important verse in the Qur'an. The major part of the verse explains the greatness of God. The verse asks the critical question: "Who can be the intercessor between man and God?" There is no one who can be perfect, no one to be intercessor without God's permission. This is a great moment to share with our friend that God chose Jesus, not Muhammad, to be the only intercessor since Jesus was sinless, born only from a woman, and did not carry the sin of the line of Adam. These things are not true of Muhammad. There is no human who can be intercessor. Muhammad is a human. Theologically, a Muslim cannot say that Muhammad is an intercessor, but in folk Islam and in most Muslim minds, Muhammad is the intercessor.

No Compulsion in Religion: Verse 256

This verse was written at the beginning of the foundation of Islam, when Muhammad was not yet politically strong. It clearly says that everyone can have his or her own religion. However, this verse was abrogated by 8:39 and 8:65, which state that the only religion is Islam. Use of this verse depends on a Muslim's theological position. More open or moderate Muslims will quote this verse; the more fanatic will use the verses from sura *al-Anfal* referred to above.

Abraham: Verse 260

This verse records a conversation between God and Abraham, during which Abraham asks for proof that God can raise the dead. The miracle of the four birds is not in the Bible, but the background of it could be God's

---

44.   1 Sam. 8–10.

45.   1 Sam. 17.

covenant with Abraham found in Genesis 15, when the Lord asked him to split the sacrificed heifer, goat, and ram and lay the pieces opposite one another. That night a lantern passed between the pieces, signifying that God had made his covenant with Abraham. It is a great parallel to lead our Muslim friend to a deeper knowledge of the truth of God and his desire to be in relationship with us.

Good Deeds/Charity: Verses 267–271

These verses teach that God sees our good deeds. It is better if we do them secretly, for if we do so, the good acts will remove some of our stains of evil. We can relate this to the teaching of Jesus from the Sermon on the Mount.[46] The difference, however, is that our good deeds will not remove sin but will gain us rewards from God.

Usury/Borrowing with Interest: Verse 275

The Qur'an strongly forbids loaning money with interest (the Islamic banks provide the same service but use different terms). This agrees with the Old Testament practice of no interest between fellow Israelites; however, Israelites were allowed to charge interest to foreigners.[47]

Assurance of Salvation: Verse 277

Many Muslims use this verse to claim the security of salvation. However, the verse does not state clearly that they will go to heaven when they die; it merely says they will have their reward from the Lord.

No Burden More Than We Can Bear: Verse 286

The last verse of this sura is parallel to 1 Corinthians 10:13, which says, "No temptation has seized you except what is common to man. And God is faithful; he will not let you be tempted beyond what you can bear. But when you are tempted, he will also provide a way out so that you can stand up under it."

The verse in the Qur'an is understood very materialistically. The "burden" is viewed in terms of material wealth. However, we can still use the commonality of phrasing as a bridge, explaining the Christian understanding in terms of the spiritual realm and how God helps us to face temptations and provides ways of escape by his grace.

---

46.   Matt. 6:1–4.
47.   Deut. 23:19, 20.

Al-i-'Imran

The Family of 'Imran

SOME PARTS DATE TO BATTLES OF BADR AND UHUD

Overview

Al-i-'Imran starts with the same letters (*aleph*, *lam*, and *meem*) as the previous sura. Some commentators say that these letters are an abbreviation of a certain text from the throne verse *(ayat al-coursi)*, which is found in sura *al-Baqara* 2:255.[1] Others refer to them as evidence of the miraculous way in which the Qur'an was given. As mentioned in the previous sura, there is no consensus as to the meaning or significance of these letters.

Some of the text of this sura was revealed to Muhammad during the seventh year of the *hijra* and is referenced to the time of the battles of Badr and Uhud. As with sura *al-Baqara*, we find here many stories shared in order to help the people understand theological truth. We read stories about God's creation, which reveal his law and ethics, showing how a good Muslim is to behave, including in male-female relations. This sura also provides some rules for debating with persons from other religions. Because it describes both the victories and defeats in battle, there is an emphasis on jihad and how martyrs (holy warriors) will have a certain status on the end day. Also, stress is given to the manner in which the Israelites went astray and corrupted the faith.

---

1. Ibn Kathir, *Tafseer al-Qur'an al-Azeem*, 1:3.

The title refers to 'Imran, who is seen as the father of Moses; thus the sura shares some of the story of Moses and connects it to the birth of Jesus.

Comments and Possible Bridges

Furqan: Verses 3–4

Another name for the Qur'an is *Furqan*, which means "the divider between the redeemed and lost" (or between heaven and hell). People have to believe in the Qur'an, or God will prepare hellfire for them.

Verse 3 is a very important verse for building bridges, because God says to Muhammad that he gave to him a true book, agreeing with the two books he already had in his hand, the *Tawrat* and *Injil*, which were light for people before. Most of the commentators look at this verse in a very subjective way. However, the actual meaning of this verse is that when Muhammad got the Qur'an, it was in agreement with the books in his hand. This means that Muhammad had these books in his hand at the time—if not literally, he still knew something about them. Some scholars look here to prove that Muhammad was able to read or was educated. Most Muslim scholars say that Muhammad was *ommi*, which could mean that he was not able to read or write or that he was a Gentile (not Jewish). A lot of material from the Torah and Gospels was translated into Arabic at the time. Some commentators read this verse very simply to say that the Qur'an agrees with the books. But some others, like Ibn Kathir, one of the most important Muslim scholars, read this verse as saying that the Qur'an proves that the *Tawrat* and *Injil* spoke about God sending Muhammad as a prophet. However, many Muslims, in searching for proof of this statement, have examined the Law and Gospels, finding it mentions nothing about Muhammad. From this, the whole theory of the corruption of the *Tawrat* and *Injil* takes place, though there is no linguistic basis for it.

God Speaks to Muhammad and Allegory in the Qur'an: Verse 7

This verse tries to prove again that the Qur'an is the Word of God. He (God) is the one who gave the book. This statement is mentioned many times as proof that the Qur'an is from God. However, nobody ever heard God speaking to Muhammad. All these verses are Muhammad testifying on his own behalf that God spoke to him. We can use this verse to open a conversation with our Muslim friend by asking if anyone ever heard God speak to Muhammad. We can then share that in the Bible, many times when

God spoke to the prophets or Jesus, he was heard by those around them. Sometimes it was by just a few people, while at other times it was by an entire nation. When God spoke to Moses, the Israelites saw, heard, and were afraid. When God spoke to Samson's mother, her husband heard too. When Jesus spoke to Saul on the Damascus road, the men traveling with him heard the voice. At the baptism of Jesus, the crowd heard the voice of God coming from above.

This verse also mentions that some of the verses in the Qur'an cannot be understood. The commentators' argument here is that this will encourage the religious leaders to study the qur'anic text more. The words *fundamental* and *allegorical* relate to the parables. We can share that even though Jesus sometimes spoke in parables, he had a purpose in doing so and many times shared the meaning of the story to those who were truly seeking God.

End Day: Verse 9

This verse indicates very clearly that in Islam there is a day of judgment or end day, and it is a very precise day. After this day the nonbelievers will go to hell (v. 12). The believers will go to a physical paradise where they will live forever with gardens and rivers of water and surrounded by clean (pure) women (companions), who are clean from wickedness, harm, and monthly periods (v. 15). This could be a good opportunity to ask a Muslim about his concept of heaven and then be able to share the biblical view for those who believe in Christ.

Best of Goals: Verse 14

It is very important to explain the first phrase of this verse by saying that Satan is the one who made these things appeal to man, not God. We see that the Qur'an here is saying that God had in mind more important things for man than this lust for things. We can share with a Muslim that God indeed has much more for us than the world can offer—he has everlasting life, with pleasures beyond all physical understanding. Then we can explain to our friend how to get there. "Nearness to God is the best of goals."

No Compulsion in Religion: Verses 19–20

These verses say that the only true religion is Islam, and the ones who have the books refused the Qur'an because of the differences between the books. Muslims are discouraged from arguing with Christians and Jews; they are simply to tell them they need to be Muslims. If they refuse, that is their choice; God has hell for them. It is important to note here that the Qur'an does not encourage Muslims to kill those they disagree with, as it does in other verses.

Day of Judgment: Verses 24–25

Verse 24 expresses the view that was common among Jews—that they will go to hell for a temporary time and then be sent to heaven. The Qur'an takes a strong stand against the idea of a purgatory, as we see the next verse proclaiming that there is one day for final judgment. Again, we can share what Christians believe about the idea of purgatory and the Day of Judgment, leading to the importance of the assurance of salvation.

Samson and His Riddles: Verse 27

This verse is very similar to the riddle of Samson, which we know from the book of Judges, chapter 14. We can share with our Muslim friend that we have a similar phrase in the Bible. This may lead to the opportunity to share the story of Samson in full.

Non-Muslims over Muslims: Verse 28

The Qur'an is indicating clearly that a non-Muslim cannot be in charge of a Muslim, though in today's world we do not see this universally applied. However, in many Muslim countries it is accepted that a non-Muslim cannot be in charge over Muslims, even though he may be more educated or can do the job better. This is why in countries where there are minority Christian groups, you will never see them in high positions within the military or government. The reasoning is that since government is the domain of God, leadership should only be for Muslims.

Commentators on this verse advise Muslims that exceptions can be made if there is no other choice. However, though a non-Muslim may be over a Muslim, the Muslim only has to look like he is giving him control, so as to put the Muslim at peace over the issue.

Please note that Yusuf Ali's translation of "friends and helpers" is not correct but should read: "Do not let blasphemers be over believers."

Muhammad's Elevation as Prophet: Verse 31

In this verse Muhammad is told to say, "If you love God, follow me." Jesus says, "He who loves me will be loved by my Father."[2] We can see in this verse

---

2.   John 14:21.

that Muhammad wants to put himself in Jesus' place and is asking for total obedience to him. Even though Islam in general considers God the ultimate being and Muhammad only a prophet, in many situations we can see this is not the case.[3] From what is happening around us in the world, we can see that Islam takes a very harsh stand against anything that comes against Muhammad or any blaspheming against him. Blaspheming against God, however, is well known in the Muslim world.

Separating the Sin from the Sinner: Verse 32

This verse reveals a great gulf between Christianity and Islam. In Islam, God does not love blasphemers. We need to share with Muslims that God loves sinners, even blasphemers, but he does not love their sin. It is this separation between a person and his acts that is foreign in Islam but vital for understanding the way of Christ. This statement of God not loving blasphemers is mentioned many times in the Qur'an and is a great bridge to use in sharing about God's love for all mankind.

Mary: Verses 33–44

In the next few verses we see the story of Mary, the mother of Jesus. We can use these verses and those in the Bible to show our Muslim friend the differences between the two accounts. The Qur'an says that Mary used to stay in the temple all the time, where God gave her fruit to eat. Zechariah the priest went to her in the temple and found in her hand a lot of fruit. The Bible teaches us that Zechariah and Elizabeth lived a distance from Mary and there was not really a close relationship between Zechariah and Mary.

We also read in these verses the story of how God gave to Zechariah John the Baptist. Zechariah asked God to give him a miracle to prove that he would have a son in his old age, so God told him that he would be silent for three days. In reality, Zechariah was silenced all the way through Elizabeth's pregnancy with John. It was not a miracle, but a punishment because he did not believe what God told him.

We read in the Qur'an that God chose Mary among all the women of the world and cleansed her (v. 42). Even though Mary is the highest elevated woman in the Qur'an, Muslim commentators hold three other women at the same level: Khadija (Muhammad's first wife), Fatima (Muhammad's daughter), and Asia (the wife of Pharaoh).

---

3.   Like the cartoons of the Prophet that caused riots in 2006.

Jesus, the Word of God: Verse 45

The angel's announcement for Mary was that God was bringing her good news. He called Jesus here the Word of God. Jesus had a very unique status on earth and in heaven. We can share with a Muslim that Jesus is the Word of God and that God reveals himself only through his Word. If we want to have a personal relationship with God and be able to hear his voice clearly, we have to be willing to accept Jesus as his Word. In explaining the Word of God with the meaning that Jesus does not separate from God, a Muslim will understand the example of an honorable man who has to keep his word, even when it costs him his life. Man's word equals a man. God's Word equals God.[4]

Jesus, from Childhood to Maturity: Verse 46

Verse 46 offers something we need to stop, look at, and discuss with our Muslim friend. We see here one of the two miracles attributed to Jesus in the Qur'an that are not in the Bible—Jesus spoke as an infant. Also it says in the same verse that he spoke to the people as a very old man.[5] Since Jesus died on the cross at about age thirty-three, he never spoke as a "very old man." This will open a discussion about Jesus' death as seen in the Qur'an and the Bible.

Jesus, Full of Wisdom: Verse 48

"And God will teach him the books and give him wisdom." We can share with our Muslim friend from this verse that all the wisdom was present in Jesus from the beginning. A parallel can be made to the story in Luke, when the twelve-year-old Jesus was found by his parents in the temple conversing with the religious teachers, and "everyone who heard him was amazed at his understanding and his answers." The passage ends by saying, "Jesus grew in wisdom and stature, and in favor with God and men."[6]

Jesus' Miracles: Verse 49

We find in this verse a collection of miracles performed by Jesus, including a second one not found the Bible, when he made birds of clay, blew in them, and they flew. This is a very unique verse, and dealing with

---

4. John 1:1.
5. Translated as "maturity" by Yusuf Ali.
6. Luke 2:47–52.

it is very complicated. Even though we can see a lot of truth in this miracle and that it places Jesus on the same level with God, it is not found in the Bible. It says Jesus "created" a bird from clay, and we can see the parallel in God's creation of Adam from clay. God is the only one who has the ability to create. Here the Qur'an is using the same word, "to create." God breathed into Adam's nostrils, and he became a living soul. Here Jesus is breathing into the clay a living spirit for a bird. We need to deal with this verse very wisely, because it could be argued that if we are using this as an example, then we are implicitly agreeing with the Qur'an that the miracle occurred.

We can, however, share with our friend that all the miracles Jesus did were for a specific reason—to show himself as God Incarnate. We can then relate the story of the healing of the paralytic from Luke 5. When the paralyzed man was dropped from the ceiling, Jesus told him first, "Your sins are forgiven." The people in the room thought in their minds: "Only God can forgive sins." They were right, but they could not see the change of the man's heart. The man was still paralyzed and lying on the mat. In order to prove his first "miracle," the forgiveness of sins, Jesus did a second one: "I tell you, get up, take your mat and go home."[7] When the paralyzed man started walking, the people saw it and only then believed that Jesus had the ability to forgive sins as God does.

Law and Grace: Verse 50

It is very clear from this verse that Jesus allowed his followers some things that had been forbidden in the Old Testament. This is a great bridge to draw a parallel between the Law of Moses and the grace of Jesus. Muslims will look at the parallel from a physical point of view (i.e., what a person can or cannot eat), but we need to take it the next step and show that Jesus is the new covenant and it is through only him that we can receive God's grace and mercy.[8]

Disciples: Verse 52

This verse describes briefly the calling of Jesus' disciples and says that they referred to themselves as Muslims. Of course this does not mean that they were Muslims with the understanding of the word today, because we know that Islam came some six hundred years after Jesus. However, we can compare this story to that found in the Bible and talk about how the disciples were submitted to God, as the word *muslim* implies.

---

7. Luke 5:24.
8. See John 1:17 and Gal. 5.

Jesus' Ascension and the Superiority of His Followers: Verse 55

Here God, in speaking to Jesus, says, "I am lifting you up to me and I will make the people follow you above the blasphemers in the end day." Muslim scholars debate the timing of when God led Jesus to himself. Some say that Jesus died for a few hours (it varies how long, since they do not agree about the crucifixion itself), then God took him to himself. Others say that God lifted Jesus up without death, based on the word *mutawafik*, which has many different meanings in Arabic but basically means, "I will let you die" or "I am coming to you." Some other commentators say, "I am giving you to die in your right time." They refer to the verse that reads that nobody (i.e., Jews) killed him.[9]

This verse also makes an interesting statement about the superiority of those who follow Jesus. While some commentators might say Muslims are true Christians, we can still use this point as a bridge by sharing the following: "If you wanted to get from here to my house, you would need someone to help you. Would you choose someone who has never been to my house before and admits that they do not know the way? Or would you say that the best person to help you get to my house from here would be me?"[10] We know that Jesus came from heaven and is living there now. Is it not logical that he would be the one who could show us the way to God?

God Does Not Love the Unjust: Verse 57

This verse reads that God will reward those who work righteousness but that he does not love the unjust. This is a good opportunity to explain how this differs with Christianity, which says that God hates the sin but loves the sinner. How can God hate what he himself created and that which has life from himself?

Jesus and Adam: Verse 59

We have read in the verses prior to this many godly characteristics applied to Jesus. However, here we see the comparison lowered to that of Adam. In the same manner in which God created Adam, he also created Jesus. We need to explain to our friend here the correct parallel between Adam and Jesus.[11]

Adam brought sin to mankind; Jesus is the only one who cleanses sin. The parallel the Bible gives us between Adam and Jesus has nothing to do with

---

9.   Sura 4:157.
10.   Greeson, *CAMEL*, 70.
11.   See 1 Cor. 15:20–23, 45–49.

the way they were created. We know that Adam was created from the dust of the earth and Jesus was born of a woman. However, Jesus existed before the year of his birth. This would be a good place to share with our Muslim friend Jesus' appearances in the Old Testament.[12]

It is important to emphasize the difference between the Qur'an and the Bible in regard to the issue of Jesus and Adam. Also note that these verses (33–63) were given by Muhammad when some Christian bishops from Najran, near Yemen, were visiting him.[13] They tried to prove to him that Jesus was the Son of God since he had no human father. Of course, they meant Son of God in the spiritual sense, not the physical sense. Muhammad did not immediately reply but told them to wait and come the next day. When they returned, he was ready for them with these newly revealed verses.[14]

Common Terms Between Christians and Muslims: Verse 64

This verse lists three areas of agreement between Christianity and Islam:

1. We worship God alone.
2. He has no partners (popes, priests).
3. We do not make lords or patrons (saints) from among men.

In general we can use this as a great bridge of commonality between us and our Muslim friends, though it is important to make sure the understanding of the meaning of each point is the same.

Abraham: Verses 65–67

Muhammad is told to ask the people of the Book to stop fighting over Abraham. His argument is that Abraham was before Judaism and Christianity and was in reality the first Muslim. Here would be a good place to explain to your friend the continuity of Judaism and Christianity.[15] Jesus did not come to change Judaism but to fulfill it. While we can agree that

---

12. I.e., the one with Shadrach, Meshach, Abednego in Dan. 3:25; the blazing torch among Abraham's sacrifice of covenant with God in Gen. 15:17; the visitor to Abraham before the condemnation of Sodom and Gomorrah in Gen. 18:13–33; the commander of the Lord's army in Josh. 5:13–15.
13. Gabriel, *Jesus and Muhammad*, 97.
14. Ibn Kathir, *Tafseer al-Qur'an al-Azeem*, 1:323.
15. See also sura *al-Baqara* 2:113.

Abraham was neither a Jew nor a Christian, he also was not a Muslim. In sharing the biblical story, we can show how he was one of the prophets God used to bring his message to the people.

Abraham and Muhammad: Verse 68

This verse attempts to make a parallel between Abraham and his followers of that time and Muhammad and his followers. Abraham was purely submitted to God. Muhammad was purely submitted to God. A brief comparison of Muhammad and Abraham in the physical sense will bring our friend to realize the great difference between the two.

Veracity of the Bible: Verse 84

God is asking Muhammad's followers to believe in all that is given in the books revealed to Abraham, Ishmael, Isaac, Jacob, the tribes, Moses, Jesus, and the prophets. He says there is no difference in them. This is another opportunity to speak about the veracity of the Bible as God's Word.

One Religion: Verse 85

This verse is clear in stating that the only acceptable religion is Islam. This proves to be a great contradiction, for if there was agreement with all the religions before, how could only Islam be the acceptable one? We can look at this from another way as well: If there are contradictions between Christianity and Islam, how can they both be from God?

Assurance of Salvation: Verses 90–91

Here we see clearly the theology of Islam that a believer can lose his salvation. If a person believed but then blasphemes, God will never accept his repentance. After a person dies, nothing can change his destiny. Even with this very precise doctrine, we know in reality that Muslim family members and friends will do everything possible to get a person who has denied Islam to say the *shehada* (word of witness) again, and this clearly contradicts what we have here.

Straight Path: Verse 101

The expression of the straight path, as seen in this verse, is applied to the Muslim life on earth. Once a person becomes a Muslim, that person will start on the straight path. The same expression also can be used in relation to the Day of Judgment. A Muslim will pass over to either heaven or hell through the straight path. We need to share with our Muslim friend that Jesus said, "I am the way (straight path)."[16] Without Jesus, neither a Muslim nor a Christian can find the straight path. Only through Christ are we able to subject our human nature and live a holy life, pleasing to God. After death, only Christ can be the straight path, because he is the only one who came back from death to show us the way to God.

Umma *(The Holy Muslim Nation): Verse 103*

Here the Prophet is encouraging Muslims to be united in *umma* (the holy Muslim nation). The basis for their unity is God bringing them back to himself, making their hearts unified, making them brothers, and saving them from hell by his grace. However, if we look at Islam in general today, we can see that the conflict inside the *umma* theologically, politically, and physically is far greater than the conflict between Islam and other religions or political entities. Here it is very important to share that if God gave that order or unity and it did not last, can we say this is really a godly order?

Faces in Heaven and Hell: Verses 106–107

We find here an unusual description of the people going to heaven and hell. On that day some people's faces will be white (those going to heaven), and others will be black (those going to hell). Though some commentators explain this allegorically, if we go to the Arabic text, there is nothing that makes it read in anything but a literal way.

We can make a comparison to what Jesus said: "When the Son of Man comes in his glory, and all the angels with him, he will sit on his throne in heavenly glory. All the nations will be gathered before him, and he will separate the people one from another as a shepherd separates the sheep from the goats. He will put the sheep on his right and the goats on his left."[17]

Jesus was talking about the essence of the person, the person's heart, not about the color of the skin. In heaven, will all the faces be white and in hell all the faces black? In heaven, we will find faces of all colors—people of all nations who have accepted Jesus.

Muslims, the Best of Peoples: Verse 110

The Qur'an is very clear in stating that Islam is the best social structure in the world and that it keeps the people in the nation in perfect status with

---

16. John 14:6.
17. Matt. 25:31–33.

God. If we look today at the effect of Islam socially, it will not take much to realize it is not the best structure as the Qur'an says, but that instead it could be the most devastating. In comparison, this verse claims that while some Christians and Jews have faith, most are "perverted transgressors."[18]

God's Wrath and the People of the Book: Verses 111–112

Islam takes a very harsh stand against Christianity and Judaism as it points out the nonviolent reaction of these peoples when wronged. Islam sees the return of hatred by love as weakness and a major downfall. Verse 112 reads that the people of the Book will receive the wrath of God and be forever in a state of destitution. However, if we look at the world today, we find the people of the Book (as long as they are abiding by God's Word) among the most prosperous and advanced peoples in the world.

Paradise and the People of the Book: Verses 113–115

Ironically we find that the attitude completely changes here to say that some of the people of the Book worship God, read the Book all the night, believe in the end day, and do good; thus they are among the righteous. Paradise is a reward for such people.

Thus, in the same sura we find the Qur'an condemning the people of the Book and calling them blasphemers and at the same time saying they can make it to paradise. Still, this is evidence that a non-Muslim can go to paradise.

Relationship with Non-Muslims: Verse 118

This verse is a warning for Muslims not to make friends with non-Muslims or to trust them. This helps us understand why, when we are talking to a Muslim, that person does not trust us or seems to have a hidden agenda. We need to pray that the Holy Spirit will soften that person's heart toward us as non-Muslims so that we will be able to reach that Muslim with the message of God's love.

God's Help: Verse 124

At the battle of Badr, the Muslims were outnumbered by the enemy, so God sent three thousand angels to help them win. We can find parallels to Old Testament stories that also show God's help to his people. However, we

---

18.   Ali, *The Holy Qur'an*, 151.

can then share that by the time of Jesus' coming, God no longer used the same methods. He laid down the sword of wrath and extended his grace through Christ. We will then typically hear our Muslim friend ask, "But what about the Crusades?" We need to explain that this was not a Christian solution for taking Jerusalem but the wrong use of religion by an earthly kingdom simply because it was ambitious for power.

Omniscience and Omnipotence of God: Verse 129

This verse states that God is omniscient and that everything in heaven and earth belong to him. He forgives and punishes whomever he chooses. In order for God to forgive and punish, he should be all-just, but this is not mentioned. Thus we find the essence of Islam—God is Master. He is ultimate in judging, and man can do nothing about it. Man is completely predestined.

Muhammad's Elevation as Prophet: Verse 132

Though a short verse, this is a very dangerous statement, which puts Muhammad on equal standing with God. Since no Muslim can talk to God, he or she has to be obedient according to Muhammad. Therefore, if Muhammad fails, a Muslim will fail. We know that Muhammad said of himself that he is just a slave of God. He has no divine powers to protect himself from failing. But how can we obey God directly without Muhammad, if all that we have from God is only what Muhammad said? We should not rest our eternal destiny on one human being. In many areas of the Muslim world, we find that the people have elevated Muhammad far higher than God. Our friend may object to such a statement, but if we really take a wise look around us, we can see how true this statement is.

Forgiveness: Verse 135

This verse makes it clear that when a Muslim does wrong, all he has to do is ask God's forgiveness and he will be forgiven, no matter the nature of the sin. However, there is no assurance of forgiveness in Islam, and there is a certain way a Muslim has to ask in order get his sins forgiven. Therefore, most Muslims will never have confidence or peace in the knowledge that he or she has been truly forgiven. This is a good opportunity to talk about the forgiveness we have through Christ.

Harm to God; Love Suffers: Verse 144

We read here that Muhammad is just a prophet like all other prophets and that God does not care if he dies or lives, nor would it hurt him. This presents a great contradiction to the statement that Muhammad is the seal of the prophets.

The expression "hurt (harm) to God" is used many times. If all mankind is destroyed, this will not harm God, with the meaning of hurting him. We need to share that in Christianity the relationship between God and man is based in love. God suffers and hurts when he sees people suffer and hurt, and that is the essence of love. Then we can share with our Muslim friend that God suffered when Adam sinned.[19] Also prior to the flood when God saw the wickedness of the people, he was very hurt or grieved.[20] The Bible even compares God to a loving, caring mother who breastfeeds her baby, thus illustrating his sympathy and care for his people.[21] We can also share how Jesus suffered through the incarnation by being reduced to the form of man (slave) even though he was God and how he ultimately suffered on the cross as he took on the sin of mankind.[22] The Holy Spirit suffers, or is grieved in the heart, when the believer sins.[23] The Holy Spirit's work in the world today is to limit the effect of Satan by containing evil until the end of the days.

If God Is for Us: Verse 160

We have a great parallel to this verse in the Bible. Even though all the commentators refer this to the godly triumph in the physical sense (the battle of Badr), we can, however, take it to a higher level spiritually and share with our friend, "If God is for us, who can be against us?"[24]

How to Judge Prophets: Verse 161

This verse reads, "No prophet could ever be false to his trust, but even if he is, he will make amends on the day of judgment." In Islam, a man of God is not to be judged with the same standard as a normal man. In God's eyes there are various grades of men. Muslims are not to question their leader (Muhammad). Would God allow a man who claims to be a prophet to do wrong? Christians judge their leaders by God's Word and anyone who claims to be a prophet by whether their words come true. "You may say to

---

19.   Gen. 3:8.
20.   Gen. 6:6.
21.   Isa. 49:15; 66:13.
22.   Mark 8:31; Luke 24:26; Heb. 2:9, 18; 1 Peter 2:21.
23.   Eph. 4:30.
24.   Rom. 8:31.

yourselves, 'How can we know when a message has not been spoken by the LORD?' If what a prophet proclaims in the name of the LORD does not take place or come true, that is a message the LORD has not spoken. That prophet has spoken presumptuously. Do not be afraid of him."[25]

Temptations: Verse 165

Though once again the Qur'an is speaking of a physical battle (Badr), the words used are very close to those found in the book of James in relation to temptation. "When tempted, no one should say, 'God is tempting me.' For God cannot be tempted by evil, nor does he tempt anyone; but each one is tempted when, by his own evil desire, he is dragged away and enticed."[26] The Bible meant for this to be applied to the battle for the human soul (good versus evil). It can be a great bridge to take our friend to a full understanding of the concept.

Death in the Way of God: Verse 169

This is another of the verses that triggers the justification for killing in fundamentalist Islam. Anyone who gives his soul defending God will go directly to heaven. We need to share with Muslims that God does not want us to die defending him. He wants us to die to our sins and to live in the Spirit for him, serving mankind.

Harm to God; Love Suffers: Verse 176

Here we find another reference stating that God will not get hurt when people go astray and blaspheme, but instead he will simply give them a harsh punishment. We can talk again about how love suffers and refer to the verse that reads: "The Lord is not slow in keeping his promise, as some understand slowness. He is patient with you, not wanting anyone to perish, but everyone to come to repentance."[27]

Muhammad's Justification as a Prophet: Verse 183

Even though he was not able to bring fire from heaven, Muhammad is justifying his role as prophet by saying that even when prophets did such miracles, the people did not believe them. This is a good opportunity to share the story of Elijah and talk about what makes a prophet a prophet.

---

25. Deut. 18:21–22.
26. James 1:13–14.
27. 2 Peter 3:9.

Nature Gives Witness to God: Verse 190

This verse finds a great parallel in the verse that says, "The heavens declare the glory of God; the skies proclaim the work of his hands."[28] The wise will remember God in all situations and take time to meditate on God's Word. We can share with our Muslim friend that while we can know there is a God from his works, it is most important to know of God's redemption of nature and people. Nature is in stress because of sin until the end day when we will have a new universe spiritually. Ultimately we cannot know God only through the creation; it has to be through his Word and the work of the Savior.

Paradise and the People of the Book: Verse 199

This is a very important verse because it says non-Muslims (Christians/ Jews) can satisfy God. The tricky part is that it says they can please God because they believe in the books and also in the Qur'an. We need to share with our Muslim friend that a true Jew or Christian cannot agree with the Qur'an because of the fundamental differences. This may lead our friend to ask what the differences are, and allow us to share the message of the cross.

---

28.   Ps. 19:1.

Al-Nisaa

The Women

AFTER BATTLE OF UHUD

Overview

Sura *al-Nisaa* speaks generally about the family, society, and relationships between people, as well as giving some rules to govern these relationships. Family is the building block the Prophet uses to show how to build the whole society. This sura was given to Muhammad after the battle of Uhud, when many Muslim men were killed, so it was to help reorganize the family structure.

Muslim scholarship refers to this sura by saying that all people have one father and one mother, Adam and Eve (made from one spirit), so there is a common brotherhood in Islam. They say that Islam is calling for peace among the earthly tribes. However, if we look at the reality of life, in most of the Muslim lands, equality does not exist and peace is very rare.

Comments and Possible Bridges

Origin of Sin: Verse 1

This verse is the source of a great theological debate in Islam. The most common understanding is that God literally created all souls from Adam. They want to give the understanding that all mankind is equal. Therefore, man should fear God. We can share with our Muslim friend that we are not created from Adam's soul, but we are the children of Adam and God takes the time to create each individual soul. If all are created from Adam's soul, we would be photocopies of him, which is not true. However, we do inherit a lot of characteristics from Adam and Eve, especially the sinful nature. It is for this reason we need a Savior. This is a great bridge from which we can talk to our friend about the origin of sin, the fall of Adam and Eve, and the redeeming plan God has for mankind.

Marriage Issues: Verse 3

This verse literally reads, "You can enjoy sexually in marriage whosoever you like of women, two, three, or four, and if you cannot be just, only one or whatever you have in your hands." It is helpful to recognize here that it says you can marry two. It starts with two, not one, so it gives men the choice to have more than one wife. In the Muslim world today, multiple marriages are common, especially in the poor areas and among the low class in society. This is primarily because Islam allows it.

The irony is that at the same time the verse reads, "You can marry up to four, but you have to be just among the four." The verse continues, however, and says that a man will never be just. The dilemma is that within the same verse, the Qur'an tells the Muslim to marry up to four women while at the same time it limits it to one in order to ensure justice. So what will a good Muslim choose—four or one? Some commentators refer to Judaism and Christianity as encouraging polygamy. This is not true. God's plan from the very beginning was one husband and one wife for a lifetime. When Jesus was asked, he took the issue all the way back to the beginning of creation. "'Haven't you read,' he replied, 'that at the beginning the Creator "made them male and female,"' and said, "For this reason a man will leave his father and mother and be united to his wife, and the two will become one flesh"? So they are no longer two, but one. Therefore what God has joined together, let man not separate.'"[1]

They become one body. One man and four women are not one body. This is not God's original plan for mankind. In the Garden of Eden, God made one Adam and one Eve. It will be amazing to see our friend's reaction when we ask him, "Do you think if God made Adam in the garden and four Eves, it would still be called paradise?" Any sound Muslim, with a big laugh, will say of course not.

---

1.   Matt. 19:4–6.

Orphans: Verses 6–10

For the next few verses, the Qur'an is focusing on orphans and how harshly God will punish anyone who takes advantage of them. The Qur'an deals with two important sociological issues resulting from the war: the number of women remaining after the war was more than the number of men; and there were many orphans. The Prophet is scaring them to death so that they will not take advantage of the orphans. Verse 10 says that if you eat up (take) an orphan's money, it is as if you are taking fire into your belly. We can build a bridge here to the verse that reads, "Religion that God our Father accepts as pure and faultless is this: to look after orphans and widows in their distress and to keep oneself from being polluted by the world."[2]

Inheritance: Verse 11

Here Muhammad is dealing with the issue of inheritance. Because there were so many dead from the war, they had to find ways to handle inheritances. It is very clear from the beginning of the verse that a male receives double the portion of inheritance of a female. Later we will look at the judicial ramifications of such a concept. The verses that follow continue in giving guidelines for inheritance. We can build a bridge here in talking, not about the amount received, but about what we do with inheritance and tell our friend the story of the prodigal son.[3] This, of course, can lead to the importance of having an eternal inheritance, which far outweighs anything we can receive here on earth.[4]

Adultery: Verse 15

If a woman is charged and found guilty of adultery by four male witnesses, she is to be locked in her house until she dies or God finds another way for her. This is understood by scholars as meaning that another husband will be found to take her. In another place in the Qur'an, however, the punishment for this crime is the application of a hundred lashes.[5] We can discuss this issue by asking our friend what happens to the man in such situations. The usual response is nothing. We can tie this to the time when Jesus was asked what should be done to the adulterous woman.[6]

---

2. James 1:27.
3. Luke 15.
4. Heb. 9:15; 1 Peter 1:4.
5. See sura 24:2.
6. John 8.

Marriage Issues: Verses 22–24

A Muslim man is prohibited from marrying his father's wife, his mother, nieces, aunts, or the girl who was nursed from his mother. Nor can he marry two sisters at the same time. This list of prohibitions developed into another practice in later Islamic theology called "nursing the elder." If a man wants to make sure that other men will not take sexual advantage of his wife, he will let his wife nurse the man, making it then illegal to approach her sexually. It is a bizarre practice but one that continues to get attention in the press and society of the Muslim world today.

The Qur'an calls married women "the protected ones" or "the fortresses," and Muslims are prohibited from marrying them. It is very important here to notice that these "protected women" are only those married to another Muslim, while the ones married to non-Muslims are not protected. Therefore, the women they win in war (whatever you hold in your right hand) are yours, married or not. Even if she is married to the enemy, as long as she is captured in the war, it is lawful to take her as a wife.[7] The Bible clearly states that we are to love our enemies, protect their belongings, protect even their animals, and, much more, protect their friends and wives. The Bible does not give us any right to kill someone and take his wife as a trophy. We can begin a bridge here with the story of how King David desired the wife of Uriah and sent him to die in battle in order to take her.[8] God showed his displeasure in this by sending the prophet Nathan to confront him of his sin.

Sinful Nature of Man: Verse 28

The Qur'an says that God created man weak. Commentators explain this as meaning weak against man's desires. We need to share with our Muslim friend that the flesh and the fallen human nature will never be able to be subdued. He will agree with us that man is very weak and cannot stand up against his desires and the wicked nature of his heart. Here we can share that the only way a man can be strong enough is when he is born again and takes a new nature, different from the fallen nature of man.

Men over Women: Verse 34

This verse reads that men are *qawwamun* over women, which means, as Ibn Kathir says, "that the man has more value than a woman."[9] This implies

---

7.   Gabriel, *Jesus and Muhammad*, 170.
8.   1 Sam. 11–12.
9.   Ibn Kathir, *Tafseer al-Qur'an al-Azeem*, 1:435.

that he is her boss, is greater than she is, and is the ruler over her; he is the one who punishes her when she does wrong. The reason for this superiority is because the men spend money on women. However, if we look at the Muslim world today, we find that many women make more money than their husbands. (This is true even in the poorest segments of society.) Therefore, the fundamental meaning of the verse vanishes. On the other hand, the Bible says that God created them male and female equally. They both sinned and have the same fallen nature, and they both need the same Redeemer. In Christianity, man and woman are perfectly equal, yet different in gifts and office.

Another part of the verse advises the man, as the protector of the woman, on how to handle a wife whom he *thinks* is not obedient. He can admonish her verbally, which in many cases is a daily occurrence in the Muslim home. He can punish her sexually, by refraining to sleep with her. (He, however, can enjoy himself with other wives while letting her suffer.) If she is still not obedient, he can beat her until she obeys. We need to share with Muslims that the Bible teaches us to deal with our women as our own body. We will never beat up our body but will take care of it and respect it and build it up. The more we show love and respect to our wives, the more willing they are to obey and honor us by their actions.[10]

Prayer, Purification: Verse 43

This verse literally says that you do not pray when you are drunk; so there is an indirect connotation that a Muslim can drink, but he cannot pray when he is drunk. This explanation will never be accepted in Muslim realms, because in other places drinking is completely forbidden. Therefore an explanation developed that says that when a Muslim prays to God, he should not be *like* a drunk; he needs to understand what he is saying.

This verse lists several things that cause impurity in prayer:

1. Drunkenness
2. Illness
3. Traveling
4. Having gone to the bathroom
5. Touching a woman

---

10. Eph. 5:22–33.

If a person is impure, he must wash before prayer, that is, wash just the hands and face. The understood meaning is that after washing, God will forgive and then prayers can be offered. The concept is that washing before prayers cleanses the person and enables him to be before a holy God. We need to share with our friend that water does not wash away sin (that is, if we considered touching a woman or going to the bathroom as a sin or unholy). The only way to wash away sin is by confessing it to God and asking his forgiveness through Christ alone. It will be helpful also to know that a lot of these purification practices were taken from pre-Islamic practices.[11]

It will be proper here to also talk about what defiles a person by sharing the words Jesus spoke to the Pharisees: "'Are you still so dull?' Jesus asked them. 'Don't you see that whatever enters the mouth goes into the stomach and then out of the body? But the things that come out of the mouth come from the heart, and these make a man "unclean." For out of the heart come evil thoughts, murder, adultery, sexual immorality, theft, false testimony, slander. These are what make a man "unclean"; but eating with unwashed hands does not make him "unclean.""[12]

It is not going to the bathroom or touching something that defiles, but the sin that comes out of a wicked heart, like lying, slandering, gossiping, and so on. For this reason a person's heart needs to be changed in order to be holy for God.

Corruption of the Bible: Verses 46–47

The Prophet takes a very strong stand here against the Jews because they refused the message of the Qur'an. They basically said, "We heard your Qur'an, Muhammad, and we do not want it!" According to this verse, they misrepresented the words of the Qur'an given to them by Muhammad, but it is very important to note here that it does not say that they changed the words of the Old Testament. The next verse gives proof of this, because it says that the Qur'an proof-texts what they (the Jews) have in their book. God then threatens them by saying that they do not believe the Qur'an, and he will make their faces as if they have no features.

For the wise reader, however, these two verses do not prove that there was any change in the Old Testament, but actually proves the opposite—that the word of the Qur'an was proof to what was in the Bible, including that

---

11.   John 2:6.
12.   Matt. 15:16–20.

A Christian Guide to the Qur'an

Muhammad is the seal of the prophets. A bridge could be drawn here for if the words of the Qur'an prove what the Jews had in their hands, it would be helpful to compare the stories in the two books. Such a comparison will lead our Muslim friend to find many differences. Names and places are different, and the sins of the prophets are not mentioned in the Qur'an. Thus, a wonderful biblical-qur'anic study could be developed with our Muslim friend based on these verses.

Shirk, *Unforgivable Sin: Verse 48*

The unforgivable sin in Islam is *shirk*, which means "to put any partners with God." We also have only one unforgivable sin. We can share with our friend that the unforgivable sin in Christianity is almost the same—it is blasphemy against the Holy Spirit, which is the refusal to accept the work of the Spirit in our hearts by accepting Jesus as Savior. "Anyone who speaks a word against the Son of Man will be forgiven, but anyone who speaks against the Holy Spirit will not be forgiven, either in this age or in the age to come."[13] We need to be aware of the dilemma right there—talking about Jesus and the Holy Spirit is *shirk* in Islam.[14]

God Curses Man: Verse 52

This verse contains a very prolific statement: God curses men. Here we need to share with our friend that in Christianity, God does not directly curse mankind. Because his essence is holy, he cannot curse a person; but the absence of his holiness in one's life is itself a curse on that person. In the Garden of Eden, God told Adam and Eve not to eat from the fruit of the Tree of the Knowledge of Good and Evil, for if they did, they would die. The death they faced was separation from God. They discovered the meaning of God's command when they ate from the tree. They no longer had a close, intimate relationship with their Creator, which is why they suffered when cast out of the garden. The absence of God is suffering and a curse.

Hell: Verse 56

This verse offers a very descriptive picture of hell. God will put those who do not believe in Muhammad's verses in a fire; and once their skin is burned, he will put another skin on them, and they will burn again. We can

---

13.   Matt. 12:32.
14.   See also verse 116.

talk about how Jesus described hell in the Bible: "And if your eye causes you to sin, pluck it out. It is better for you to enter the kingdom of God with one eye than to have two eyes and be thrown into hell, where 'their worm does not die, and the fire is not quenched.' Everyone will be salted with fire."[15]

We need to take time here to explain the difference between the concept of a physical hell and a spiritual one. The Qur'an describes both hell and paradise in a physical sense. While the Bible uses similar descriptive words, the meaning is clearly spiritual. The best way to explain this is by sharing that hell is the eternal absence of God in man's life, which brings total lostness, eternal hopelessness, and complete spiritual darkness. This truly is the ultimate hell. The soul of the person would be tormented—not his earthly, physical body (which returns to dust at death), because we will be spiritual beings in eternity.

Muhammad's Elevation as Prophet: Verse 69

We find this statement repeated many times: "Obey God and the Apostle." Through such obedience a person receives the final approval for heaven. The people of that day never heard God speaking to Muhammad. They never saw God speaking to Muhammad. Muhammad brought the message and said it was from God. With no witnesses to prove that these are words from God, wise-thinking Muslims would not agree with the statement that we have to obey God and Muhammad. Jesus made many statements about testing his words and about the prophets proving what he said. Before a crowd of witnesses, God the Father also spoke on behalf of Jesus.[16] Many heard God speaking to Jesus, and that is why we have a logical reason to believe in Jesus and obey his words.

Kill in the Name of God: Verse 76

This verse separates people into two schools: those who kill for Islam and those who kill for Satan. Because of this distinction, the Qur'an orders Muslims to kill everyone who is not killing for Islam. We can share that Jesus never ordered his followers to kill, because he came to give life. He did not kill but raised the dead. When one of his followers cut off the ear of the high priest's servant, Jesus healed the cut ear. We can ask: "Do you want to kill or bring life? Whom do you want to serve?"

---

15.   Mark 9:47–49.

16.   Matt. 3 and 17.

Jihad: Verse 77

The Prophet tells his followers that it is ordained from God for them to kill. When the people questioned his words, he explained that even though one's life is shortened, the obedient one will receive in paradise far more than what he has on earth. He continues to make his argument by saying that death will come to every person eventually, even if one is in the strongest fortress. We can contrast these words to the commands for the Christian found in passages such as Colossians 1:3–17 and Romans 12:9–21.

Muhammad's Elevation as Prophet: Verse 80

We can see how this and other verses shape Islam and put Muhammad in the highest place—sometimes even higher than God. In this verse, Muhammad is the voice of God when he says, "He who obeys the Apostle obeys God."

Greetings: Verse 86

If a person is greeted in any fashion, he or she must return it with an even greater greeting. Muslims greet one another with the words *salaam alekum*. It will be imperative that when we meet a Muslim, we greet him in peace, because his book tells him he has to return our greetings back to us. We can use this practice to talk about real peace, not just greetings, and how we have peace in our hearts when we talk together.

Killing Fellow Muslims: Verses 92–94

The Qur'an warns that a Muslim should not kill another Muslim believer. If a Muslim kills another Muslim intentionally, he will be destined to hell. He is also warned to be careful when attacking another city, watching whom he kills. It is important not to rush into killing people to take their possessions. First, one must listen and see if they are Muslim or not. If they are Muslim, they should not be killed. God will provide many spoils.

Jihad: Verse 95

The Qur'an encourages people to make literal application to jihad (holy war). It is clear in this verse that the one who actually takes part in the physical holy war is higher than the one who supports it with his money and position but does not engage in warfare, unless he is sick or cannot do it for some specific reason. This brings us to the essence of jihad. For any Muslim, the ultimate obedience to God is actual participation in holy war.

Some scholars read this differently and explain jihad intellectually; however, the actual, physical war for a Muslim remains theologically the highest form of obedience to God. We need to share with our Muslim friend that our real war is not with flesh and blood, not with our fellow human, whether a believer or not, but against Satan and the principalities of darkness. We also can talk about how we separate the sinner from his sin. We take a stand against sin, yet we love the sinner as our Father did.

Non-Muslims over Muslims: Verse 97

We see the Qur'an discouraging Muslims from living under the submission of a non-Muslim country and telling them to move to a land governed by the Muslim *umma*. We see today the direct opposite of this happening, as Muslims are willingly traveling to the West and to openly non-Muslim nations because of what those nations can provide in terms of a better life materially and personally.

Entry into Heaven: Verse 124 This verse indicates that paradise was made equally for men and women, but in other places, we hear Muhammad saying that the majority in heaven will be men. As the verse says that those who have faith and do deeds of righteousness go to paradise, we can make a good connection with the faith of Abraham, which is far closer to this reality than that of Muhammad. Those who go to heaven are those who do deeds of righteousness as a result of following the faith of Abraham, a faith that was in the promise of the one to come.

Marriage Issues: Verse 128

In this verse we find a great difference between a man deserting his wife and a wife deserting her husband. As we saw previously, if the wife deserts her husband, he can rebuke her with a loud voice, refrain from sexual privileges, and beat her physically.[17] This verse, however, prescribes no punishment for the husband who deserts his wife. We can share with our friends that God created men and women equally but different. Because a man and woman are equal, they need to have equal rights. We can share with them how equal rights are taught in the Bible.[18]

---

17.   Sura 4:34.
18.   Eph. 5:25–33; Col. 3:18–19; 1 Peter 3:7.

Blasphemers: Verse 150

The Qur'an gives a definition of blasphemers in this verse. A blasphemer is one who does not believe in all the prophets and will differentiate between them. A Muslim asks, "Do you believe in Muhammad, the Prophet of Islam?" If our answer is no, we will be blasphemers according to his book. As Christians, of course, we recognize that God's Word was completed by the end of the book of Revelation. Therefore, we need to answer our friend wisely in order to build a bridge and not a wall. We can share that we know a lot about Muhammad and that he is the Prophet of Islam. There are a lot of things that Muhammad said that agree with the Bible. We can agree with those. But we also must say that he said some other things that do not agree with the teachings of Jesus. As Christians, we cannot agree with them. The immediate thought for a Muslim will be, "What are these things?" We can then take the time to study the Bible with our friend, pointing out the areas of disagreement.

Muhammad's Justification as a Prophet: Verse 153

God is telling Muhammad not to worry that the people of the Book are asking for proofs for his prophecy. He tells him that they asked Moses to show them God (face-to-face), but God denied that for the Israelites and burned them with thunderbolts. We need to share with our friend that the Israelites in reality asked Moses to speak to God for them and not let them see God, because they were so afraid of him.[19] The thunderbolts did not kill the people, but they heard the thunder and saw the lightning from a distance and trembled. If anyone wants to see God, God does not kill them but takes the time to reveal himself to them. We are living in the age of grace—the ultimate revelation came in Christ, for whoever wants to see God. We can share with our Muslim friends that if they really desire to see God, they need to look at Jesus.

Jesus' Crucifixion: Verse 157

This verse reads that the Jews claimed they killed Jesus, the Son of Mary, but in reality they did not kill him or crucify him. So many stories and sayings try to explain this verse. The best way to build bridges here is to look deep into the verse to agree on what is true in it and try to keep our Muslim friend from listening to human explanations. We can share that

---

19. Exod. 20:18–21.

it is true that the Jews did not kill Christ. Jews did not crucify him. We can agree with this, because a Muslim is thinking about the one who held the hammer to drive the nail into Jesus' hands. Jews did not do it. It was forbidden for Jews to use the cross for punishment. Instead, the actual act of crucifixion was performed by the Roman army. It was plotted for by Jews but implemented by Romans.

The verse says, "it appeared to them" that he was crucified. We can tackle this point on several different levels. First, on the cross Jesus was so deformed by the abuse of the Roman soldiers that he looked different. Isaiah shows us the picture of the suffering Christ on the cross.[20] His appearance does not alter the fact that he was crucified. Second, the Bible as a historical book clearly records the crucifixion of Jesus, and there are many other historic sources as well that prove the crucifixion.[21]

Jesus, the Word of God: Verse 171

Here the Qur'an is calling on Christians, as the people of the Book, not to call Jesus God, because God has no physical son, and God is not three but only one. They are told not to brag about their religion. We can share with our friend that this verse talks about Jesus as the Word of God. We can then explain that we will never understand a person without his word. The honor of a person is to keep his word, even if it costs his life. We cannot separate the word from the person. The word reflects personality and the essence of that particular individual. The Word of God equals God. Jesus is the Word of God and is from his Spirit. The Spirit of God cannot separate from him. We need to take time here to explain that the Spirit of Jesus was different from the spirit of man. The spirit of man was created; the Spirit of Jesus was not created but entered the world through the miraculous virgin birth. The Spirit of God is one Spirit.

---

20.   Isa. 53.

21.   Strobel, *The Case for Christ*, 73–91.

Al-Maida

The Table Spread

LAST PILGRIMAGE TO MECCA

Overview

This sura, the Table or *al-Maida*, is one of the last suras given to Muhammad. Its basic teaching is on how to fulfill a deed or contract either between man and God or between men. It also gives some restrictions as to the kinds of food Muslims should or should not eat and explains how to perform the ablutions (washing before prayers). Some verses also refer to how the Christians and Jews changed the biblical text. It explains that Jews and Christians are enemies of Islam and that Muslims should never submit to them. There is a very strong verse that says that whoever calls God three is a heretic and that all who believe this are blasphemers.

Al-Maida also gives instruction about how to perform the pilgrimage, declares that liquor is completely forbidden, and ends with verses about 'Isa (Jesus) declaring to those who worshiped him his innocence as to the accusations against him by saying that he was just a slave and is not to be worshiped.

Because this sura ends with a very harsh stand against Christians, we can see a big difference between this and suras from the beginning of the revelations, which were very friendly toward the Jews and Christians. The Prophet was hoping to get them to enter into Islam, and thus Judaism and

Christianity would be diminished. However, when they failed to comply and become Muslim, Muhammad turned against both Jews and Christians and called them infidels.

There are some amazing stories surrounding this sura. Some commentators say that Muhammad received this sura in one setting, while riding a camel. Because the sura was one of the biggest texts and contained a lot of important information, it became so heavy that the camel had to lie down.

Comments and Possible Bridges

Food Restrictions and Perfection of Religion: Verse 3

Here God gives to the Prophet a list of the foods Muslims should not eat. However, if one must eat one of these forbidden foods in order to stay alive, God will forgive him. This verse holds a very important expression from God to Muhammad: "Today I perfected your religion . . . and have chosen Islam as a religion for you." Commentators say that God preferred Islam to all other religions, as it was the best religion. Some commentators claim this is one of the last verses of the Qur'an because of the verse's meaning. There are, however, many differing opinions about the length of time between this verse and the death of Muhammad.

The best way to draw a bridge here is to share that if God is saying to Muslims that he perfected Islam, it is the time to take a good look into the moral and ethical standards of Islam in order to see that they are truly superior. The Qur'an draws from many Old Testament laws, as found even in a few verses at the beginning of this sura, in which legalistic requirements are made as to what Muslims may eat and drink. The Bible, however, while it contains rules for living, enables a believer's conscience, under the leadership of the Holy Spirit, to be the guide for his behavior, especially in areas that are not clearly defined in Scripture. We can observe in many Muslim countries Muslims themselves looking up to Christians in relation to their marriage relationships, love for enemies, interpersonal relationships, and trustworthiness. Many Muslim businessmen select Christians to be their treasurers, because they know they can be fully trusted. We can encourage our friend to choose one principle and discuss it from the standpoint of the two books.

Food Restrictions and Marriage Issues: Verse 5

This verse allows the Muslim to eat meat slaughtered by the people of the Book, which means they approve the way of butchering an animal for food.

However, today in the Muslim world this is not widely accepted because in killing any animal for food, Muslims have certain rituals that need to be done in order to call the meat *halal* (allowed by God to be eaten). These rituals include reciting the Qur'an, using a certain knife with three bolts in the handle, and repeating "God is great" three times. Only then can the meat be consumed by a Muslim. What is interesting to note here is that no mention is made of pork; rather, all things good and pure are made lawful to the Muslim.

The other allowance the Qur'an gives in this verse is that Muslims can marry women of the Book. This verse has been understood in two ways: they can marry Christian or Jewish women as long as they are not married to someone else (*muhassanat* or protected), or, based on a reference from sura *al-Baqara*,[1] they can marry the blasphemers after they believe. Based on that sura, the people of the Book are blasphemers, and Muslims are forbidden to marry them unless they convert.

We have to mention here that while a Muslim man may marry a Christian or Jewish woman, a Muslim woman is punished by death if she marries anyone outside of Islam. We can use this as a bridge by discussing this as a totally unfair social rule. Then we can share that the Bible is very clear about marriage—both partners must be believers, no matter what the background previously.

Prayer and Purification: Verse 6

Here we find more details about purification before prayers. The Muslim is to wash his face and hands, up to the elbows. With a wet hand he is to wipe over his head and then wash his feet up to the ankles. If prior to prayer the believer touches a woman or has a bowel movement, he must wash again. If no water is available, he can perform the ablutions with the dust of the earth. See notes on sura 4:43 for bridge.

Twelve Tribes of Israel: Verse 12

The Qur'an mentions that God appointed twelve leaders for the Israelites. It does not name the twelve or even refer to Jacob. However, it does use the word *Israel*. This would be a great opportunity to bridge by sharing with our Muslim friend the story of the twelve children of Israel (Jacob) and how these tribes are mentioned in detail in the Old Testament.

---

1. Sura 2:221.

Corruption of the Bible: Verses 13–14

The Qur'an says here that the people of the Book (Jews) changed the words of their Book and even forgot some parts of what God gave them. The Christians did the same thing. Because they did this, God put a great distress among them. These verses provide a great opportunity to share with our Muslim friend that we have text of the Bible from the second century, only 125 years after Jesus,[2] which, of course, predates what we have of the Qur'an.[3] However, the best point can be made by reminding our friend that Muhammad mentioned some other place in the Qur'an that the Bible is proof text for what he said. This means that the Bible of his time was intact.

Blasphemers: Verse 17

The Qur'an is very straightforward in saying that Christians are blasphemers. "Whoever says that God is the Christ" falls into this category. It is important to note in this verse that it does not say, "Whoever says that the Christ (Jesus) is God," but "whoever says God is the Christ" is a blasphemer. Muslims cannot conceive of reducing God to Jesus, but if we reverse half of the verse, we can elevate Jesus in his deity to be equal to God by first telling our friend that we agree with the statement written and that this would in fact be reducing God to one facet of his being. We can then share how we believe the opposite is true by taking the time to explain that Jesus is not God the Father, but the Son. At the same time, Jesus and the Father are one. When we say to a Muslim that Jesus is God, it is as if we are taking away the Father and are putting Jesus Christ in his place, which is incorrect from the theological point of view. We need to explain to our friend the office of God, the office of Jesus, and eventually the office of the Holy Spirit. The Father cannot destroy Jesus, because in destroying Jesus, he is destroying himself, and God is limited by his own nature.

Sons of God: Verse 18

Muhammad is taking a strong stand against Christians and Jews when they say that they are the sons of God and beloved. In response to their

---

2.   John Rylands 52 Codex, discovered in Fayoum, Egypt, in 1935, contains excerpts from the book of John. The oldest full text of the entire Bible is around AD 350.

3.   The first revelation came from Muhammad in AD 611. The biblical material we have is from three hundred years prior to Muhammad.

assertion, Muhammad tells them they are only human and God still punishes them for their sins. We need to take some time here to explain that if the people of the Book make such a statement, they are not talking in the physical sense but in the spiritual sense.

Wandering of the Israelites: Verses 22–26

These verses vaguely refer to the story of Joshua and Caleb, who were among the spies sent into the Promised Land. In their report to Moses, they said the land could be taken, but the majority of those who went in put fear into the people by saying the inhabitants of the land were very powerful. Thus God had them wander in the wilderness for forty years as a result of their fear.

We can share with our Muslim friend that the reason God let them wander in the desert for forty years was not simply because they were afraid of the people in the land, but also because they had been disobedient to God in the wilderness and worshiped the golden calf. The Lord also used those years to prepare the land for them. Each of these reasons can be used as a bridge to reach out to Muslims, and allow us to tell them the Bible stories so they can gain a fuller understanding of how God was working.

Cain and Abel: Verses 27–31

We jump back to the story of Cain and Abel (*Qabil* and *Habil*), though their names are not mentioned. It is reduced to five verses. We see a dialogue between Cain and Abel that is not in the Bible. Verse 30 states that Cain killed his brother. Then, in verse 31 we read that God sent a raven to show Cain how to bury his murdered brother. This raven story is from old Jewish legends.[4] We need to explain that the main issue was not the burying of his brother but the consequences of what he did. We can then share from the biblical narrative the complete story, including the curse he was forced to live under and the way he was cast out from his people.[5]

Worldly Gain Versus Faith: Verse 36

This verse says that if a person has everything on earth (all earthly goods) and he blasphemes or rejects God, he will not have any benefit on the end day and will go to hell. It provides a great parallel to the verse that says,

---

4. Ginzberg, *The Legends of the Jews.*
5. Gen. 4.

"What good is it for a man to gain the whole world, and yet lose or forfeit his very self?"[6]

Punishment Leads to Repentance: Verses 38–39

These verses present us with a great contradiction. Verse 38 reads very clearly that both male and female thieves must be punished by the cutting off of their hands. Verse 39, however, says that God will forgive the one who confesses his sin and does good. This raises a question for our Muslim friend: How will God forgive the thief after his hand has already been cut off? Cutting off the thief's hand is not God's way. The Bible does not include any punishment that takes away body parts. We can discuss how sin should be dealt with from the inside, not the outside. We need to talk about how we can change our hearts in order not to steal. Cutting off a person's hand is not going to stop him from being a thief. It will only make him a very angry thief.

Veracity of the Bible: Verse 43

The Qur'an is clear here that the *Tawrat* contains the Word of God, his law, and can be used for judgment. This proves that the Bible in Muhammad's time was not changed.

Law Confirmed by Gospel: Verse 46

It is a very important fact, according to this verse, that Jesus followed the previous prophets of the *Tawrat* and that God gave him the *Injil*, which is considered a light and way for the lost. The Gospels confirm the Old Testament. We will easily be able to agree with this and share more with our friend about the relationship between the Old and New Testaments in the light of history and salvation.

Veracity of the Bible: Verse 47

God tells the Christians that they must use the *Injil* as their law. This again proves that Muhammad considered the Bible in his time true. There are four questions we can ask our friend about the alleged corruption of the Bible, as we try to open his mind to the truth of this issue:

1. Who changed it?
2. Why was it changed?

---

6. Luke 9:25.

3. When was it changed?
4. What parts were changed?

God's Indifference: Verse 54

The Prophet is warning the Muslims that if they lose their faith, God does not really care, for he will replace them with another people who love him more. We need to share with our friend that God cares for each individual, because he created each person unique. God does not replace one with another.

Hezballah: Verse 56

Whoever considers God and Muhammad his superiors will become believers and will be *hezballah*, which the Qur'an here refers to as the triumphant ones. As we look around today and see those who call themselves *hezballah*, we can see how much blood they shed, even as they blow themselves up in order to win a war. In this we are able to understand the heart of the message of Islam when applied.

Non-Muslims over Muslims: Verse 57

We see the strong stand against Christianity and Judaism at its epoch, as the Prophet clearly states that these people mocked Islam and are the enemy of Islam. He strongly forbids Muslims from putting themselves under their authority.

Created in the Image of God: Verse 60

We read here that God is telling Muhammad that in his wrath he will change the people of the Book into monkeys and pigs. This provides a great opportunity to share with our Muslim friend that man is made in God's image, so he would never change the one he made in his image into a pig or monkey. We can share that in many places in the Bible, God strongly condemns any sexual contact between man and animals.[7] Such an act disgraces God's image in man, and he tells us to be holy as he is holy.

Human Characteristics of God: Verse 64

Muhammad is reporting that Jews have said God's hands are tied, meaning that he does not give blessings. The Prophet answers them by saying God's

---

7. Lev. 18:23; 20:15, 26; Deut. 27:21.

hands are not tied but are spread out wide. He spends and gives as much as he wants to, which means that he is mighty and blesses all.

What is interesting for us in this verse is that he talks about God's hands at all. This means he deals with God as a person or gives him human characteristics. Elsewhere in the Qur'an he talks about God sitting on the throne.[8] In the meantime Muslims are forbidden to try to imagine what God looks like. It is blasphemy for a Muslim even to start to think of God as a person, because that will lead to the yearning to have a personal relationship with him. So when it comes to this area, Muslims are very quick to quote the verse that says, "There is no one like him." Even though we could explain this in a deeper way by saying there is no one equal to God, this verse has been used more often with this understanding of forbidding the imagining of God.

Paradise and the People of the Book: Verses 65–69

These verses say that if the Christians had believed, among other things, in what God gave Muhammad, they would have been able to go to paradise. This means that the Christians took a stand and did not believe in the message of the Qur'an during Muhammad's time. Neither do they believe in the Qur'an today, because there are major contradictions between the Qur'an and the Bible.

We find a completely contradictory verse at the end of this strong stand against Christians and Jews. It implies that all Jews, followers of John the Baptist (Sabians), and Christians who believe in God, the end day, and do good will not be sad (i.e., they will make it to heaven). Yet this comes after so many verses that make it clear that Christians, Jews, and other non-Muslims will go to hell, and that they need to believe in the Qur'an to go to heaven.

When we deal with Muslims today, we need to be aware that they will respond to this paragraph in one of two ways. Muslims who believe that Christians and Jews are good and will make it to heaven will concentrate on the "friendly" verses from the Qur'an. Others will disregard this verse and sentence all non-Muslims to hell. It helps to know which we are dealing with before using this verse as a possible bridge.

Murder of Prophets: Verse 70

This can be a very nice bridge, because even though God made a covenant with the Israelites and sent them many prophets, they did not believe some and

---

8.   Sura 7:54.

killed others. We can share with Muslims that we agree with this verse and quote Jesus' words, when he said, "Woe to you, teachers of the law and Pharisees, you hypocrites! You build tombs for the prophets and decorate the graves of the righteous. And you say, 'If we had lived in the days of our forefathers, we would not have taken part with them in shedding the blood of the prophets.' So you testify against yourselves that you are the descendants of those who murdered the prophets. Fill up, then, the measure of the sin of your forefathers!'"[9]

Jesus came to fulfill the prophecies and to be the direct connection between God and man. He proved that in so many different ways even in the Qur'an: he raised the dead, made the blind see, and made the lame walk. Only God can do that. Jesus came to tell people there is no need anymore for an indirect relationship between God and man. God himself came in the form of a man. Although most of the Jews rejected Jesus, any person who believed in him would be assured of going to paradise. Jews, just like everyone else, have to accept Jesus as Savior in order to make it to heaven.

Blasphemers: Verse 72

Blasphemers are those who say God is Jesus. The verse reads similarly to that of verse 17 of this same sura, but here it is added that Jesus denies his deity and tells the people to worship God, their Lord and his Lord. If they worship Christ, they will be blasphemers. These words are very strange in comparison to what he said in the Bible. Jesus said God was his Father and our Father, but in the meantime, when people worshiped Jesus, he did not stop them.[10] All of Jesus' miracles were designed to demonstrate his deity.

Jesus told Philip: "Don't you know me, Philip, even after I have been among you such a long time? Anyone who has seen me has seen the Father. How can you say, 'Show us the Father'? Don't you believe that I am in the Father, and that the Father is in me?"[11] Jesus and the Father (God) are one. It is very important to explain this to our Muslim friend.

Trinity: Verse 73

As with calling God Jesus, Christians also are considered blasphemers for their belief in the Trinity. It is important to share here what *trinity* really

---

9. Matt. 23:29–32.
10. Matt. 14:33; 28:9, 17; John 9:38.
11. John 14:9–10.

means. It is not a numerical differentiation but a division of offices. We can address it by describing first the human personality, which is made up of three parts: body, mind, and spirit. We cannot separate one from the other, yet each has a distinct role. We do not say, "I love you from all my spirit," or "I eat food with my mind." Each is a unique part of our personality, as are the Father, Son, and Spirit in relation to the person of God. We are made in God's image.

Perhaps we can use the illustrations of water (liquid, steam, and ice), the sun (the star, rays, and heat), and the triangle. There are many things around us that have three dimensions yet are indivisible as one thing. Such illustrations may demonstrate the three-in-one idea, though they cannot fully parallel the biblical Trinity of one God in three distinct persons, which in the end is a mystery.

Jesus' Humanity: Verse 75

The Qur'an stresses the point of Jesus' humanity by referring to the fact that he and his mother both ate food. The Galileen commentary explains that if one like this "eats food," he will be similar to animals and therefore could never be God. The result of eating food is to produce urine and stool, and this shows that he is inferior and not God.[12] The Qur'an mentions all the miracles Jesus did, but it strongly denies his deity. We can bridge this by saying that there was a purpose in Jesus coming to earth and living as a man. He modeled for us the life of devotion to God and also was able, through his humanity, to identify with our weaknesses.

"Therefore, since we have a great high priest who has gone through the heavens, Jesus the Son of God, let us hold firmly to the faith we profess. For we do not have a high priest who is unable to sympathize with our weaknesses, but we have one who has been tempted in every way, just as we are—yet was without sin. Let us then approach the throne of grace with confidence, so that we may receive mercy and find grace to help us in our time of need."[13]

Jesus—Blessings not Curses: Verses 78

This verse says that David cursed the Israelites who rejected faith and that Jesus cursed those who disobeyed. We can share with our Muslim friend that even as Jesus hung on the cross, knowing full well who crucified him, he was blessing them and asking God to forgive them. He did not curse them. The only thing Jesus cursed was a fig tree.[14] He never cursed a person

---

12.   Mahali, *Tafseer al-Galileen*, 120.
13.   Heb. 4:14–16.
14.   Mark 11:14.

or anything made by man. Jesus came, knowing that mankind was already under the curse of sin and death. He came to remove the curse by becoming the curse for us.[15]

Christians Closer to Muslims than Jews: Verse 82

This verse separates Christians and Jews and categorizes Jews as the highest enemy of Muslims. Christians are viewed as the closest in the family of faith to Muslim believers. The reason Christians are closer to Muslims is because they have priests and pastors and are humble. The next verse says that when the Christians heard people quoting the Qur'an, their eyes filled with tears and they said that they believed in the almighty God and so wanted to be included with the Muslims.

Many moderate Muslims will quote this verse in order to show friendship to Christians. However, if we take a deeper look into it, we must recognize the contradiction. How can a Christian who hears the Qur'an heartily agree with a message that so sharply contradicts the Christian's own? Maybe we need to take a deeper look in order to understand why their eyes were filled with tears. We can share with our friend that perhaps it was because as believers in God, they looked at the Muslims with deep grief and cried because they knew that it is only through belief in the deity of Christ that anyone can make it to heaven.

Past Sins: Verse 93

Once a person becomes a Muslim, all previous history is eradicated. Some go as far as to use this verse to say that once a Muslim believes, he will make it to heaven. However, the verse literally means that once a person becomes a Muslim, all previous sins will be eradicated. We can build a bridge here by sharing the story of Zacchaeus.[16] When he accepted Jesus and became a believer, even though in the spiritual realm he became a new creation in Christ, he told Jesus that he would make restitution up to four times to anyone he had cheated. When we accept God through Christ, we are immediately made holy and acceptable for entering paradise. However, the process here on earth is to grow to become like Jesus in following his example.

This does not mean that we will never sin again; on the contrary, because of the continued struggle with the natural man in us, we do sin and those

---

15. Gal. 3:13.
16. Luke 19.

sins can be held against us—not for eternal damnation but for hindering our growth in Christ. We need to strive each day to live in a way that pleases God and confess to him anytime we commit a sin, knowing that he will forgive us now because of the sacrifice of Christ on the cross.

Justice and Mercy of God: Verse 98

This verse says that we should know that God is a harsh punisher, yet he is also very merciful. Here we can take the time to explain the concept of the mercy and justice of God.

Without the death of Christ on the cross, God's justice could never be satisfied and his merciful essence could not exist. The concept of mercy is the greatest obstacle in a Muslim's coming to understand the Christian concept of the forgiveness of God through Christ.

All Muslims hold to the belief that God is just and merciful. We can ask our friend how God can be just and all-merciful at the same time, and then give the illustration of the court. If the court is a court of justice, and a person comes in having committed a murder, justice demands that he be punished equal to his crime. Thus, one who has committed murder must die. That is justice. However, if it is a court of mercy, then when the man comes to the court having committed murder, the court in mercy will pardon his crime. That is mercy. Of course, this could never be the case, because our friend will admit that someone who commits a sin such as murder must be punished by God.

A Muslim may argue that small sins do not merit severe justice as something like murder does. While that is true, we must draw attention to the nature of God. God is holy (pure light), to which our Muslim friend will agree. If God is holy, then he can have nothing in his presence that is not holy. Even the smallest sin is impure in the face of God, thus it must be punished. We are held responsible for all that we do that is contrary to the nature and will of God.

So, we can ask Muslims, "How can God be both just and merciful at the same time?" (It is good to give them some time to think about this—their religion does not offer them an answer.) Share with them the verse from the Qur'an that says that if one has doubts, he should ask the people of the Book.[17] We can then say, "We are some of them. Would you like for us to offer you a solution to this dilemma? In order for God to show mercy to man

---

17.   See sura 10:94.

and allow him to stand in his presence on the Day of Judgment, the price for his sin has to be paid. Only in the cross of Christ can both the justice and the mercy of God meet.[18] Christ took upon himself the sin of mankind, allowing God to look with favor on all those who accept his sacrifice for their sin."

Oath-Taking: Verse 106

This verse talks about a person who is near death. He tells his will to two witnesses, and once these two swear in God's name, they can write or deliver his will. Jesus said we are not to swear even by our head, because we cannot change even one hair from black to white.[19] Instead, he says, "Let your 'Yes' be 'Yes,' and your 'No,' 'No.'" Even if we are at our last breath and writing our will, our words should be consistent and truthful. What a great bridge to share with Muslim friends. Many places in the Qur'an encourage them to swear on God's name. A Muslim uses God's name to make oaths in everything in his life—when he marries, when he divorces, when he kills an animal to eat, and even before war. It would be a good opportunity, every time we hear them swearing, to build the bridge about speaking the truth.

Jesus' Miracles: Verse 110

The Prophet reminds us that God supported Jesus by the Holy Spirit, and then he lists all Jesus' miracles, including some not in the Bible, such as when he made birds from clay and spoke in his infancy. There is evidence that these two nonbiblical miracles were in circulation from extrabiblical sources during Muhammad's time.[20]

Disciples: Verse 111

This verse makes all the disciples of Jesus Muslims. Here we need to share with our friend that the word *muslim*, with the qur'anic understanding as one who submits to the teachings of Muhammad in Islam, never existed before Muhammad. The disciples of Jesus lived more than six hundred years before Muhammad. Logically, they could never be Muslims, as Islam had not yet come into being. The same thing goes for Abraham and others Muhammad claims as Muslims. Of course scholars try to justify such verses by going to the actual meaning of the word, "to submit to God," but this is

---

18. Ps. 85:10.
19. Matt. 5:33–37.
20. "The Gospel of the Infancy of Jesus Christ," in the second century and "The Gospel of Thomas the Israelite." See Thomas, "Muhammad, the Qur'an, and Christian Sources."

not the way the Qur'an intended the words to be used or the implication drawn when read by Muslims around the world.

Jesus' Feeding of the Multitude: Verses 112–115

These are the only verses that relate to the title of the sura, *al-Maida*, and they refer to the miracle of Jesus' feeding the multitude. The dialogue we have here is the disciples asking Jesus to bring a tableful of food from heaven. The purpose of bringing this table from heaven is that their hearts will be at rest and that they will believe in God's power. Jesus asks God to bring the table down.

As we bridge this passage to that in the Gospels,[21] we can begin by explaining that when Jesus fed the multitude, it was not at the request of the disciples. In reality the disciples asked Jesus to have the people sent home, since there was no food to feed them. It was then that Jesus told the disciples to give them food to eat. The main purpose for the multiplication of food in Jesus' hands was to feed the hungry. Because of Jesus' compassionate heart, he did not want to send them home hungry, as they might faint on the way. The picture here is not a table coming from heaven above, as most Muslims imagine, but that Jesus very simply took the bread, gave thanks to God, and broke it, and as the people started eating, the food multiplied.

This is a great opportunity also to refer to Jesus' temptation in the wilderness, when Satan told him that if he was the Son of God, he should make bread out of the stones.[22] We know that Jesus was capable of making bread out of stones—we have seen that from this miracle. However, Jesus chose not to sin, though tempted by Satan. He does not perform miracles on a whim but for a specific purpose—to demonstrate his deity. The verses following this miracle in the Qur'an again refer to Christ denying his deity. (We notice that every time the Qur'an states a big miracle of Jesus, it is also quick to reduce him to just a mere human again.)

Trinity: Verses 116–118

It makes no sense that God would ask Jesus a question about what he had done if he really knows all things. The Trinity most Muslims think that Christians believe in consists of God, Mary, and Jesus. When the Qur'an takes a strong stand against three gods, it usually refers to these three

---

21.   Matt. 14:13–21; 15:29–38.
22.   Matt. 4:1–11.

persons. We need to take the time to explain to our friend the Trinity we believe in, which is God the Father, Jesus, and the Holy Spirit.

In verse 118, Jesus says it is up to God to punish or forgive. We can share with our friend that the Jesus we know cared greatly about his disciples, the lost, and even the people who would come to belief because of our witnessing today. Read to them some of Jesus' prayer before he went to the cross, as found in John 17.

Omniscience and Omnipotence of God: Verse 120

This is a very nice verse with which to end the sura. We can agree that God has all dominion in heaven and earth. He is powerful over all things. What a statement we can use to lead our friend to think about how God owns heaven and earth and all that is in it. He owns each and every one of us. We can compare this with a reading together of Psalm 145.

Al-An'am

Cattle

MECCAN

Overview

Tradition says that the sura *al-An'am*, or the chapter of the cattle, came to Muhammad in one setting and that when Muhammad received this sura in Mecca, it was surrounded by seventy thousand angels coming down from heaven. In general, the sura presents bits and pieces of the stories of the prophets, beginning with Abraham and how he developed the worship of one God. There is also a description of how God created living things from the dust and of how amazing the universe is. As well, this sura provides directions on what is permitted and forbidden to eat.

In the area of ethics and practical rules for living, this sura deals with several issues. The most important value in Islamic ethics is stated clearly in this sura: the worship of only one God (*Allah*). To add Jesus, the Holy Spirit, Mary, or any others to him is blasphemy. Fornication, killing a human soul, and taking an orphan's money are strictly forbidden. Muslims should be just in buying and selling, work toward justice, fulfill their oaths, and take care of parents. Also forbidden is the practice of killing girl babies while saving boys.

Cattle in the land of the Islamic revelation were very important. The word includes not only cows, but also all grazing animals, such as camels, buffalo, goats, and sheep. They were used for transportation; people built homes from their skin; they were the main source of food (meat and milk), and clothes were made from them. Thus cattle were a very important commodity. Before and after the coming of Islam, they carried the same weight of importance, leading Muhammad to share an entire sura under their name.[1] The meaning of the word *an'am* comes from *na'am* (plural), meaning "blessings." In the Arabic language it means "the grazing money."

Comments and Possible Bridges

God the Creator: Verse 1

This verse is very similar to several verses found in the Bible, such as: "The fool says in his heart, 'There is no God.'"[2] Here, the Qur'an reads that though God created the heavens and earth, darkness and light, there will be some who reject Islam and worship other gods. This is a good opportunity to create a bridge in drawing them to the biblical passage that reads,

> For since the creation of the world God's invisible qualities— his eternal power and divine nature—have been clearly seen, being understood from what has been made, so that men are without excuse. For although they knew God, they neither glorified him as God nor gave thanks to him, but their thinking became futile and their foolish hearts were darkened. Although they claimed to be wise, they became fools and exchanged the glory of the immortal God for images made to look like mortal man and birds and animals and reptiles. . . . Because of this, God gave them over to shameful lusts.[3]

The Qur'an just states that these people worship other gods. The Bible says that when one looks at creation, it is utterly foolish to say that there is no God and that all these things were created by themselves. We can then move to the subject of God's judgment.

Creation of Man: Verse 2

Here we read that God made man from clay, though it does not go into detail as to how. This verse also makes no mention of God breathing his

---

1. Abd-el-Karim, *Al-Jabour al-Tariqiya lil-Sharia al-Islamia*, 33.
2. Ps. 14:1.
3. Rom. 1:20–23, 26a.

spirit into man's nostrils. The clay cannot truly become man without a spirit, so we can share from the biblical record the details of how God created man from clay and breathed into his nostrils the breath of life from his spirit.

We can continue the story by sharing how God created both man and woman in his image. The Muslim says that a person is not complete religiously before marriage. Some Muslims may call the wife the other half, but in the teachings of the Qur'an, we cannot find this implied in any way. As we share how God made Adam and Eve in his image, we can begin to talk about the characteristics of the image of God. His "fatherly" characteristics are implied as he is the Father of all mankind. He is the one in ultimate control. He deals with all mankind in a just way. He is ultimate justice. However, we also can share that God has motherly characteristics as well. He is the loving one, full of tenderness and care. He is the provider for all needs—physical, emotional, and spiritual. He is not only the merciful one but also gentle and compassionate, which are characteristics that a mother would have toward her children.[4]

Incarnation of an Angel: Verse 9

When people doubted the Prophet's message, God says in this verse that he could have sent down an angel to give a testimony on Muhammad's behalf. An interesting point to note is that if an angel had been sent, God says he would have made him like a man and would have him dress as the people on earth. Remember, this verse was used as an answer for the doubters, who said, "If you really want us to believe Muhammad, let God bring an angel to confirm your testimony." God ends the argument by saying he did not send the angel because it would have caused them more confusion.

In the Bible, there are many appearances of angels—to Abraham, Joshua, and others. While some of the angels in the Bible stories were clearly heavenly in appearance, others were not. However, the interesting point to note here is that God is telling them that if he brought an angel, it would not be in his heavenly form but in that of a man. What a wonderful bridge and parallel we can draw to God's sending Jesus to earth. Jesus also came like a man, dressed liked us. If Jesus had come in all his heavenly glory, no one on earth could have looked at him and lived.

---

4. Biblical references could include: Deut. 32:10–11; Ps. 91:4; Isa. 49:15; 66:13; Matt. 23:37.

God Speaks Through Muhammad: Verses 11–19

Here we have a series of verses that start with the word *tell*, indicating that God is speaking to Muhammad, who then tells the people. As the Prophet speaks, God's sayings will come. It implies that God is speaking through Muhammad's tongue. This reflects the way the Qur'an was inspired—Muhammad is reciting the exact words written on the stone tablets in heaven. All the words of the Qur'an are therefore God's words. The background of these verses is not mentioned, as is often the case in the Qur'an, leading us to sometimes run into fragmented sayings; thus we have to go back to other writings like the *Hadith* or commentaries to see what is meant by certain statements.

God Does Not Need: Verse 14

This verse states that God is the one who feeds but does not eat. The best understanding of this is that God gives, but he does not take; he has no need. We can build a bridge by sharing that in Christian theology God seeks a relationship and dialogue with man out of love. As man enjoys this relationship, so does God.[5] This is a very complex concept to understand, but we can see that it is even more fully fulfilled in the incarnation of God in Christ. Though Jesus had the power as God to provide for his own needs, he chose to wait on men and women to provide for and minister to him.[6]

God Speaks to Muhammad: Verse 19

Muhammad answers the people who doubt his message. This verse says that God gave Muhammad the Qur'an "as a miracle," and this is the greatest evidence that it is from God. A good question we can ask our friend here is: How can we be sure that God has given this Qur'an to Muhammad? No one ever heard God speak to Muhammad.[7]

Qur'an, Repetition of Stories of Old: Verse 25

This verse reads that those who say that all things in the Qur'an were mentioned before are blasphemers. We can point out to our Muslim friend that if we closely examine the stories in the Qur'an, we will find that many have been previously told in the Bible, but in greater detail. We can ask him

---

5. Prov. 8:31.
6. Mark 15:41; John 4:6–7.
7. See also sura 3:7.

to share any particular story and help him to compare it to what we have in the Bible.

Veracity of the Bible: Verse 34

The apostles (prophets) before Muhammad also faced rejection. God came to their aid and gave them comfort, saying, "No one can alter (change) the words of God." If this statement is true, then how can we not have the original revelation in the Jewish and Christian Scriptures? This would be a good opportunity to remind our friend of the fact that God is capable of protecting his Word, which we have in the Bible.

God Seals the Heart: Verse 46

This unique verse contains a very prolific expression: "God . . . sealed up your hearts." This phrase is used here to illustrate the point that if God were to make you blind and deaf and seal your heart, what other god could help you? What a difference in the way we use the same expression in Christianity: God puts his seal on man's heart upon acceptance of Jesus as Savior. His seal is the Holy Spirit, who is a guarantee of our faith. We can draw a great comparison by sharing that God's seal is not to make us blind and deaf but to make us blind and deaf to sin and to be able to live completely for him.[8]

Justice and Mercy of God: Verse 54

God says that if someone comes to Muhammad, and says, "Peace be on you," this means he is coming to Islam. Even if he is a sinner, God will forgive him immediately when he asks for forgiveness. From this verse, we need to refer again to the mercy and justice of God. Even if God does forgive him, how can we account for God's justice in relation to the sins prior to forgiveness?[9]

Keys of the Unknown: Verses 59–60

This verse talks about the omniscience of God, saying that he has the keys of the unseen and unknown. We can build a bridge here by sharing about the keys given to Peter by Christ. "Simon Peter answered, 'You are the Christ, the Son of the living God.' Jesus replied, 'Blessed are you, Simon son of Jonah, for this was not revealed to you by man, but by my Father in

---

8.   See 2 Cor. 1:22 and Eph. 1:13.
9.   See sura 5:98.

heaven. And I tell you that you are Peter, and on this rock I will build my church, and the gates of Hades will not overcome it. I will give you the keys of the kingdom of heaven; whatever you bind on earth will be bound in heaven, and whatever you loose on earth will be loosed in heaven.'"[10]

The keys given to Peter were truly unknown prior to the coming of Christ; they were the great mystery kept until the appointed time.[11] That mystery is that Christ is the Son of the living God. Now through Christ's coming, we can share in that which was previously unknown. Also, through the gifts of the Holy Spirit, God also allows many Christians to have the gift of knowledge, which enables them to share with lost people things that no one could know except through God's revelation. God remains ultimate in knowledge, but as believers in Christ, we are blessed in having received understanding of what many are yet to know.

God Saves from Land and Sea: Verse 63

This verse reminds us that God is mighty and is the one who saves us from catastrophes at sea. We can build a nice bridge here by sharing the story of Jonah.

Satan's Effect upon Muhammad: Verse 68

In this verse God is discouraging Muhammad from getting drawn into debates with the blasphemers who speak against the Qur'an. He adds, however, that if Satan ever makes him forget and he starts arguing with them, once he comes back to his senses, he should then leave the council of the blasphemers. This verse provides us with insight into Satan's effect on Muhammad. He can make the Prophet forget or do something against God's will. We can build a bridge by contrasting Muhammad's weakness in temptation with Jesus' strength in facing Satan in the wilderness.[12]

Intercessor: Verse 70

In this verse God is telling the followers to leave blasphemers alone. Muslims are to proclaim to nonbelievers what awaits them on the end day if they do not believe, for no one will intercede for them. God is the only intercessor. We can ask our Muslim friend how God can intercede with

---

10. Matt. 16:16–19.
11. Eph. 3; Col. 2.
12. Matt. 4:1–11; Heb. 4:15.

himself? An intercessor is one who stands between two parties and speaks or prays on behalf of one to the other. Who would God be interceding to? The Bible says: "For there is one God and one mediator between God and men, the man Christ Jesus."[13] The only intercessor between man and God is Jesus.

End Day: Verse 73

This verse gives a very limited explanation for the end day, but it does say that the trumpet will be blown. We do not know who will blow the trumpet or how or when. This would be a good opportunity to talk about what the blowing of the trumpet means for Christians.[14] In talking about the end day, we can turn to the last three chapters of the book of Revelation for a very vivid picture of what is to come.

Abraham: Verses 74–79

We find here an explanation of Abraham's experience of knowing God. Abraham saw his father worshiping idols and questioned this practice, thus God showed him the kingdom of heaven and earth. The Qur'an uses a very Christian term, *kingdom of heaven*, but adds to it the term *earth*. After God revealed this to Abraham, the night came, and he saw the stars and said, "This is my Lord." Then, when the moon appeared, brighter and bigger than the stars, Abraham proclaimed, "This is my Lord." Yet, when the moon disappeared, he said, "Woe to me, this cannot be God." Again, when Abraham saw the rising sun, he said, "This is my Lord." When the sun went down, he said, "Woe to me, this cannot be my God." Finally, when he realized that the creation was weak, he turned his face toward God.

There are many things we could discuss in relation to this story, but perhaps it is best to share the complete story of the call of Abraham in the Bible, showing how God spoke to Abraham to draw him to himself. Abraham did not find God; God found Abraham.

Prophets: Verses 84–86

We find here a list of prophets. Some names are changed from the Hebrew into an Islamic form of Arabic, while others are the same as found in the Arabic version of the Bible. The chronological listing is not accurate. For example, verse 85 speaks of *Zakariya*, John, Jesus, and *Elias* (Elijah). In

---

13.   1 Tim. 2:5.
14.   1 Cor. 15:52; 1 Thess. 4:16.

going over this list with our friends, we can take the time to put them into proper order and share their stories.

God, Giver of Life and Death: Verse 95

We can bridge here to the Muslim mind by sharing something from Samson's life, when he gave his riddle, "Out of the eater, something to eat; out of the strong, something sweet."[15] Jesus brought many dead people to life, which shows his divinity, since only God can bring life from death. Also, we know that a fig tree died immediately upon the word of Christ.[16] When Jesus comes back, a sword will come from his mouth. He will be the Judge, passing the sentence of life or death on each soul, according to what each person has done in his life. If he accepted Christ as Savior, he will gain eternal life; if he has rejected Christ, he will be condemned to eternal destruction.

Stars to Guide Us: Verse 97

God made the stars in order to serve as our guide on land and sea. We can compare this with the following verses in the Bible in leading a Muslim to a greater understanding of creation: "And God said, 'Let there be lights in the expanse of the sky to separate the day from the night, and let them serve as signs to mark seasons and days and years, and let them be lights in the expanse of the sky to give light on the earth' . . . God made two great lights. . . . He also made the stars. God set them in the expanse of the sky to give light on the earth, to govern the day and the night, and to separate light from darkness."[17]

Jinn: Verse 100

This is the first mention of jinn, and it says God created them. God is blaming the blasphemers, Christians and Arabs, for saying that God has sons and daughters. All commentators blame the Christians for saying God has sons and the Arabs for saying he has daughters. We need to share with our Muslim friend that God did not create jinn, whom we understand to be evil spirits. Most Muslims, however, think that jinn are serving spirits, and there is a great deal of confusion between the seraphim and the jinn, who were made out of flames in order to serve God. They also served King Solomon.

---

15. Judg. 14:14.
16. Matt. 21:19–20.
17. Gen. 1:14–18.

As for the sons and daughters, we can share that when a person accepts Jesus as Savior and is born again, that person is adopted into God's family. We are not the physical sons and daughters of God, but we are his spiritually.

Son of God: Verse 101

The Qur'an asks, "How can this great Creator have a physical son? He has never had a companion." However, we find that the Qur'an sometimes calls Abraham "the companion" of God. We can share that God loves to have fellowship with man, because man is the only one created in his image and with free will. When we come to God on our own to love him, that makes him very happy, for this is the kind of relationship he seeks.

Understanding God: Verse 103

Even though we cannot see God, as this verse says, we can still have a relationship with him. Though the Qur'an says God is above all comprehension, we can share that he provides us many ways to know and understand him.

God's Lack of Responsibility for Man: Verse 107

Though God is in total control of man's destiny, he is telling Muhammad here that he is not responsible for men when they choose wrong; neither is he the judge of their deeds. We will want to share that Jesus is responsible for his people. He is so responsible that he died for them. Jesus said, "For I have come down from heaven not to do my will but to do the will of him who sent me. And this is the will of him who sent me, that I shall lose none of all that he has given me, but raise them up at the last day. For my Father's will is that everyone who looks to the Son and believes in him shall have eternal life, and I will raise him up at the last day."[18]

Testimony of the Angels and Dead: Verse 111

God says that even if he did send angels and the dead to speak on Muhammad's behalf, many people still would not believe. We can make a parallel to the story Jesus told of the rich man and Lazarus.[19] Jesus said that even if someone rose from the dead, the rich man's brothers would not believe. It is good to draw the story from here to share that we do have an

---

18.   John 6:38–40.
19.   Luke 16.

actual example of one rising from the dead—Jesus. We can then ask, "What is hindering your belief in him?"

Veracity of the Bible: Verse 115

The Qur'an states that no one can change God's Word. Most arguments with Muslims will center on the veracity of the Bible. This verse could be used as proof from the Qur'an itself that if no one can change God's Word, which here refers to the Qur'an, then this has to be true for the Bible too, or God would be unjust or weak.

Hell: Verse 128

Hell is real and is made for blasphemers and jinn. It is eternal. We can agree, as Christians, that it is real and eternal and share some of the biblical passages regarding hell.

Jinn: Verse 130

The Qur'an reads that God sent messengers to man and jinn (fallen angels). It will be helpful to bring our friend's attention to the fact that God sent messengers (prophets) only to mankind, not to fallen angels. Fallen angels already were condemned to hell before Adam came into the picture; thus there was no need for their redemption.

Human Sacrifice: Verse 137

We can compare this verse to the sad statement in the Old Testament about the Israelites sacrificing their children to Molech. "They built high places for Baal in the Valley of Ben Hinnom to sacrifice their sons and daughters to Molech, though I never commanded, nor did it enter my mind, that they should do such a detestable thing and so make Judah sin."[20] Even today in various places in the world, there are people who practice human sacrifice. Through Christ we must take a stand against such an evil practice.

Cattle and Food Restrictions: Verse 146

The last verses of the sura provide more information about cattle (from which comes the sura's name) and regulations for food. Verse 146 is a unique verse, as Muhammad is explaining the food restrictions God placed upon the Jews in the Old Testament. There are certain animals they cannot eat at

---

20. Jer. 32:35.

all, and others of which they cannot eat their fat, except for the fat on the back of the animal around the intestines.

Muhammad says God gave these restrictions to the Jews as punishment for their embezzlement (taking something by force that did not belong to them). We need to explain that this was not God's punishment for the Jews but that it was for the well-being of their bodies and to set them apart as a people. Today we understand even more that animal fat is not good for one's health.

However, Muhammad was speaking of Old Testament restrictions. We need to bridge between the Old and New Testaments by noting that the New Testament says the word of the Law kills[21] and by then sharing what happened to Peter when he had the vision of the clean and unclean foods prior to the visit from those sent by Cornelius.[22] It is not what we eat that makes us unholy but what comes from our hearts.

God's Indifference: Verse 149

This verse says that if God so desires, he can lead everyone onto the right path, but he does not want to. We can share here the verse that says God wants all people to be saved.[23] He desires all people to know him personally and has made the way possible through Christ.

Individual Responsibility: Verse 164

The main core of this verse is that every soul is responsible for itself and no one can take on anyone else's sins. This verse seems to be protesting the fact that Jesus takes our sins away. Many places in the Qur'an stress that every soul is responsible for itself or for its own sins and that no one can redeem another. This is a great opportunity to share the fact that man cannot even redeem himself from his own sins. He needs a redeemer. We can forgive another, we can pay a penalty for someone else, and we can even save a human body by offering our own. However, we cannot save a human soul by our own soul, because we do not own our own soul—God gives it to us. Jesus, however, is owner of his soul, and he is the only one who can redeem a human soul. In the Qur'an the concept of redemption is nonexistent. Using a verse like this can build a bridge in helping Muslims understand the concept of redemption.[24]

---

21.   2 Cor. 3:6.
22.   Acts 10.
23.   1 Tim. 2:3–4.
24.   See Rom. 3:21–26; Eph. 1:3–10; Heb. 9:11–14.

Al-A'raf

The Heights

MECCAN

Overview

The beginning of this sura is an extension of the previous sura, *al-An'am*, as it discusses the beginning of mankind, including the creation of Adam and his ejection from Paradise. Some of Satan's temptations of man are mentioned in this sura, as are various stories of prophets, including Noah, Lot, and Pharaoh. As in the previous sura, some prophets are referred to by an Islamic name, while the names of famous prophets such as Abraham, Noah, Moses, and David are the same as in the Arabic Bible. Though Jesus is a famous prophet, his Islamic name is used (*'Isa*, instead of the biblical *Yesua*).[1] *Al-A'raf* also includes a description of Muslims who have become apostate by the delusion of Satan.

Comments and Possible Bridges

Mystical Letters: Verse 1

This verse begins with the letters *aleph, lam, meem, saad*, and like all the other suras with a similar beginning, there is no clear meaning. Commentators have numerous opinions as to what they really mean.

---

1. See appendix B for a list of biblical names found in the Qur'an.

Muhammad, Ashamed to Proclaim: Verse 2

The sura begins with God telling Muhammad not to be ashamed when giving the Qur'an to the people. The words are for warning nonbelievers and encouraging believers. This is a very good point on which we can draw a bridge. When God gave his word to the prophets in the Old Testament, he told them many things, such as these words spoken to the prophet Jeremiah: "You must go to everyone I send you to and say whatever I command you. Do not be afraid of them, for I am with you and will rescue you,"[2] and, "Go and proclaim in the hearing of Jerusalem."[3] But never did he tell any prophet of the Old Testament, "Do not be ashamed of my word." God's Word never makes us ashamed. All revelation in Islam came through one person, so for him to be ashamed to share it is a problem. In the Bible God's revelation is given through many; and even though at times it suggests some were *shy* about proclaiming the revelation, this does not carry the same implication of being ashamed of what one has received.

Sodom and Gomorrah: Verse 4

This verse asks the rhetorical question of how many villages were destroyed while the inhabitants were sleeping. It is referring to Sodom and Gomorrah, but neither the details nor the names are given. We can ask our friend, "Would you like to know the rest of the story about Sodom and Gomorrah and why God's wrath came upon them?" This provides a good bridge to talk about sin and sin's consequences, among other issues.

Omniscience and Omnipotence of God: Verse 7

God says in this verse that he knows all, for he was never absent. We can agree with our Muslim friend about the omnipresence of God and share parallel verses from the Bible.

Day of Judgment: Verses 8–9

Here we have a glimpse of what is going to happen on the Day of Judgment—the works of each person will be put on the scale. If one's good deeds are great enough, he will make it to heaven. We can share with our Muslim friend that the allegorical scale was mentioned in the Bible centuries earlier, when Isaiah said, "Surely the nations are like a drop in a bucket; they

---

2.   Jer. 1:7–8.
3.   Jer. 2:2.

are regarded as dust on the scales; he weighs the islands as though they were fine dust."[4] In saying this we can then bring them to the ultimate scale or measure of our worth before God, when Jesus said, "Anyone who says, 'You fool!' will be in danger of the fire of hell."[5] According to the Islamic scale, one atom over 50 percent makes the difference between heaven and hell, as good deeds are weighed against the bad. However, on the Jesus scale, one atom over zero will keep a soul from eternity in heaven. One sin will keep us from the presence of God, because a holy God cannot be in the presence of sin. This will lead us to share about the need for a Redeemer.

Origin of Evil: Verse 11

We will discuss the creation of Adam in another place,[6] but here we need to consider the origin of evil in Islam. In the Qur'an the origin of evil comes after the creation of man, not before. This verse tells us that God asked all the angels to bow down and worship Adam. All the angels fell down and worshiped Adam except *Iblis* (Satan); therefore, God cast Satan down.[7] Here a good bridge could be drawn with this question: Would God really ask angels to worship man? Bowing down in worship is intended only for God. We can share that throughout the entire Bible when man was worshiped and not God, the result was destruction and wars. During the great temptation in the wilderness, Jesus told Satan, "Away from me, Satan! For it is written: 'Worship the Lord your God, and serve him only.'"[8]

Satan's Purpose: Verse 16

Satan says to God, "Since you tempted me, then I will be watching and doing my best to get mankind out of your way." Here we can share the biblical story of Satan's fall. While we can agree with Muslims that Satan is active in leading mankind to turn from God, we cannot agree with how Satan became the epitome of evil. God did not tempt Satan; rather, Satan himself began to look around at all the angels and creation. He was the first among the creation

---

4. Isa. 40:15.
5. Matt. 5:22.
6. See sura 15:26–44.
7. Note: The reason Satan gave for not worshiping Adam was that Satan was created from fire, which is superior to the material Adam was created from, which was clay.
8. Matt. 4:10.

and the greatest angel. And he started thinking, "I'm even better than God." This was the first evil pulse in God's creation. God himself had nothing to do with the Morning Star's thoughts, because when God created the Morning Star, he was perfect as was all God's creation.[9] It is important to note that the fall of Satan occurred before the creation of Adam, not after.

Hell: Verse 18

God speaks to Satan, saying that he will fill hell with him and all his followers from mankind. We can share with our friend that hell was made the moment Satan was cast from heaven. Hell was not made for mankind but for Satan and the angels who followed him. The addition of humans to the population of hell would come later, when Adam sinned and opened the way for all mankind to be infested with sin. The sentence was passed on Satan first—a long time before Adam came into the picture.

Fall of Man: Verses 19–25

These verses contain the story of man's fall. God tells Adam and Eve not to touch the tree. It is very important to notice that here it is not the Tree of the Knowledge of Good and Evil but the Tree of Immortality. Many discussions and bridges could be drawn right there. When mankind was begun with the creation of Adam, God blew his spirit into him, and thus Adam was already immortal. Therefore the forbidden tree for Adam and Eve was that of the knowledge of good and evil, not immortality. There was another tree in the garden, however, called the Tree of Life—this was not the immortality tree. If someone ate from this tree, apparently that person would stay in the same status without change. God stopped Adam and Eve from eating from this tree after they sinned because he had a plan for them for salvation. They needed to die physically in order to be raised again spiritually into a new, perfect form.

According to the Qur'an, the reason Adam and Eve ate from the tree is because Satan tempted them to eat from it. While we can agree with this, we have disagreement over Satan's purpose for leading them into sin. His main purpose, as understood by Muslims, was to show their nakedness. We need to share with our beloved friend here that the main purpose for Satan was not to show their nakedness but to get them out of Paradise, as verse 16 mentions. Satan did not even know they were naked, because for an angel

---

9.   Isa. 14:12–15; Ezek. 28:11–19.

this would have no bad meaning. It was not shameful. We can share that if we go to the Bible for the real story, all the parts of the story will make more sense. First, Satan tempted Adam and Eve to eat from the Tree of the Knowledge of Good and Evil, and when they ate, because it was the Tree of Knowledge, they realized that they were naked. The shame was not so much because of their nakedness as it was because they had become sinful beings in comparison to the Holy God. They felt shame before God.

Once Adam and Eve discovered their shame, according to the Qur'an, they began to pile over themselves the leaves of the garden; and at the same time God called them and told them, "Didn't I tell you not to eat from the tree? Didn't I tell you that Satan is your enemy?" A great parallel can be made here with the biblical account. After they ate from the tree, God did not come immediately, though we know he would have known exactly what happened. He gave them some time to consider their deed. He came in the perfect cool of the day and took his time to restore the relationship. First, he called them: "Where are you, Adam?" And we can hear in the dialogue between God and Adam, a loving Creator trying to reach out to a sinful, hiding humanity. It is very important also to take time here to say that when God asked, "Where are you?" it was not because he did not know where Adam was but because he was trying to restore the relationship by getting Adam to confess his sin. We can see God using this same method in many places in the Bible, such as Nathan's visit to King David, Saul on the road to Damascus, Ananias and Sapphira, and Peter after his renunciation of Jesus.

In verse 23 in the qur'anic story, Adam and Eve ask God's forgiveness, and he casts them out of the garden. Then in verse 25, he says, "On earth you will live, die, and from it be resurrected." We can agree with this reminder that man's soul lasts forever. Though sin leads to certain death, we can have hope in an eternal life, but must of course make a choice in order to spend that eternity in heaven and not hell.

Dress of Righteousness: Verse 26

This is a very important verse, as God tells Adam and Eve, "We give you dresses to cover your shamefulness and feathers and the dress of righteousness." A beautiful bridge can be built from the phrase, "dress of righteousness." Our Muslim friend needs to understand what this means. We can take him to the parable of the prodigal son and share how the father covered his wayward son with a costly robe, accepting him back home without question.[10] We can relate this as well to the words of Isaiah about the robe of righteousness.[11]

Second, we need to notice that it was never mentioned here that God ever covered them with garments made out of leather, as recorded in the biblical account.[12] The issue of sacrifice is not mentioned in the qur'anic account of the fall, so it is important to share with our friend that as a result of man's sin, blood had to be shed—a sacrifice made—for his shame to be covered. However, the cover (clothes) given him was a temporary or outward fix, and an even greater sacrifice would be required to cover the shame of sin in man's soul. This will lead us to share about the necessity of the coming of Christ.

Eye of the Needle: Verse 40

This verse declares that those who do not believe Muhammad's verses will never enter heaven until a camel can pass through the eye of a needle. This analogy is given in reference to the impossibility of either a criminal or an unbeliever entering the kingdom of God.

Jesus used the same allegory in a completely different setting. When a wealthy man turned away from following him, Jesus said to his disciples, "I tell you the truth, it is hard for a rich man to enter the kingdom of heaven. Again I tell you, it is easier for a camel to go through the eye of a needle than for a rich man to enter the kingdom of God."[13] However, this was not the end of the discussion. "When the disciples heard this, they were greatly astonished and asked, 'Who then can be saved?' Jesus looked at them and said, 'With man this is impossible, but with God all things are possible.'"[14]

We understand from this that though it is impossible for us to imagine a camel going through the eye of a needle, the amazing grace of God can go beyond the impossible and make a way for a sinner to enter the kingdom of God. We can then share how God made the way for the impossible to happen through Christ.

Great Gulf Between Heaven and Hell: Verse 50

In reading this verse, we find a great point for reaching Muslims, for the verse tells us that the people in hell will ask the people of paradise to give them

---

10.   Luke 15:11–31.
11.   Isa. 61:10.
12.   Gen. 3:21.
13.   Matt. 19:23–24.
14.   Matt. 19:25–26.

some water or anything God has given them. The dwellers of heaven will answer by saying that God forbids it for the blasphemers. We can share with our Muslim friend the parable Jesus told about the rich man and Lazarus.[15] This story gives us an idea of what will happen in heaven. When the rich man calls on Father Abraham and asks a little comfort from Lazarus, Abraham replies that there is a great gulf between the two places, and thus no crossing from one to the other can occur. While Jesus' story was an allegory used to illustrate the fact that the ultimate destiny of a person is determined in this life, not beyond it; in this sura, we see that a connection between the two places is implied by the people of hell being able to communicate with those in heaven. Returning to the more important conclusion, the biblical story says that the rich man asked Abraham to send one from the dead to go to his family, that they might avoid his destiny. Abraham told him that they had the prophets, meaning they had all it takes in order to make their own decision.

The main theme of this parable is that man's final destination will be determined before he dies based on his own decision. Nothing can change his destination after death. A relationship between hell and God's kingdom is impossible. Inhabitants of neither place can talk to each other or cross to each other. We need to encourage our Muslim friend to make a decision now before it is too late.

Human Characteristics of God: Verse 54

We can notice two things in relationship to this verse. First, God created the universe in six days. Many places in the Qur'an mention six days, but some other places mention a different number of days for Creation.[16] We need to share with our friend that God made his creation in six days, and on the seventh he rested. The Qur'an says here he created it in six days and then sat on his throne, but it does not mention when.

Second, we can point out the part of the verse that says that God sat on the throne. When we ask our friend, "What does God look like?" he will be quick to say that there is no one like him. We need to understand that when a Muslim makes such a statement, he has in mind that God is so mighty and so great that we cannot compare him with anyone. In reality, a Muslim is forbidden to even imagine what God looks like. A verse like this and some others we will mention later can be used to challenge his mind to start to

---

15.   Luke 16:19–31.

16.   Sura 41:9–12.

consider and think about how God looks. If God has a throne and sits on it after the Creation, was he standing before he sat down? Was he tired and needed to sit? We know these are hypothetical questions for Christians, but for a Muslim it will bring the reality to him in a shocking manner. Some other places in the Qur'an mention the mighty arm of God. Does this imply he has a body? How does his body look? Maybe only in the incarnation of Christ can we even fathom the arm of God and sitting and being tired. When the Qur'an says, "He is the one who does not sleep," does that mean he is watching all the time? If we succeed in getting a Muslim to even start to think on such questions, it is the first step toward his salvation.

Lot: Verses 80–84

We read in this passage the story of Lot in a very condensed form. He was sent as a prophet to his people to call them to leave their sinful practices of homosexuality, but they rejected his message. In verse 82, it says that the village refused, and they cast Lot out. However, the plural is used in referring to Lot, leaving a question in the mind of the reader as to who was with him. The Qur'an gives no indication who was with Lot but says they were pure. The next verse reads, "But we saved him and his people, except his wife." In verse 84, the literal words say, "We rained over them a rain and watched what happened to the criminals."

It is important for us to put this story into perspective for our Muslim friend. We need to share here that, in the first place, Lot chose to live among these people when he left Abraham. To the best of our knowledge, he did not try to change them. He was suffering as he lived among them, but we have no record that he was preaching morality to the people. When he asked the people of the city to leave his guests (angels, or messengers of God) alone, they did not respect Lot; they did not remember that at one time his uncle, Abraham, saved their king and city from King Kedorlaomer.[17] No, they wanted to attack his house. We can share the full story from the Old Testament—how God saved Lot and his daughters and why his wife became a pillar of salt.[18] All these details are not given in the qur'anic version but will interest a Muslim.

It is very important to note, however, that the Qur'an does not tell about any of the sins of the prophets. It makes them look almost perfect. This is a good place to share about the many faults Lot had, for example, arguing with

17.   Gen. 14.
18.   Gen. 13–19.

Abraham over the sheep and land; choosing to live among sinful people, offering his daughters in order to protect his guests, not trusting God's protection, and, of course, sleeping with his girls, causing great grief for the whole nation of Israel in creating the Moabite and Ammonite races. The point in sharing Lot's weaknesses is to reveal that as much as we see his sins, by so much do we appreciate God's grace.

Moses: Verses 102–129

In this passage, we can read about Moses going before Pharaoh to ask him to release the enslaved Hebrew people. The story centers on the miracle of Moses' staff becoming a serpent and swallowing the magicians' snakes. As a result of this, the Qur'an says in verse 120 that the magicians bowed down before Moses and said, "We believe in the Lord . . . of Moses and Aaron." Pharaoh became angry, telling the magicians, "How did you believe in him before I gave my permission?" Then he threatened to cut off their right hands and left legs and crucify them all. The problem with this statement is that there is no record of the use of crucifixion during this time. The first to use crucifixion were the Persians around the seventh century BC. In sharing the biblical account of this story, we can point out to our friend that there is no indication that Pharaoh's magicians ever accepted the God of Moses.[19]

Plagues: Verses 130–135

As we read about the plagues God sent upon Egypt, we find two of the plagues mentioned in the Qur'an are not in the Bible—the flood and lice. And only five plagues are included in the Qur'an, not the ten recorded in the Bible. This is a good opportunity to share about the plagues from the book of Exodus.[20] One plague mentioned in the Qur'an is the blood, but no details are given. As we share about the blood, we can focus on the issue of blood in general, moving to the blood of the firstborn and then to the blood the Hebrews had to put on the two sides and mantel of their doors. This can lead to the deeper meaning of the requirement of blood for redemption.

Moses: Verses 136–150

The crossing of the sea is mentioned, though briefly, in the Qur'an. Once the children of Israel arrived on the other side of the sea, it says they came

19.   Exod. 7:8–13.
20.   Exod. 7–12.

to another nation, which had idols.[21] The people asked Moses to give them an idol, and he replied that they were an ignorant people. We can use this to talk about the weaknesses in the Hebrews while emphasizing God's patience for his name's sake.

In verses 142–145, we see the story of the giving of the Ten Commandments. Though the Qur'an mentions that God gave tablets to Moses, we are not told what was written on them. We, however, can tell our Muslim friend what was written on these tablets.

The record of the golden calf is given in verses 148–150. When Moses caught his brother, seizing him by the head and dragging him, Aaron said the people pushed him to do it. The Qur'an says Moses then threw the tablets; it does not mention, however, that they were broken. We can share with them the rest of the story.[22]

Muhammad in the Bible: Verse 157

This is one of the most crucial verses in the entire Qur'an, for from it has come the whole Muslim theory that the Bible is not true.[23] First, God talks about the people who follow the unlettered (*ommi*) Prophet, meaning either that the Prophet could neither read nor write or that he was from the nations (i.e., not Jewish). Many non-Muslim scholars agree that Muhammad could at least read. The Qur'an says the people who follow the *ommi* Prophet will find things written about him in their own books (*Tawrat* and *Injil*).

We need to be very firm with our friend in explaining that the Bible never mentions or even remotely refers to Muhammad as a prophet coming from God. In reality, the Bible tells us that after Jesus, we should be aware, because false prophets will come. By the end of the book of Revelation, all God's Word for mankind was complete, and the work of redemption had already been completed on the cross, when Jesus said, "It is finished."

Some Muslim scholars look to some verses in the Bible that speak about the Holy Spirit, who will come after Jesus' ascension, as referring to Muhammad, the Prophet of Islam. We can take our friend to the Bible and point out the great difference between the person of the Holy Spirit and the person of Muhammad, the Prophet of Islam.

---

21.   Sura 7:138.
22.   Exod. 19–34.
23.   Also in sura *al-i-'Imran* 3:50.

Wilderness Wanderings: Verse 160

This verse mentions that Moses struck a stone, producing twelve springs of water for the people. God also gave them manna and quail for food. The verse indicates that the Israelites struggled in the wilderness, yet without clarity as to the real situation. We can therefore share with our friend why they had to stay so long in the wilderness as we read the biblical account together.

Mountain Miracle: Verse 171

This verse records a miracle not mentioned in the Bible, as God tells the people to remember the many miracles he did for them and how he took the mountain and put it over their heads like a cloud. This is not described here allegorically, but as a true miracle. While the Bible does not speak of any such miracle, we do know that in many places God brought a cloud to provide shade or protection, either literally or allegorically.[24]

Dog as Example of a Sinner: Verse 176

God gives a comparison between a person who follows his own desires and that of a dog. If you chase a dog and he runs, he pants with his tongue hanging out. Even if you leave him alone, he still pants the same way. We can draw the parallel here with an example of a dog found in the Bible. The dog is compared to the sinner, who after hearing the truth, returns to his wicked ways. The sinner is like a dog that returns to his vomit.[25]

Eyes Blinded, Hearts Hardened, Ears Deaf: Verse 179

This verse is talking about jinn and men who are destined to hell. It uses the phrase "They have hearts which do not understand, eyes that do not see, and ears that do not hear." We have a similar saying in the Bible, when Jesus spoke to his disciples.

The disciples came to him and asked, "Why do you speak to the people in parables?"

> He replied, "The knowledge of the secrets of the kingdom of heaven has been given to you, but not to them. Whoever has will be given more, and he will have an abundance. Whoever does not have, even what he has will be taken

---

24. Exod. 13:21; 14:19; 40:36–38; Isa. 4:5.
25. 2 Peter 2:22.

from him. This is why I speak to them in parables: 'Though seeing, they do not see; though hearing, they do not hear or understand.' In them is fulfilled the prophecy of Isaiah: 'You will be ever hearing but never understanding; you will be ever seeing but never perceiving. For this people's heart has become calloused; they hardly hear with their ears, and they have closed their eyes. Otherwise they might see with their eyes, hear with their ears, understand with their hearts and turn, and I would heal them.'"[26]

It is important in making such a comparison that we make it clear that man still has a choice in his eternal destiny. Because some chose to refuse the message of Christ, he continued to share the truths of the kingdom in public but in such a way (parables) that those who rejected him would no longer understand. Those who were open to his message, however, were able to gain insights into his purpose and kingdom even through the stories.

Names of God: Verse 180

Mention is given here to the beautiful names of God. While a list of all the ninety-nine names of God is never given in the Qur'an, they are produced from various statements about him in the book. The names of God for a Muslim are not God, but they help the Muslim to know the characteristics of God. We can agree with some of the names and disagree with others.[27]

Predestination: Verse 186

Islam is very strong on predestination. We find this in many different places. The first part of this verse reads literally: "Whosoever God misleads, he will never be saved." The verb "misleads" refers directly to God, as if God intentionally brings a human to life and then misleads him. We need to emphasize the free choice all mankind has, which even goes to the extent that God might change his mind in response to man's choice. God is dynamic, not static in his will.

Creation of Man: Verse 189

The first part of this verse states that God created all mankind from one breath or spirit and made from it his companion (wife). The great question we

---

26.   Matt. 13:10–15.
27.   Geisler and Saleeb, *Answering Islam*, 23–28.

need to discuss with our Muslim friend is, Whose spirit is all mankind made from? Is it the spirit of God or another spirit? Here we can share that God breathed into Adam's nostrils, and then out of Adam's rib, he made Eve. The important point is to realize that the spirits of all mankind come from God.

Temptations: Verse 200

This verse says that if Satan whispers something to us, we should seek refuge from God. A *hadith* records that the Prophet told his wife Aisha that he was troubled because of a spell a Jew had cast on him. After being bothered by the influence of the spell for several days, the following verse came to him.[28] Here we can talk about Satan's influence on mankind in general and then on those who profess Christ as Savior.

Prayer: Verse 205

At the end of this sura, we find an unusual verse for a Muslim. It says, "Remember your God in your own spirit humbly, in secret (or quietly)." This stands in opposition to what we find with the Muslim prayers today. Muslims stand on every corner or in the street of the mosque praying to God in a very loud and obvious way. We need to remind our Muslim friend here of the words of Jesus to his disciples: "But when you pray, go into your room, close the door and pray to your Father, who is unseen. Then your Father, who sees what is done in secret, will reward you."[29] Talk to your friend about the closet prayer and how when we give with the right hand, the left should not know what the right had does. This is a great bridge.

---

28. Gabriel, *Jesus and Muhammad*, 104.
29. Matt. 6:6.

Al-Anfal

Spoils of War

AFTER BATTLE OF BADR

Overview

Sura *al-Anfal* centers on the battle of Badr, which was fought on Friday, the seventeenth of Ramadan, in the second year of the *hijra*. It is seen as a great victory for Islam, as Muhammad's followers defeated the Meccan pagans, even though Muhammad's army was much smaller. Because Muhammad wanted his followers to understand why he left Mecca and needed to wage war, the content of this sura focuses primarily on the reasons for and laws of war. It gives Muslims directions for waging and winning war. It instructs them on how to deal with the profits of war and how to deal with captives. In order to fulfill the greater purpose of Islam, justification is given for migration from a place where they are persecuted to another land, allowing Islam to spread all over the world. The final target for Islam is to bring the whole world into the Muslim nation, using all power and means possible. In Islam the purpose justifies the means.

As we work through the beginning of the sura, we need to remember that God did allow war in the Old Testament for very important reasons. Humanity was in its infancy. People groups fought one another in a savage way, as sin spread from the time of the fall. As with Sodom and Gomorrah, God sometimes moved to wipe out an entire city because of the inhabitants' sinful nature and to keep evil in check. In settling the people of Israel into the Promised Land, God allowed wars to be fought in order to cleanse the land from sin and provide a place where those called his could make a fresh start as a nation devoted to God. However, sin is never completely wiped out, and Israel failed in their devotion to God's laws. As humanity developed and civilizations grew, God's prophets made it very clear that his ultimate purpose centered in the coming of Christ. War could not eradicate sin; only a change of heart in the depth of each person could give victory over sin. Jesus told his followers to refrain from fighting,[1] and the New Testament says that wars begin because of the lust and jealousy in man's heart.[2] We still live in a fallen world, controlled by sin, but we find far fewer wars and inner strife in Christian societies than we do in Muslim ones.

Comments and Possible Bridges

Spoils of War: Verse 1

This sura begins with God telling the Prophet what to say in response to people's questions regarding the spoils of the war. The answer is that spoils are at the disposal of God and his Prophet.[3] The Prophet will get the best share first, then whatever is left is to be distributed among those who participated in the battle. We will see this happen on several occasions following battles. Sometimes the Prophet's spoils would include certain horses or women he liked and took as part of his initial percentage.

Fighting over Spoils of War: Verse 9

When the believers started to fight over the spoils of the war, God reminded them through this verse that he sent thousands of angels to help them win this war. We can bridge this to the ways in which God helped the children of Israel at times of war in the Old Testament. (For example, God caused the sun to stand still and sent huge hailstones to help Joshua[4] and terrified the Midianites with just the jars and torches of Gideon's men.[5]) Yet we will want to move from this topic to that of the purpose and outcome of the battles. We also can share about the times God told the children of Israel to destroy all the spoils, leaving nothing to tempt them or cause division.

---

1. Matt. 26:50–56; John 18:36.
2. James 4:1.
3. See verse 41 as to the percentage received by Muhammad.
4. Josh. 10.
5. Judg. 7.

The story of Achan from Joshua 7 is excellent in illustrating the seriousness with which God took the matter of obedience to his word on spoils. We need to share that the reason for the war was not the spoils, but to control sin.

Mutilation of Enemies in War: Verse 12

We see God's direction to the believers to aim at the heads of their enemies and cut off their fingers, preventing them from ever again holding swords. We see the echo of these verses applied today in modern conflicts, when Muslims take hostages and publicly decapitate them. We know it hurts even the hearts of moderate Muslims to see such cruelty. We can share with our Muslim friend that the God of the prophets never gave such an order to those who took the Promised Land or to its later kings. The only incident in which a leader used such action was when the young David killed Goliath with a sling and stone. Proving the death of Goliath, he then cut off the Philistine's head.[6] This one decapitation saved the lives of many, many heads on both sides of the war. How different is the motive and outcome here from what we see among Muslims. It is important to note that David did not normally approve of using decapitation. Following Saul's death, some of David's men killed and decapitated his son Ish-Bosheth while he was in bed. David was furious for this low act and had his own men killed as a result.[7]

Muhammad's Elevation as Prophet: Verse 13

We find many verses in the Qur'an that place Muhammad on the same level with God. Here it warns believers not to argue with either God or his Prophet; otherwise, God will inflict fearful punishment. No one dared to take a stand against Muhammad or even to question his actions out of fear of God's wrath. Within this same sura, verse 20 says not only to obey God and his Prophet, but also to not turn away from him when he is speaking. Verses 24 and 46 also exhort believers to obey God and the Prophet, while verse 27 forbids stealing from them, thus betraying their trust. More than six times within this sura alone, the same point is emphasized: obedience to Muhammad is as obedience to God.

Facing Death in War: Verse 16

A Muslim in battle has to stand up and face death. If he turns his face back to run, he is doomed to hell.

---

6.   1 Sam. 17.
7.   2 Sam. 4.

Furqan: *Verse 29*

Commentators refer to the battle of Badr as a *furqan*, or criterion, by which Muslims could judge their faith, as it was the first real trial of their allegiance to Muhammad and his cause. As a result of the battle, those who were not sincere in faith were separated from those who obediently followed the Prophet into war. We can relate this to the criterion Christ gave as the sign for those who follow him: "A new command I give you: Love one another. As I have loved you, so you must love one another. By this all men will know that you are my disciples, if you love one another."[8]

God Is Cunning: Verse 30

This verse states that the blasphemers were cunning and plotted to catch, imprison, or kill Muhammad. They may have been cunning, but there was no need to be afraid because God is more cunning. We need to explain to our beloved Muslim friend that we cannot apply this characteristic of the blasphemer to God. If the blasphemers were cunning toward Muhammad, God cannot be more cunning, for this is attributing to God a negative character trait and evil motives. However, in the Qur'an we find this as one of the ninety-nine names of God.

Qur'an as Repetition of Old Stories: Verse 31

God is saying to Muhammad that when he tells the blasphemers the Qur'an, they will tell him, "We heard that before; all these stories are before you." We need to challenge our Muslim friend by agreeing that the Qur'an did not really bring anything new.

Kill in the Name of God: Verse 39

God tells Muhammad to inform the believers that the blasphemers should be killed so that they will not corrupt others. A question could be asked: Does God really want to eliminate the wicked now, or does he want to give them more time, allowing both the wicked and good to grow? We can share with Muslims the parable of the wheat and tares.[9] If it is really God's desire to destroy the wicked now, why would he not kill all the evil people and Satan too? But good logic shows us that this is not God's way or desire.

---

8. John 13:34–35.
9. Matt. 13:24–30.

We cannot kill people because of their belief, because God created man and gave him the right to choose, even against God's own way.[10]

Spoils of War: Verse 41

The Qur'an says a fifth of the spoils are to go to God and his apostle, which means a full fifth will go to Muhammad, and he will spend it the way he sees God leading him. However, this also illustrates the continued rise of Muhammad in the eyes of himself and the people. By saying a fifth is to be given to God *and* Muhammad, Muhammad is put on the same level with God.

Angels and Punishments of Blasphemers: Verse 50

This verse gives us a picture, possibly of the end day or death of blasphemers, of angels slapping the faces and bottoms of blasphemers in order to mock them and give them a taste of the torment and fire of hell. Many questions could be raised in relation to this subject: Are the angels leading the blasphemers to hell? Are they giving them a taste of hell? Can angels really slap their faces and bottoms? Are angels going to be in heaven or hell? We can share with our Muslim friends the biblical view of heaven and help them to understand that angels would never be allowed to perform such acts of evil.

Predestination or Free Choice: Verse 53

This verse presents us with a paradox for the Qur'an: God's blessings cannot be bestowed on a people until they change themselves. Since the main theology of the Qur'an is predestination, it is confusing to see this verse, which clearly states that God is asking man to change himself. We can use this opportunity to share with our friend that God's grace is unconditional and not based on man's acts. Once a person is saved, he is always saved. God's grace is given to all mankind (he shines his sun on the wicked and righteous),[11] but his ultimate grace of salvation is in Christ—once it is given, it cannot be removed. This leads to perhaps a long discussion about grace and the law, using Romans 5 and 6 as a reference to help our friend understand that grace comes after sin, not before; if it did not, it could not be grace, for grace is something we do not deserve or merit.

---

10.   Verses 8:39 and 8:65 cancel out verses 29:46 and 2:256, which present a more tolerant view toward non-Muslims.

11.   Matt. 5:45.

Preparation for War: Verses 60–65

These are some very important verses, for Muslims quote them in preparation for or in going out to war. God tells Muhammad to get the Muslims ready for war, preparing whatever it takes to terrify their enemy in battle. He reminds them not to worry, for whatever they spend in the cause of war, God will bless them with many times more. Verse 65 finds God telling Muhammad to persuade the believers not to worry about the number of warriors they face—twenty followers of Islam will overcome two hundred of the enemy.

Jesus tells us in the *Injil,*

> Settle matters quickly with your adversary who is taking you to court. Do it while you are still with him on the way, or he may hand you over to the judge, and the judge may hand you over to the officer, and you may be thrown into prison. I tell you the truth, you will not get out until you have paid the last penny. . . . But I tell you, Do not resist an evil person. If someone strikes you on the right cheek, turn to him the other also. And if someone wants to sue you and take your tunic, let him have your cloak as well. If someone forces you to go one mile, go with him two miles. Give to the one who asks you, and do not turn away from the one who wants to borrow from you. You have heard that it was said, "Love your neighbor and hate your enemy." But I tell you: Love your enemies and pray for those who persecute you, that you may be sons of your Father in heaven. He causes his sun to rise on the evil and the good, and sends rain on the righteous and the unrighteous.[12]

The Bible consistently teaches us to be at peace with people as much as we can. One of God's main purposes for mankind is that they live in peace. He is the one who created Adam and Eve. All mankind in a way is one family, with Adam and Eve as the parents. The Bible says that Adam is the son of God in the spiritual sense. God looks at all mankind as his own children. Yes, we went astray and need to be adopted again, but God loves and cares for every individual. It is hard to imagine a human father killing one of his children. How utterly unimaginable it would be for a holy, loving God to encourage us

---

12. Matt. 5:25–26, 39–45.

to war with one another. We need to lead our friend to the Prince of Peace, who said, "I have told you these things, so that in me you may have peace. In this world you will have trouble. But take heart! I have overcome the world."[13]

Minority Victories in War: Verse 66

This verse gives comfort to Muslims who feel outnumbered by their enemies, reminding them that God will give them the victory. We can bridge this to Old Testament stories of victories the children of Israel achieved with God's help, even when they were outnumbered.

Migration Affirmed: Verse 75

God praises the ones who migrate from Mecca with Muhammad in order to enter battle. In being obedient to Muhammad's war cry, they are guaranteed many benefits, because God knows everything. We can affirm the omniscience of God, while questioning whether he would be so pleased with believers entering into battle (based on verses we have discussed previously).

---

13.   John 16:33.

Al-Tauba *or* Baraat

Repentance or *Immunity*

GIVEN SEVEN YEARS AFTER SURA 8

Overview

Some commentators say this was the last sura revealed to the Prophet Muhammad,[1] and because of some confusion as to whether or not he intended it to be added to the previous sura, it is the only sura without the *bismillah*[2] at the beginning. The main theme of the sura reflects the core of Muslim belief—to love God and his messenger, Muhammad. Blasphemers are forbidden to enter the mosque, as they are viewed as unclean. Muhammad encourages Muslims to fight the Jews and Christians until they pay the ransom, and he clarifies the idea of giving a four-month grace period to non-Muslims before killing them. Also, *al-Tauba* describes the judgment to be passed on those who do not repeat the word of praise for Muhammad. A short reference is made to the mosque the non-Muslims built to compete with that of Muhammad.

It becomes clear in reading this sura that God accepts the repentance of some, though not all. Even though "repentance" is the title of this sura, most of the material in it refers to war and the laws concerning how wars are to

---

1. Ibn Kathir, *Tafseer al-Qur'an al-Azeem*, 2:303.
2. In the name of God, the most Gracious and Merciful.

be executed, instead of explaining that repentance is when a person tries to make peace with God through confession of sin. There were some who had not gone to war alongside Muhammad,[3] but they later repented of their lack of obedience. The Prophet accepted the repentance of some, while rejecting that of others, but his general reaction was to refuse any repentance offered for not following him in battle. This reveals to us the true heart of jihad in the Qur'an and also gives us insight into why so many young men today are fighting in jihad—they fear either going to hell or being ostracized from the community.

Comments and Possible Bridges

Broken Alliances: Verse 1

Though commentators dispute the meaning of nearly every word in this verse, we understand it to mean that God and Muhammad broke the covenants with those nonbelievers with whom the Muslims had previously made alliances. The literal translation of the verse is "God and his Prophet broke the covenant of the blasphemers with whom you had a covenant before."

It is not clear whether these people had been believers and were now blasphemers or they had been blasphemers from the very beginning. The main point we need to focus on and share with our Muslim friend, however, is that when God cuts a covenant, he does not regret it or change it, because he is all-knowing—he knows the past and the future. When he makes a covenant, he knows what the outcome of that covenant will be. Here we can share about the many covenants God made in the Old and New Testaments and how they were fulfilled, beginning with the covenant with Abraham and leading to the ultimate covenant God made with mankind through the blood of Jesus.

Four Months of Grace and Then Slaughter: Verses 3–5

Other sources shed light on God's reason for breaking his covenant with the nonbelievers. The sacred mosque had been defiled by blasphemers making pilgrimage and entering it naked. Muhammad sent Abu Bakr, as the prince of hajj, to straighten them up. He was to imprison the guilty and watch every step they made. If they came back to Islam, they were to be set free. Muhammad said to give the blasphemers four months to repent

---

3.   Verse 118.

and then kill them wherever they are found. Orthodox Islam considers all non-Muslims blasphemers. We need to ask whether it makes sense that they should kill all the non-Muslims in the world if God's main message is supposed to be that of peace?[4]

Loving Family More Than God or Muhammad: Verse 24

We see a great parallel for this verse in the Gospels, when Jesus said, "Anyone who loves his father or mother more than me is not worthy of me; anyone who loves his son or daughter more than me is not worthy of me."[5] The comparison in the Qur'an is made with one's love for God *and* Muhammad. We need to take time to explain the paradox. When Jesus spoke of himself, he did so as one equal with God. Muhammad, on the other hand, always referred to himself as merely a servant of God. He never claimed deity; so, to love him and God equally should be considered blasphemy and in reality *shirk* (putting partners with God).

Non-Muslims Unclean: Verses 28–29

Muhammad declares blasphemers unclean, and therefore they should be kept from coming close to the sacred mosque. This uncleanness is not considered like that of the sick or lepers; rather all non-Muslims are considered unclean or impure in the sight of God. In contrast, we see Jesus not only loving the real unclean (lepers) but also touching them and making them clean. He also was not ashamed to be in the company of sinners and, again, with his loving touch, he brought inner cleansing.

Christians and Jews are specifically included among the blasphemers (unclean), because they did not pay the ransom (*jizya*) to the Muslims. There is a *hadith* that says, "I heard the Apostle of Allah say, I command by Allah to fight all the people till they say there is no god but Allah and I am his apostle. And whosoever says that will save himself and his money."[6] This illustrates the choices non-Muslims had in relation to Islam: accept it by saying the word of testimony, pay the *jizya*, or be killed by the sword.

Son of God: Verse 30

Christians and Jews are lumped together for condemnation because "Jews call 'Uzair (possibly Ezra) a son of God, and the Christians call Christ

---

4.   See sura 8, *al-Anfal*, as well.

5.   Matt. 10:37.

6.   Gabriel, *Jesus and Muhammad*, 127–28.

the Son of God." In both cases, the word *ibn* is used for "son" in Arabic. This word means "from" but not in the physical sense. Another word, *walid*, is used of a physical son and is found more often in other verses in reference to God not having a son. However, here, even the Qur'an does not say *walid* but *ibn*. Though it claims that the Jews referred to 'Uzair as a "son of God," we need to explain that this phrase was not known to be used by Jews during Old Testament times. Only the book of Luke uses the phrase in reference to Adam, when giving the genealogy of mankind, but it would never have been understood there in the physical sense of son.[7]

Light of God: Verse 32

In saying that Christ is one with God, the Qur'an says Christians want to quench the light of God. Commentators say that the light of God is Islam, but the Qur'an does not make that clear. What a wonderful opportunity this verse gives to share with our Muslim friend about the true Light of God. Jesus said, "I am the light of the world."[8] When we share about Jesus, we will be the light of God for others.

Four Months: Verse 36

Muhammad calls on Muslims to kill nonbelievers, except during four specified sacred months, known in Islam as Rajab, Zul-qa'd, Zul-hajj, and Muharram.[9] Though they are not supposed to fight during these four months, if someone attacks them, Muslims are allowed to fight back.

The Outcome of War: Verse 52

The outcome of war is always positive for a Muslim—either martyrdom or victory. It is helpful to raise several questions about this position, asking about the effects of war on others and on nations as a whole. It will be easy to find modern-day examples as illustrations. We can also ask about Muhammad's defeat at the battle of Uhud. The Prophet was wounded and neither died nor had victory.[10] Does this, then, contradict this verse?

Equality of the Sexes: Verse 71

The Qur'an says in this verse that male and female believers are protectors and encouragers for each other. This is in striking contrast to the teaching of

---

7.   Luke 3:38.
8.   John 8:12.
9.   Committee of the Qur'an and Sunna, *Al-Muntakhab*, 310.
10.   Sura 3:121. See Yusef Ali's note on the same verse. Ali, *The Holy Qur'an*, 154.

Islam as a whole, which insists that woman is inferior to man. However, we can use such a verse to build a bridge on the topic of the equality of men and women in Christ and our need for one another.

Paradise for All: Verse 72

This is a very good verse, though a rare one, which says both men and women are promised the everlasting paradise. We can use this as a point of agreement but also to ask questions as to how women will be blessed in the life to come, since most descriptions offer encouragement to the male audience.

Unforgivable Sin: Verse 80

According to the Qur'an, the unforgivable sin is to blaspheme God and Muhammad. We can share that for Christians, the unforgivable sin is to ultimately reject God. However, we need to explain that this is when a person completely rejects God's grace, which could have led him to heaven. This is why we as Christians continue to reach out to nonbelievers rather than seek to kill them. We want people to have maximum opportunity to accept the good news of God's grace through Christ.

Unforgiving Spirit: Verses 81–84

There is a harsh rebuke for those who gave excuses instead of following the Prophet into battle. Even though some later came to him to fight, Muhammad refused to take them with him. In later Muslim wars, he allowed them to come but humiliated them by making them stay back with the women, children, and handicapped. The climax of punishment for one who would not fight alongside Muhammad would come when that person died. The Prophet would not pray over him or stand at his grave, allowing him to die in his sin. We can tie this to our call as Christians to be reconcilers between man and God.

> So from now on we regard no one from a worldly point of view. Though we once regarded Christ in this way, we do so no longer. Therefore, if anyone is in Christ, he is a new creation; the old has gone, the new has come! All this is from God, who reconciled us to himself through Christ and gave us the ministry of reconciliation: that God was reconciling the world to himself in Christ, not counting men's sins

against them. And he has committed to us the message of reconciliation. We are therefore Christ's ambassadors, as though God were making his appeal through us. We implore you on Christ's behalf: Be reconciled to God. God made him who had no sin to be sin for us, so that in him we might become the righteousness of God.[11]

No Forgiveness for Repentance: Verses 95–96

The great paradox of this sura is reflected in these verses. Though "repentance" is its title, here God is telling Muhammad that no matter how many excuses the people give him for not following him into battle, and even if they swear on God's name, he is not to forgive them or have any relationship with them. They are unclean, and their eternal destiny is hell. We can share Jesus' response to Peter, who asked, "'How many times shall I forgive my brother when he sins against me? Up to seven times?' Jesus answered, 'I tell you, not seven times, but seventy-seven times.'"[12] When a person repents, that person should be forgiven and accepted, not refused and condemned to hell.

God continues by saying that even if Muhammad accepts their repentance, God will not forgive. We must ask our friend, "Can people be more merciful than God? Can people forgive, and God not?"

Salvation by Works: Verse 105

This verse says that God will observe the work of the believers, thus stressing salvation by works. We can share about the way of faith and grace for salvation as we know it.

Unworthy Mosque: Verse 107

This verse is about some people who built a mosque, not for worshiping God, but for their own ambition and to bring disunity among the believers. God tells Muhammad not to pray in this mosque but to pray in a mosque that is built only for the worship of God. A great parallel can be drawn here between the temple in Jerusalem and the temple in Samaria, as we share about Jesus' conversation with the Samaritan woman about worshiping God in spirit and truth.[13]

---

11. 2 Cor. 5:16–21.
12. Matt. 18:21–22.
13. John 4:1–26.

God Purchases Believers: Verse 111

This verse contains some interesting concepts we can discuss with our Muslim friend. First, it says that God bought the believers from themselves. Many questions could be raised from this one statement. Does the believer have the power to sell his own soul? If the believer sells his own soul, what will he do with the price?

Also, it says that God bought not only the souls of the believers but their money also. Must we really pay God with our souls and money in order to go to paradise? Here we need to share with our friend that it was the complete opposite that actually happened. God did not buy the souls from mankind, because they were already sinners. He paid the ransom price to save them, because they could not pay the price themselves. The price was paid to appease the justice of God and open the door for his grace to flow forth.

The verse continues by explaining that the price God paid people is paradise. If a Muslim kills and dies in God's name, he is destined for paradise. This verse qualifies this by saying that Judaism and Christianity taught the same. We need to explain here that the God of the Old Testament and the New Testament never rewarded killing in his name with paradise but condemned killing from the first soul killed by Cain till the last soul taken today.

Unforgiving Spirit: Verse 113

This verse says that once they are sure that a person will not convert to Islam, neither the Prophet nor the believers should pray for their forgiveness, even if they are related to them. Again we see the contrast to the title of this sura and an opportunity to share about the forgiveness we have in Christ and our need to always pray for those who have yet to give their hearts to him.

Abraham: Verse 114

This verse says that Abraham did pray for his father's forgiveness, but only because he had made a promise to him. However, it continues by saying that Abraham disassociated himself from his father, because he saw him as an enemy of God. There is nothing in the biblical account to indicate that Abraham ever disassociated himself from his father, for Terah traveled with Abraham from Ur to Haran, where Terah died at the age of 205.[14] We can

---

14. Gen. 11:31–32; Acts 7:1–4.

move to the example of Jesus, who also did not disassociate himself from sinners. In fact, many despised Jesus because he sat with sinners, ate with them, and loved them.

No place in the Old Testament shows us that Abraham's father was a blasphemer. Even though we can agree that we cannot ask forgiveness for the dead, as some commentators see this verse arguing, it is not clear here that Abraham's father was actually dead when Abraham quit praying on his behalf.

We can go one of two ways with this verse. We can point out either that we have to love sinners, no matter what, or that we are to love God even more than a father and mother. However, we need to be careful before we take either direction, that we do not distort the historical/biblical truth about Abraham's father.

Kill Your Neighbor: Verse 123

God is ordering the believers to kill their nonbelieving neighbors and to do so harshly. Here we find the paradox in Islam, because in some places the Qur'an says to be good to your neighbors, while here we find God telling Muslims to kill them. We need to reiterate here the command of Jesus to not only love the lost, but also to reach out to them in missions (Jerusalem, Judea, Samaria, ends of world).[15]

Blasphemers: Verse 124

Those who questioned the ability of the Qur'an to increase a person's faith were considered blasphemers and unbelievers. According to the previous verse, these people should be killed. Jesus said, "Love your enemies and pray for those who persecute you. . . . If you love those who love you, what reward will you get? . . . Do not even pagans do that? Be perfect, therefore, as your heavenly Father is perfect."[16]

Lord of the Great Throne: Verse 129

The sura ends with a wonderful phrase that says God is the Lord of the great throne. We need to consider what sentence he will give us if we really stand before that great throne. Indeed, we could ask on what basis we would be allowed to stand before the throne of God.

---

15. Matt. 28:18–20.
16. Matt. 5:44–48.

Yunus

Jonah

LATE MECCAN

Overview

The main focus of sura *Yunus* is stories from the prophets, including Jonah, from which the chapter gets its name. There are also references to the creation of the world, the Day of Judgment, and how people act as believers and nonbelievers. The sura also speaks of the Qur'an as the greatest miracle given to Muhammad. The letters *aleph, lam,* and *rey* begin this sura, as they and other letters do in many others, yet still without an understood meaning. Some commentators say the unknown or mysterious things prove the miracle of the Qur'an.

Comments and Possible Bridges

Mystical Letters: Verses 1–2

The sura begins with reference to the wonder of the Qur'an. As stated previously, there is no known meaning for these freestanding letters. We can ask our friend what he or she thinks is the purpose of these letters. We do know that some commentators say *aleph, lam,* and *rey* mean, "I see God." Other commentators refer the letters back to pre-qur'anic writings, like the Bible. The Qur'an is here referred to as a book of wisdom. It is a miracle God has given through Muhammad.

Sun and Moon: Verse 5

This verse says that God made the sun and moon in order for us to know the number of the years. We can compare this with Genesis 1:14.

Superiority of the Qur'an: Verse 38

God is telling Muhammad to challenge the unbelievers to provide even one sura like that of the Qur'an, if they believe his message is not from God. The best way to answer this challenge is to share about writings that existed prior to the Qur'an that are linguistically superior, even according to the evaluation of Arabs themselves, including some very important Muslims.[1] To write poetry or prose equal to the Qur'an is not difficult. The *Shi'ite* believe in a Qur'an that consists of 115 suras, while the *Sunni* believe in a Qur'an of 114 suras. We can ask our friend, "What is the difference in this on extra sura, and where did it come from?"

Eyes Blinded, Hearts Hardened, Ears Deaf: Verses 42–43

The rhetorical question is asked: "Can you (Muhammad) make the deaf hear or the blind to see?" Here we need to share how Jesus not only guided the people, but also healed people, including those who were blind and deaf. Furthermore, Jesus healed the heart of the blind by granting forgiveness of sins and providing salvation. Refer to the story of the paralytic[2] as well to that of the man born blind.[3]

Apostles Sent from God: Verse 47

We need to explain to our beloved Muslim friend that, contrary to this verse, God did not send a specific messenger (apostle) to every nation. All the messengers God sent were from the Jewish race. While some of them tried to reach out to non-Jews, they themselves were all from the Jewish

1. "Is the Qur'an Miraculous?" http://www.answering-islam.org/Quran/Miracle/mirac1.html (accessed May 29, 2008) and "Mu'allaqat," http://inthenameofallah.org/Mu'allaqat.html (accessed May 29, 2008).
2. Mark 2:1–12.
3. John 9.

race. God did this because the original covenant was made with Abraham, and it would be through his descendants that all nations would be blessed.[4]

Salvation by Works: Verses 54–57

These verses state very clearly that a soul cannot be ransomed by earthly possessions but must depend on repentance and God's mercy. If this is true, we can ask our Muslim friend why, therefore, there is the need for the scale at the end day to weigh the deeds of man? Sharing the verses of the Roman Road would provide a clear solution for his dilemma.

Veracity of the Bible: Verse 64

According to this verse, God's Word cannot be changed. Therefore, we need to ask our friend how the *Tawrat* and the *Injil* can be changed when the Qur'an is not? If the nature of God is to protect and keep his Word, then the Bible could not be changed. Another question presents itself here: How does this verse fit with the idea of abrogation in the Qur'an? Would abrogation not be considered a change in God's Word?

Son of God: Verse 68

Some people say, "God has a son." It is interesting to note that the word used before was *ibn*,[5] but here the Qur'an uses the word *walid* (physical son). This is a great opportunity to make a parallel between these two verses from the Qur'an. The verse continues by providing a reason for God not having a physical son—because he is rich and owns everything in heaven and earth. However, a person can be rich and have a lot and yet still have a son. Does the richness of heaven and earth release God from having his own beloved Son? Which is more valuable?

Noah: Verses 71–73

The Qur'an puts the whole story of Noah into these three verses. We can share with our friend the biblical story, including how long it took Noah to build the ark, what he was telling the people while he was building the ark, the great story of the flood, which killed everyone, and the reason God chose Noah (not because he preached to the people, but because he was found pure in God's eyes).

---

4. Gen. 22:18.
5. Sura 9:30.

Moses: Verses 74–92

We can compare the account here with both that of the Bible and that found in other sections of the Qur'an.

Pharaoh: Verses 90–92

Here we read something new in the story of Pharaoh. When he started to drown in the sea while chasing Moses, he professed his faith in God and said, "I am a Muslim." It is important to note to our friend that Islam came long after the time of Moses. It did not exist during the time of the early fathers. There is no record that Pharaoh ever claimed faith in the God of Moses prior to his death. In reality, he rejected Moses all the way. There is a contradiction in the Qur'an about how God deals with Pharaoh. Verse 92 says that God saved Pharaoh's body, but according to sura 17, verses 102–103, he died as a blasphemer.

Muhammad and Doubt in God's Word: Verse 94

This is a pivotal verse, and we need to take a long stop there. God is telling Muhammad, "If you doubt my word, ask the Christians and Jews." Many questions present themselves here. Did Muhammad doubt that these words were from God? Is the word of the Bible higher in authority than the Qur'an (as a proof text to the Qur'an)? If we get our Muslim friend to even think about these things, he has taken a step on the road to salvation.

God's Will: Verse 99

If God so willed, he would be able to make all mankind believers. We can share that God is limited by his characteristics. Because he is just, he cannot make all people righteous. Because he made man in his own image and with the power to choose, he cannot bend man's will to make him a believer. The Bible makes it clear that God does desire that all people accept him as Savior, but he cannot disregard the way he made man.

Hud

The Prophet Hud

LATE MECCAN

Overview

Hud begins with a proclamation of the Qur'an as the Word of God and a warning for those who do not believe. The sura encourages evangelism and says that those who do not accept the Qur'an are blasphemers, while those who believe will be rewarded. The earthly punishment for blasphemers is described as well.

This sura reveals Noah's story in more detail, as well as that of a prophet called Salih and his people, the Thamud. There is also more of the story of Abraham and Lot found here. At the end of the sura, Muhammad reminds the people that God is ultimate in his knowledge.

This sura is named for the prophet Hud, who is known from Arabian tradition to have been a prophet to the 'Ad people in southern Arabia, descendants from Shem, son of Noah.[1]

Comments and Possible Bridges

Condemnation for Unbelief: Verses 1–24

These verses encourage Muslims to preach Islam, while condemning nonbelievers to eternal damnation. This could provide an opportunity to

---

1. Ali, *The Holy Qur'an*, 358.

share with our Muslim friend that Christians are also commanded by Jesus to share the good news of the kingdom, opening a door to explain in detail what that good news is.

Noah Ridiculed: Verse 38

While Noah was building the ark, people mocked him. Noah responded by telling them that he would ridicule them as well. Here we can share from the biblical account that Noah was a righteous man, and therefore would not speak in a way that would not bring honor to God.[2]

Noah Acting in Faith: Verse 40

According to this verse, when the rains came, God ordered Noah to bring into the ark a pair of each animal, his family, and other believers. We need to explain here that according to Genesis 7, God had Noah fill the ark with animals and his family long before the waters came. There were at least two of each of the animals, but for some kinds there were seven. After seven days, God then sent the waters to flood the earth.

This would provide a good opportunity to talk about the faith of Noah. To not only build the ark on dry land, but also to fill it with animals and his family before the rains came were great acts of faith. He was obedient to God even though those around him must have thought him crazy. We can then talk about how following God (through Christ) can seem crazy to others and may bring ridicule, but God will reward us as we obey his Word.

Noah's Disobedient Son: Verses 41–48

The Qur'an gives us here a dialogue between Noah and God. Noah is asking his son to come into the ark, but the son refuses. Noah then argues with God for the sake of this wayward son. God refuses Noah's argument, and the son perishes in the flood. The biblical account clearly states that Noah's entire family was saved from the flood. Here the two books differ, as the Qur'an not only talks about this son who is lost, but also adds other believers outside of Noah's family to those who avoid death by being on the ark.

Noah, Newly Revealed Story: Verse 49

This verse reveals God telling Muhammad that Noah's story was previously unknown but has now been revealed only to the Prophet. He is

---

2. Gen. 6–7.

telling the Prophet this story so that Muhammad and future Muslims may be patient through suffering. While we can agree that the story of Noah provides a good example of patience, we should be frank with our Muslim friend that the story of Noah was known to peoples long before the Prophet and is given in much more detail in the Bible.

Hud: Verses 50–60

A new prophet, called Hud, appears in this passage. He calls on the 'Ad people to believe in God and do good, but they refuse. God saves the prophet Hud but brings punishment on all the 'Ad people, destroying them with a strong and mighty wind.

Salih: Verses 61–68

In continuing his discourse about disobedience, God shares about the sending of the prophet Salih to the Thamud people. This prophet told them that the female camel was a sign from God and a symbol for them; thus they should let her live in peace. The people, however, were evil, and they killed the camel. Salih told them that because of their wickedness, God would smite them after three days. At the appointed time, God made them unable to move in their homes, but he saved Salih.

Abraham: Verses 69–83

This passage begins with the visit of the messengers to Abraham and Sarah. We find a conflict between two accounts of this same story found in the Qur'an. In this sura, Sarah laughs before she is told the news of the promised child, Isaac.[3] By contrast, in sura 51, Sarah laughs after the news is shared with her.[4] As we ask our friend about this difference, we can share the actual story from the biblical account.[5]

Following the news about the child, Abraham began to argue with God about Lot's (Lut) people. Verse 76 says that God's decree could not be turned back. We can relate this to the dialogue between Abraham and God, as Abraham prays for the city[6] and to how prayer can be effective in changing the mind of God.

---

3. Sura 11:71.
4. Sura 51:28, 29.
5. Gen. 18.
6. Gen. 18:22–33.

Lot: Verses 77–83

As we consider the story of Lot, it is important to help our friend understand that the people of Sodom were of no relation to Lot. He chose to go and live among them, even though they were evil. This is a good bridge to the idea of bad choices and consequences we face in making them. In the qur'anic account, we see that Lot offers his daughters to the evil men of Sodom as he does in the biblical story, but the Qur'an does not tell us what happens to Lot's wife when she turns back to look upon the city. We can share with our friend the rest of the story from the Bible.

Shu'aib: Verses 84–95

These verses present us with yet another extrabiblical prophet, Shu'aib, who went to his own people, the Midianites (Madyan). His message was this: Be fair in your selling and buying. His people refused him, and the same punishment came on them as came on the prophet Hud's people. The story of Hud is very close to that of Shu'aib. It is important to notice that when we read of the prophets not mentioned in the Bible, the Qur'an gives much more detail to their stories.

Condemnation for Unbelief: Verses 96–109

Following these various accounts of prophets who faced disobedient peoples are warnings of condemnation for all who do like those who refused these prophets.

Length of Heaven and Hell: Verses 106–108

These verses teach that heaven and hell will exist as long as the heavens and earth endure. We can share with our Muslim friend that even though the heavens and earth will come to an end, there will be a new heaven and a new earth, where God will dwell with his people forever.[7] Our destination, whether it be heaven or hell, will last for eternity and will not end. This is why we need to be sure of where we are going.

Good Deeds: Verse 114

This verse introduces a very important concept in Islam, namely, that good deeds remove bad deeds. From here the theory of the balance on the Day of Judgment came. We need to share with a Muslim that sin is not just a physical

---

7. Isa. 65:17; Rev. 21:1–4.

act; it has a spiritual dimension. When we say to a person, "You are a fool," we commit a great sin. Man was made in God's image, and in calling a man a fool, we are saying to God that he is a fool as well. Even if we pay back the hurt we caused our brother, how can we be justified before God? This makes the idea of an act or good deed removing sin (or evil) impossible.

Trust God: Verse 123

We see here a very nice verse that says God knows all mysterious things in heaven and earth, and to him all things will come back; so worship God, because he knows all you are doing. There is a great parallel to this in the final verses of the book of Ecclesiastes. There, Solomon wanted to summarize his thoughts and said, "Now all has been heard; here is the conclusion of the matter: Fear God and keep his commandments, for this is the whole [duty] of man. For God will bring every deed into judgment, including every hidden thing, whether it is good or evil."[8] Verses like this can be used very nicely as a bridge to Muslims.

---

8.   Eccl. 12:13–14.

Yusuf

Joseph

LATE MECCAN

Overview

This sura, in its entirety, is basically the story of Joseph, though it also contains some verses to prove the authenticity of the Qur'an as the Word of God (which we will discuss later). It is the most detailed biblical story in the Qur'an. Before dealing with the analysis of this sura, we encourage you to read the two accounts of Joseph's life, as found in the Bible and in the Qur'an. Then you will be able to see the differences, understand the wisdom behind the intact story in the Bible, realize how the Qur'an misses important details, and have a clearer view of the historical account.

The story of Joseph is mentioned only in this sura, and since the period for this revelation to Muhammad is late Meccan, we might assume that he heard about Joseph only later in his life.

Comments and Possible Bridges

Arabic Language: Verse 2

God gave the Qur'an in Arabic so that the people would understand.[1] We should ask our Muslim friends, "Does this mean that God does not want

---

1. "In order that ye may learn wisdom," as Yusuf Ali has, is not a correct translation.

other peoples to understand it? Should the Qur'an not be translated into other languages, as some Muslim thinkers believe?"

Throughout the Islamic world, when it comes to reciting the Qur'an in the mosque, only the Arabic language is accepted. We can share with our friend that God's plan was to diversify languages (Tower of Babel),[2] so in a sense, all languages are from God. The Lord understands them all, and we can communicate with him in any language. God also wants to speak to man in a language he will understand, so it only makes sense that he will reveal himself in English to the English, in Chinese to the Chinese, and in Arabic to the Arab. We cannot limit God to only one language.

Joseph's Unknown Story: Verse 3

God is telling Muhammad that he is giving him one of the best stories, one that no one else knew before, or realized fully. Some commentators use such a concept to justify the miraculous nature of the Qur'an, saying that Muhammad told stories that could not have been known to him previously. However, it is not difficult to know that the account of Joseph was written about 1400 BC[3] in even more detail, and was thus a well-known story.

Joseph's Dreams: Verse 4

The qur'anic story begins with Joseph telling his father about his second dream—seeing the stars, sun, and moon bow down to him. We can use this to share with our Muslim friend that, while this was in fact one of his dreams, Joseph also had an earlier dream about bundles of wheat.[4]

Joseph's Interpretation of Dreams: Verse 6

We see here Joseph's father telling him that the Lord will teach him how to interpret dreams. This is very early in the story, since Joseph at that time had just had a dream and did not attempt to make any interpretation. As we read in the biblical account, it was actually his brothers and father who interpreted the dreams or assumed their meanings.[5] God did give him the ability to interpret dreams later on in life, when he was told the dreams of his fellow inmates in prison. However, at this point, when he had his own dreams, he did not know what they meant.

---

2. Gen. 11:9.

3. *Life Application Bible*, xvi.

4. Gen. 37:5–7.

5. Gen. 37:8, 10.

Joseph Thrown into a Well: Verses 8–10

Without giving the setting, the Qur'an moves immediately to Joseph's brothers throwing Joseph into a well. It quotes one brother as he discourages the others from killing Joseph and tells them to throw him into a well so that maybe someone will pick him up. We can share with our Muslim friend that we know the name of that brother, and we can then read the incident from the Bible. We can emphasize the point that when Reuben told them to put Joseph into the pit, he did not have in mind that someone else would pick him up later, but that he himself would come and save him from his brothers and take him back to his father.[6]

Joseph, the Concept of Sowing and Reaping: Verses 12–18

This passage in the Qur'an is somewhat confusing, for it goes back to the brothers talking to their father and asking him to allow them to take Joseph with them so that he can play. They take the responsibility for being his protectors. The father expresses his fear that Joseph will be eaten by a wolf, but the brothers assure him this could not happen. However, they do return to their father with a bloody shirt to prove that Joseph has indeed been devoured by a wolf.

In the Qur'an, in contrast to the biblical account, the father does not believe his sons when they return with the bloody robe. Therefore, the whole concept of God dealing with Jacob is lost in the story. The lesson of Jacob reaping what he sowed cannot be realized if Jacob does not believe that his son died. It is a great opportunity to explain to our friend that in reality, when the brothers brought Jacob the bloody garment, he was the one who jumped to the conclusion that Joseph had been eaten by a wild beast.[7] Then we can share that God is very precise in giving us the details of this story, allowing us to see how Jacob truly reaped what he had sown earlier in his life when he was deceitful to his own father.[8] It was because Jacob deceived his father with his brother's clothes that he was later completely deceived by his own sons with Joseph's clothes.

Joseph and Potiphar's Wife: Verses 21–33

The story develops quickly as we find Potiphar's wife closing the doors on Joseph and trying to seduce him. (While her name is mentioned neither

---

6. Gen. 37:19–22.
7. Gen. 37:31–35.
8. Gen. 27:14–27.

in the Bible nor the Qur'an, Potiphar is referred to as the nobleman 'Aziz in the Qur'an.)[9] The Qur'an reports that as the nobleman's wife started to seduce Joseph, the same feelings began to arise in Joseph as well. We need to share here that even if Joseph began to have such feelings, he would be lost. The biblical account tells us, however, that he never desired her but kept his heart pure, even though she tried to trap him many times. He was able to do this because he considered committing such an act with her offensive to God, even before he thought of the offense it would be to her husband.[10]

During her attempt to seduce Joseph, the wife tears his garment. When her husband catches them, she accuses Joseph. Joseph tries to justify himself using great wisdom in his defense: if the garment is torn from the back, she is the liar; if it is torn from the front, then he would be the liar. The passage reveals that the garment was torn from the back. Thus, the nobleman not only blames his wife, but also all womankind, saying that their snares are unmatched.

Though the husband believes Joseph, the Qur'an goes on to tell us that Joseph is sent to jail. How is it, after being proven innocent, Joseph is still put into jail? We need to share here the truth of the story from this point. Joseph escaped the wife's attempts, but she raised accusations against him in private to her husband, using his cloak as evidence and without providing Joseph an opportunity to defend himself. Thus Potiphar believed his wife and had Joseph put into jail.

Returning to the Qur'an in verse 30, we find the story has developed in an unusual way, with the women accusing the nobleman's wife of fornication. So she comes up with the idea of giving a feast, where the food can be eaten only with knives, and she invites Joseph to come to the feast. As soon as the women of the city see Joseph, they go crazy over him and start to cut their hands with the knives, claiming he is not human, but an angel. As this is one of the few places in the Qur'an where we can find women lusting over a man, it is a good opportunity to share that as much as a woman can be a temptation for a man, a man also can be a temptation for a woman. When theological scholars discuss sexual issues, they do not consider this story or point at all.

Thus in verse 33, we see the reason, according to the Qur'an, that Joseph goes to prison. Joseph asks God to protect him from the lust of these women and says that he prefers imprisonment rather than being with these women. God thus guarantees him prison as a protection from the women. The central

---

9. Sura 12:30.
10. Gen. 39:8–10.

idea is to put the blame on women, when in reality Joseph was put into jail because Potiphar thought he was guilty. This could be a chance to ask our friend what is wrong with the idea of Joseph being falsely accused and imprisoned. We can then share about God's redemption in spite of injustice.

Joseph, Interpreter of Dreams: Verses 36–57

The Qur'an briefly mentions the two slaves of Pharaoh who were also in prison and their dreams, which are very close to what we have in the Bible, and how Joseph interpreted the dreams. The difference we find here is that the slave who was saved and returned to Pharaoh's service, at the time when Pharaoh is seeking a meaning for his dream, tells Pharaoh that he will provide the interpretation. Then he goes to Joseph and asks him the meaning of Pharaoh's dream. Joseph tells the cupbearer, who in turn tells Pharaoh. It is only after the interpretation has been given that Pharaoh calls for Joseph. But Joseph refuses to leave prison, telling Pharaoh that he was put there under false accusations. He desires that his name first be cleared by the nobleman's wife. Pharaoh has the woman brought in, and she confesses. While talking about the variations in the story, we can also ask a question: If the Qur'an told us earlier that Joseph basically had himself put into prison, why is he now asking for his name to be cleared and saying he was put there under false accusations?

We can share the biblical account, telling our Muslim friend that in reality Joseph was brought directly to Pharaoh to interpret the dream. Joseph never mentioned Potiphar's wife, because he already had forgiven her and no longer held anything against her. When asked to interpret the dream, Joseph did not claim the ability as his own but said that God would give the meaning to Pharaoh.[11] Seeing God's wisdom in Joseph, Pharaoh put him in charge of the land, in contrast to the version in the Qur'an, where Joseph asks Pharaoh to be made treasurer.[12]

We can use the differences in the accounts in another way as well. Joseph's refusal to leave prison until his name was cleared brings a shade of another story in the Bible—when Paul refused to leave prison quietly but insisted that the magistrates come and take them out publicly.[13] It will be a good opportunity to help our Muslim friend understand the difference between the actions of the two men.

---

11. Gen. 41:15–16.
12. Sura 12:55.
13. Acts 16:16–40.

Joseph's Brothers Before Him in Egypt: Verses 58–93

Again we move to another part of the story without receiving adequate information about the change of events or setting. The account of Joseph's brothers coming to Egypt and being recognized by Joseph, along with the incident with the silver cup, are a little different in the Qur'an. For example, in verse 69, we see Joseph telling Benjamin privately about his real identity before letting his brothers go with the stolen cup.

The remainder of the story also differs. The brothers eventually return to their father without Benjamin. The Qur'an does not show that the brothers of Joseph were changed or had matured since the time they dropped Joseph into the pit. The Bible tells how his older brothers (Reuben and Judah) pleaded with their father, begging him to allow them to take Benjamin to Egypt. Reuben even offered his own sons as a sacrifice, if Benjamin were not returned safely.[14] This act of nobility and maturity is not mentioned in the Qur'an. The Qur'an reveals that they continued to blame Joseph and even Benjamin as being bad descendants of their mother, implying they were both thieves.[15]

Joseph Proves His Identity to His Father: Verses 93–96

The story continues by saying that Joseph sends his shirt with his brothers, that his father might smell his scent and realize he is alive. Once they put the shirt over his face, Jacob's eyes become well, and he is able to see. The miracle of opening his eyes with Joseph's shirt is not mentioned in the Bible. We can share, however, that according to the biblical account, as soon as Jacob knew that Joseph was alive and he would go to see him, his soul revived in him.[16] The Bible shows that his eyes were still dim, however. When he was on his deathbed and blessing Joseph's children, Joseph thought that it was because he could not see well that Jacob put his right hand on the younger son, but in reality Jacob knew exactly what he was doing. Jacob's insight was much greater than his eyesight.[17]

We read in the Qur'an that members of his household tell Jacob that he is still thinking like the old way, lost in his old thoughts. But Jacob was the oldest and wisest in his household, and the biblical account gives no

---

14.   Gen. 42:37; 43:8–9.
15.   Sura 12:77.
16.   Gen. 45:25–28.
17.   Gen. 49.

indication that his entire household showed him anything but respect and honor. They never put him down for his grief over Joseph.

The Rest of Joseph's Story: Verse 101

We need to share the biblical truth of this story. The Qur'an indicates that Joseph's brothers were wicked from beginning to end. We need to show how God worked in their lives through time and how they developed by the end of the story. Jesus even came from the line of Judah. It is important to point out that the father blessed each and every one of his children, showing how God works through redemption with mankind and not only through punishment.

The rest of the story really needs to be told, because when the story stops in the Qur'an, it ends with glorifying Joseph and blaming Satan for all the wrongdoings of his brothers. And it portrays Joseph asking God to let him die as a Muslim. We must share the story in all its fullness!

Joseph's Unknown Story: Verse 102

Though Muhammad was not alive at the time of Joseph, God tells Muhammad that he will reveal to him a story never before told. In reality this story had been familiar to many prior to Muhammad. It was told generation after generation, and in its oral transmission, it was corrupted. It was such a corrupted version that Muhammad heard and that found its way into the Qur'an. It is our responsibility and privilege, therefore, to share the original story with our Muslim friend.

Al-Ra'd

Thunder

LATE MECCAN

Overview

The main theme of this sura is how nature gives glory to God and, more specifically, how the thunder gives him glory and testifies for his holiness. The sura also reveals how the blasphemers are not satisfied with the glorious Qur'an as the greatest miracle and ask the Prophet for another miracle besides the Qur'an. Muhammad tells them that the Qur'an is the greatest miracle that will remain to the end days. As usual, an attempt is made to prove that the Qur'an is the authentic Word of God and Muhammad is the ultimate messenger.

This sura as a whole can be paralleled to the Psalms, using it to lead our friend to join us in reading Psalm 19 in particular.

Comments and Possible Bridges

Creation: Verses 2–3

These verses tell how God made the heavens and lifted them without posts; then he made the sun and moon to circle the earth according to a certain time. As the heavens were lifted without pillars, so the earth was stretched and anchored.

With these two verses, we can begin to dialogue with our Muslim friend about the accounts of creation as given in the Qur'an and the Bible and how they differ. The Bible describes the heavens as a canopy,[1] which gives the impression that it is round, surrounding the earth. We need to be careful because many Muslim scholars have tried to read into the Qur'an the latest discoveries about creation, but in the very text before us, the Qur'an declares clearly that the earth is flat and there are anchors that hold it down. In other places we read as well that the mountains anchor the earth.[2]

Man Responsible to Change: Verse 11

This is a very important verse. It reads that God cannot change people until they change themselves. We can ask our friend how man can ever truly change without supernatural power from God. We can draw the bridge to Paul's confession in Romans.[3]

Thunder: Verses 12–13

Even though the whole sura is titled "Thunder," these are the only verses in the sura that relate to the subject. Verse 12 says God reveals the lightning so that we may be afraid, and then he brings the heavy clouds filled with water, which can be disastrous. When the Qur'an was written, electric light was not known. Thunder in the night was a very scary thing, especially in the desert, where it is rare. We need to share here the difference in attitude between Muhammad and the psalmists. The psalmists looked at the lightning, not as a scary phenomenon, but as an opportunity to magnify God and his creation.[4]

In verse 13 we can see a parallel to Psalm 19, in that thunder gives praise to God. The second part of the verse, however, is very harsh. God brings down thunderbolts and smites those who argue about his power. The literal words of the Qur'an read that God punishes those who argue with him. We need to share with our friend that God made man with free will. God loves to dialogue with man, and in the Bible we can read him saying, "'Come now, let us reason together,' says the LORD. 'Though your sins are like scarlet, they shall be as white as snow.'"[5] So God's desire for the lost is to redeem them, not to smite them with instant death.

---

1. Isa. 40:22.
2. Suras 15:19; 16:15; 21:31.
3. Rom. 7:21–25.
4. Pss. 29:7–11; 97; 144:3–10; 148:7–14.
5. Isa. 1:18.

On the other hand, we are reminded here of Sodom and Gomorrah. When the time is ripe, and when mankind drifts so far from God, God's judgment comes. He did not destroy Sodom and Gomorrah because of an argument, but because the people stopped talking to God and decided in their hearts to follow Satan. In relating this view of God's justice, we also need to remember that since Christ's sacrifice on the cross God deals with man in a much more gracious way, though the final judgment is still realized by those who do not accept Christ.

If we look at some references that explain the Qur'an, one of the *hadith* says that two men, Irbid and Amer, tried to kill Muhammad.[6] When Irbid tried to pull out his sword to smite Muhammad, his hand was frozen, so he was not able to kill the Prophet. The moment the two men left his presence and went out, a thunderbolt killed Irbid. Amer got an ulcer in his stomach and died. This is the background of this verse about God sending thunderbolts to smite people. If we consider this *hadith* to be authentic, the main idea of nature glorifying God is gone, and the only place thunderbolts are mentioned is in God's punishing one who tried to kill Muhammad.

Every Knee Shall Bow: Verse 15

This is a wonderful parallel to the verse that reads, "Therefore God exalted him to the highest place and gave him the name that is above every name, that at the name of Jesus every knee should bow, in heaven and on earth and under the earth, and every tongue confess that Jesus Christ is Lord, to the glory of God the Father."[7] We can share with our friend the deity of Jesus from such a verse. The Qur'an is very clear that every creature in heaven and earth will bow before God, whether they like it or not. When we compare this to what we have in the Bible, we can bring to our friend the reality of the deity of Christ, as every knee will be bowing before him on the end day.

Paradise, Garden of Eden: Verse 23

God promises believers the Garden of Eden (literal translation from Qur'an), where they will be with their wives, children, and fathers. Here is a good place to share that heaven will not be the Garden of Eden, because it will not be a physical place, but a spiritual place. The heavens and earth

---

6. Hafez Abu Khasim al-Tabrani as per Ibn Kathir, *Tafseer al-Qur'an al-Azeem*, 2:462.
7. Phil. 2:9–11.

will cease to exist, and a new heaven and earth will come. A new, heavenly Jerusalem will come to pass, where God will dwell with his people forever. One time the Sadducees told Jesus a story about seven brothers, each of whom in turn married the wife of the eldest brother and then died, and none produced an heir. They asked him which would be the husband of the woman in heaven. Jesus told them that in heaven there will be no marriage in the physical sense. In fact, we are not even sure how much we will recognize loved ones. Earthly relationships like father, son, wife, and daughter will cease to exist, and we will be like angels in heaven with spiritual bodies.[8]

Hearts at Rest in Remembering God: Verse 28

This is a great opening statement we can use with a lot of Muslims when we start to talk about religion, and even when the argument starts to get heated. We can quote the second half of verse 28: "When we talk about God and mention his name, our hearts will be at rest." Use it wisely.

Superiority of the Qur'an: Verse 31

This verse is an attempt to prove that the Qur'an is the most important book in the world. It is the miracle of God. It says that if there is any book that, when read, will move mountains, or shatter the earth, or make the dead speak, it will be the Qur'an. Muhammad did not say that the Qur'an does this; rather, he is comparing the Qur'an to all writings ever written (the Bible included). He continues by saying that even if there was a book that could do such magnificent things, the Qur'an is still above them.

We can share with our friend that when God speaks mountains tremble, the earth splits open, and the dead rise.[9] This already happened in the Old and New Testaments. Jesus, the Word of God in the flesh, whose words are recorded in the *Injil*, spoke to the dead and brought them back to life, and the earth trembled when he died. This shows us that the miracles of the Qur'an are very limited in comparison to what we have in the Holy Bible.

Water in Paradise: Verse 35

Heaven is always described in the Qur'an as having rivers of water flowing beneath it. This provides an attractive, physical view of heaven for a people surrounded by sand. We will talk more about this in other verses.

---

8. Matt. 22:23–32.
9. Cf. Exod. 19:18–19; Num. 16; 2 Kings 4:32–35.

Abrogation: Verse 39

This verse creates a theological dilemma. We can ask, "Does God write something and then erase it? Does he change his mind?" Refer to notes on sura 2:106 for more on this topic.

Muhammad's Justification as a Prophet: Verse 43

This sura ends with an attempt by Muhammad to prove himself as a prophet. God speaks through him by saying that it is enough that God and the Qur'an gives witness to him. Anyone who does not call him a prophet will be labeled a blasphemer.

Ibrahim

Abraham

LATE MECCAN

Overview

These verses are dedicated to Abraham, believed by most Muslims to be the one who, with his son Ishmael, built the Ka'ba in Mecca as the house of prayer for God. It is held that he traveled to Mecca in order to take Hagar and Ishmael there. He left them there for a while and then returned; then he and Ishmael built the Ka'ba.

It is important to note here, and in relation to other suras that mention Abraham, that most non-Muslim scholars refute the idea that Abraham traveled to Mecca. We have in the Bible a clear account of the places to which Abraham traveled. There is no reference to his going as far as modern-day Saudi Arabia. Geographical, physical, and political reasons lead us to maintain the strong opinion that Abraham could not have traveled to Mecca.

Even though Abraham's name is mentioned seventy times in various suras of the Qur'an, his name is mentioned only one time in the sura that bears his name. Most of the account of sura *Ibrahim* is not even about Abraham. This is why it is necessary to have an index in any qur'anic study. Suras are not grouped by subject, and titles may have little to do with content.

Overall, we do not find much information about Abraham, except that he has two sons, Ishmael and Isaac. However, we can use this as an opportunity to share with our Muslim friend God's treasures about Abraham by reading the complete story from the Holy Bible.

Comments and Possible Bridges

Predestination: Verse 4

The Qur'an reads here: "God leaves straying those whom he pleases."[1] We need to share with our friend that if this is the case, man will be totally predestined. However, we know that the heart of God, his desire, is that no one goes astray.[2] God does not lead anyone astray; otherwise he would be unfair. God's desire is not that man goes astray but that he will come to know God. Man's sin is responsible for leading him to destruction. In the Muslim mind, man is totally predestined and has no say.

At this point, Christians need to be careful about predestination. We do know that the names of believers are written in the Book of Life before the existence of the world. On the other hand, this book is sealed and no one knows its contents; therefore, our position is to share God's heart with people (that all may come to know him). From our point of view, God can change his mind if people seek him for salvation.

God Does Not Need: Verses 7–9

These verses refer to an account in the life of Moses and say that God does not care at all if he is blasphemed by man, because he is very rich. To the Muslim mind, God does not need man. We can use this to share about the essence of God, leading our friend to understand that in love we need each other. God needs man's love, not because he is not complete and is seeking to be completed in man's love, but because God is so great that he wants to share his greatness with the ones he loves. When God loves man, it does not make him less God, nor less rich. In fact, God's love and need for man will not affect his richness at all.

Verse 9 provides other examples of God's destruction to show his lack of need for man. It refers to those destroyed by the flood, and the people of 'Ad and Thamud. The understanding here is that God does not care about people. He can wipe them off the face of the earth when they disobey. It is crucial to share with our Muslim friend that when the people of Sodom and

---

1. Ali, *The Holy Qur'an*, 620.
2. 2 Peter 3:9.

Gomorrah and the flood were dying, God was grieved.[3] The sin of mankind grieved his heart so much that he planned, even before time began, to die for man (in Jesus). In doing so, he was passing the sentence of judgment. The point is that when God does bring destruction, he does care and is grieved. God is great and rich; he does not need man in the sense that he is lacking in his character without a relationship with mankind, but God loves man and counts every soul as precious in his sight.[4]

Hell: Verses 14–17

Hell is described in these verses as a place so horrible that a person can drink death and not die, even though he asks for it. We can compare this to the verse in the Bible that reads: "During those days men will seek death, but will not find it; they will long to die, but death will elude them."[5] Hell truly will be terrible, because people cannot stop the pain and agony they will be in. But the ultimate pain will be eternal separation from God. Right now, our lives are bearable because he is present in the world, whether we have a relationship with him or not; but on the end day, those who have not accepted his gift of salvation through Jesus will bear the ultimate pain of being void of God.

God Blamed for Man's Destruction: Verse 22

We find something very unique in this verse. Satan is justifying himself for leading people astray by saying that God told the people about right and wrong. Since Satan was given no power over man, he cannot be blamed for man's destruction. The way the Qur'an reads here makes it appear that Muhammad agrees with what Satan is saying. Therefore, we would be led to the conclusion that the only one to blame for man's destruction is God, leaving Satan innocent. Predestination thus relates to Satan as well, meaning God created him for the purpose of leading man astray.

Good Word: Verses 24–25

We can relate these verses to that in the book of Psalms: "The righteous will flourish like a palm tree, they will grow like a cedar of Lebanon; planted in the house of the LORD, they will flourish in the courts of our God. They

---

3. Gen. 6:6–8; 18–19; 2 Sam. 24:16; Ps. 78; Jer. 42:10.
4. Ps. 116:15.
5. Rev. 9:6.

will still bear fruit in old age, they will stay fresh and green, proclaiming, 'The LORD is upright; he is my Rock, and there is no wickedness in him.'"[6]

In sharing this passage, we can explain the meaning of the psalm by comparing a "righteous" man to "a good word," as found in the Qur'an, and share that a person is only as good as his word. This will lead us to the perfect example of a man of his word—Jesus. Then we can refer to the verses in the New Testament that talk about Jesus as the Word of God.[7] When Christ's word dwells in us, we too become like fruitful trees, for he is the vine and we are the branches.[8]

Abraham: Verses 35–37

The only mention of Abraham's name in this sura comes in verse 35. Most commentators say that Abraham is blessing Mecca after he built the Ka'ba, which is called the "forbidden house" (v. 37). The actual meaning of the word *haram* is "to be forbidden." Scholars explain this word with the meaning that God forbids people to destroy it or to cause any harm to it. We need to share with our Muslim friend that God does not live in homes, and God is not going to ask man to protect God's house. If it is really God's house, he will protect it himself.

We can compare this to the church building or cathedral in Christianity, which is sometimes referred to as a "holy place," meaning a place "set aside for sacred use." Therefore, when we are in this place, we are meeting with the holy God for worship. However, we know from the teachings of the New Testament that God has chosen not to live in man-made structures but in man's heart.[9] We ourselves need to be holy, because we are his temple when he dwells in us. We need to risk sharing with our friend that when three and a half million people circle around the black stone called Ka'ba, it is not holy at all before God. He takes greater pleasure in a humble heart that chooses to follow him, to be cleansed by Jesus' blood, and to allow the Holy Spirit to live within him. That becomes the holiest place on earth.[10] We can go further in this comparison by relating the characteristics of the Old Testament tabernacle or temple to our own bodies when the Holy Spirit comes to dwell in us through Christ.

---

6. Ps. 92:12–15.
7. John 1:1, 14.
8. John 15:1–8.
9. 1 Cor. 3:16–17; 6:18–20; 2 Cor. 6:16.
10. Rom. 12:1–2; 1 Peter 1:15–16.

Asking Forgiveness for Others: Verse 41

Abraham is asking forgiveness for his parents and the believers. We can help our friend to understand that no one has the power to receive God's forgiveness on behalf of another. We do not have the power or right to mediate between God and man. Each person is responsible for his own sins and must confess them personally to God in order to receive forgiveness. Yet, that forgiveness will still not come unless we seek the true Mediator—Jesus Christ. He alone is worthy to talk to God on our behalf.

This also provides a good opportunity to share what the Bible says and what we believe about asking forgiveness, in contrast to what the Orthodox and Catholic churches practice in relation to confession of sins to a priest.

New Earth: Verse 48

This is a great opportunity to build a bridge by sharing with our friend the description of the new heaven and new earth in Revelation 21. We can also talk about the importance of living godly lives in order to speed the coming of the day of God.[11]

---

11.   2 Peter 3:11–13.

Al-Hijr

The Rocky Tract, or Stone

LATE MECCAN

Overview

This sura describes the miraculous ways of God's creation. It also refers to the first battle between Satan and Adam and Eve and the continuation of this battle until the end of the world. The punishment of the wicked and the reward of the good are highlighted in *al-Hijr*. Personalities mentioned are Abraham, Lot, and the Thamud people, who lived in the valley called *al-Hijr* (stone).

Comments and Possible Bridges

God Protects His Message: Verse 9

This can be one of the most important verses used to prove the authenticity of the Bible. It says here that God sent down the *zikr* (God's message to man) and will protect it from corruption. The point here that we need to make to our Muslim friend is that while the word *zikr* could be understood as the Qur'an, which he will be quick to agree with, it can also refer to the Bible.[1]

Stars: Verses 16–17

God created stars and set them in the heavens. As we compare this with

---

1. Cf. suras 16:43; 21:7; 38:49, 87.

our own verses from the Bible,[2] we can share that the main reason for the creation of the stars is that all who look at them will realize the might and wisdom of the Creator. In this vast universe with its amazing constellations at unfathomable distances, God also placed the stars as a nighttime guide for man. We can thus understand a very practical purpose for his creation.

The verses continue by saying that God protects the stars from Satan. The truth is, God did not protect them, for they and the rest of creation fell under the curse when sin entered the world, and, like man, they are waiting for complete delivery from the effects of sin in the end day. The apostle Paul gives a vivid description of the suffering nature endures due to sin.[3]

Creation: Verse 19

If we take this verse literally, there are problems in its meaning. It reads that God has spread out the earth (like a carpet),[4] and, therefore, we could not view it as the sphere it has been proven to be, but as flat. Again, as in previous verses, the mountains are thrown in place to fix the earth and make it more stable.[5] We know geologically that the earth does not receive stability from the presence of mountains. On the contrary, mountains are unstable. The stability of the earth comes from its shape, rotation, and the gravitational forces of the solar system. We can use this verse to ask our Muslim friends this question: What do you mean the mountain keeps the earth stable? While they may come to see the difficulties in the verse, we can answer their questions and lead them to look to the Creator and his ultimate purpose for creating the earth and mankind.

Jinn: Verses 26–27

God created man from clay. He also created jinn (evil spirits or demons) from poisonous fire. There is much debate among scholars over the meaning of the words "poisonous fire."[6] As we look at this verse with our Muslim friend, we can ask what he or she understands jinn to be. We are not exactly sure how God created angels, but the New Testament describes them as "flames of fire."[7] We can understand the confusion that comes from the Qur'an about God's creation of jinn.

---

2. For example, Ps. 147:4–5.
3. Rom. 8:19–23.
4. Ali, *The Holy Qur'an*, 640.
5. Sura 13:2–3.
6. Yusuf Ali's translation "from the fire of a scorching wind" is not correct.
7. Heb. 1:7.

What we need to express to our friend is that God created all things good. He created a perfect man called Adam, perfect angels, and a perfect creation. If we are to relate jinn to Satan and the fallen angels, we must make clear that God did not create them from poisonous fire. This gives the connotation that the substance or essence of Satan was evil. It is a good opportunity to review Satan's fall and talk about free will.

Creation of Man: Verses 29–30

We can draw a parallel to the Genesis account in the phrase "breathed into him from my spirit" in verse 29 of this sura. We can agree that God did breathe into Adam the "breath of life" and give more details for the story.[8] It is interesting that the same phrase is used when the Qur'an refers to Jesus' birth.[9]

Verse 30 reveals God commanding the angels to bow down before Adam. We understand the very special position the Qur'an wants to bestow on Adam, but our question should be: Would God ask for worship of any other being beside himself? This is a dangerous position in which to put man, as it could lead to pride and disregard for God.

Satan's Fall: Verses 31–35

Satan refuses to bow before Adam; thus, God curses him and casts him out of his presence. We need to note here that the fall of Satan comes after the creation of Adam in the Qur'an, while in the Bible it occurs prior to the creation of man.[10]

In this passage, however, we find a dialogue between Satan and God. Satan is asking God for an extension before punishment, so God grants him freedom until the end day. A great parallel can be drawn here to the time when Jesus cast the evil spirits from the lunatic. The evil spirits asked him not to destroy them but to send them into a group of pigs.[11] We can then draw our friend to the point that God allows us a certain amount of time on earth to follow him, but at the end of our life the judgment will come and repentance will be no more.

---

8. Gen. 2:7.
9. See sura 66:12.
10. Isa. 14:12–15; Dan. 8:10–12.
11. Mark 5:1–13.

Satan Tempted by God: Verses 39–40

Satan tells God, "Because you tempted me, I will tempt the nonbelievers." We must share that God did not tempt Satan.[12] Satan himself was full of pride and wanted to take God's place.[13] Satan, however, does tempt mankind, and he uses what is within him—pride—because this is the source of all evil. It is very important to notice that temptation is for all mankind, not only the nonbelievers. The book of Revelation tells us that Satan tempts even the chosen ones, and he went as far as to tempt Jesus, the incarnated one.

Satan's Power: Verse 42

This verse reveals that Satan has power only over those in the wrong. The Bible reveals to us, on the other hand, that the sin Satan promotes has power over all people—good and bad, lost and saved, wicked and righteous. The only way to overcome this power is through the work of Christ.[14] Thus we can share that we agree that the only true power Satan has is over his children. For Jesus made it clear that we are either children of Satan or children of God.[15] Only through Christ can we become children of God: "You are all sons of God through faith in Christ Jesus."[16]

Abraham: Verses 53–60

Here we have an account of the angels coming to tell Abraham that he would have a son and that God would destroy Sodom and Gomorrah. It is good to point out that Abraham already had Ishmael by this time, so the son about whom they are bringing the good tidings is Isaac, not Ishmael. We can move from these verses to those in the New Testament about the son of the covenant and the other son.[17]

Lot: Verses 61–74

The qur'anic account of God's dealing with Sodom and Gomorrah differs from that of the Bible. There is no dialogue between Abraham and the Lord in order to assure Lot's safety, but rather the angels tell him from the beginning that Lot will be saved and that his wife will lag behind. While

12. James 1:13–15.
13. Isa. 14:12–15.
14. 1 Cor. 15:55–58; 1 John 5:1–4.
15. John 8:33–59.
16. Gal. 3:26.
17. Gal. 4:21–31.

the Qur'an gives a vague reference to a larger group of people being saved along with Lot, we can read from the biblical account that all were destroyed except for Lot and his two daughters.

Verse 74 tells how God destroyed the city by raining down stones made out of clay. The Bible refers to the destruction as coming by brimstone and fire.[18] The archaeological facts show that the cities were burned, so the biblical account, which says God rained burning sulfur, is more accurate than just stones made out of clay.[19] We can bring strength to God's Word when we challenge our Muslim friend to look to archaeology as a source to give authenticity to the Bible.

---

18. Gen. 19:24 (KJV).
19. Wood, "Is there any evidence for the biblical story of Sodom and Gomorrah's destruction by fire and brimstone (sulfur)?" http://christiananswers.net/q-abr/abr-a007.html (accessed May 23, 2008); and Craig, "Scientists uncover Sodom's fiery end," http://news.bbc.co.uk/2/hi/middle_east/1497476.stm (accessed May 23, 2008).

Al-Nahl

The Bee

LATE MECCAN

Overview

In this sura God threatens the blasphemers and shows his might and power through the evidence of his creation. His grace for mankind is demonstrated by his creation of cattle, plants, and the sea, which provides fish to eat and ornaments for decoration. This proves, therefore, that they have to worship him. He warns people against accusing the Qur'an of being just a compilation of old stories. God then tells about the great punishment that will come to the blasphemers on the Day of Judgment and of the great blessings that will come to the believers.

God tells of his power to create the poor and the rich and of how he created man, male and female. His might is emphasized through the telling of many parables. He shows the miraculous nature of the Qur'an and warns the blasphemers against taking a stand against the Qur'an. He comes close to directly accusing the Jews of being blasphemers.

Comments and Possible Bridges

God's Timing: Verse 1

Muhammad is speaking on God's behalf and warns the blasphemers not to mock God about the end of the days, because it is surely coming and they need to be aware. We can build a bridge here by sharing that God does things in his own time. Yes, people have always tried to do things in their own timing. We drink instant coffee and instant tea and see instant problem solving in the movies, but God does not work this way. We cannot rush God with what we have in our mind. We must learn to wait on him.[1]

Angels: Verse 2

In this verse we see God saying that he sent a word from his Spirit to the angels to whomever he pleased of his messengers. The message was: "Beware; there is no god except Me." Here we can ask our Muslim friend a question to stimulate his or her thinking: Is the angel the one who spoke, or was it the Spirit of God? In Islam there is no clear differentiation between the Spirit and the angel. In several places we find the words *Holy Spirit* and *Gabriel* used interchangeably.

As we discuss this issue, we can share with our friend our point of view (which comes from the Bible) that there is a difference between the angel and the Spirit of God. The angel is a created being; he is just a messenger of the Spirit of God. While the translation uses the word *inspiration*, in Arabic, the word is *ruh*, which means "spirit." Our point in this discussion is to make clear that the angels are not the Spirit, even though we can agree that the Spirit of God is the one who brings his mind and thoughts to us.

Creation of Man: Verse 4

We need to take a deep breath in order to discuss many issues here with our friend. Is man created from clay or from sperm? If the sperm is in the man's glands, the man is already a living being. God created man from the mud of the earth and then breathed life into him. He then created Eve from man's rib. In speaking about man coming from sperm, this is not creation, but the procreation that God instilled in mankind as he joined man and woman together.

We can take this opportunity to share these beautiful verses of David in the book of Psalms: "For you created my inmost being; you knit me together in my mother's womb. I praise you because I am fearfully and wonderfully made; your works are wonderful, I know that full well. My frame was not hidden from you when I was made in the secret place. When I was woven together in the depths of the earth, your eyes saw my

---

1. Isa. 40:31 (KJV).

unformed body. All the days ordained for me were written in your book before one of them came to be."[2]

This is a great bridge in referring specifically to David. He describes his beginnings in his mother's womb (lowly), and yet later on he became a mighty king. This relates to the meaning of verse 4 in this sura, which says man starts from a lowly thing (sperm) and grows to become a mighty man who can stand to argue against his enemies.

Creation for Man's Benefit: Verses 5–11

These verses describe how God subdues his creation for man's benefit, and we can compare them to the creation account in Genesis.[3] However, in talking about creation, we may want to relate this to the importance of being good stewards of what God has given us. If we look around us today, we can see Saudi Arabia's abuse of oil, Africa's abuse of gold, and fallen humanity worldwide abusing God's resources, and we can see the consequences of this deviation from God's plan in global warming, high pollution rates in many cities, increased illnesses, and even the reduction of the human life span or quality of life in many places. These are great issues for our day, and they provide an opportunity to ask our Muslim friend to look at the difference between Western countries and the Muslim world, where environmental issues are virtually ignored. We can then share biblical principles that make a difference for us in the importance we place on caring for the environment.

Creation: Verse 12

Even though it sounds very good, the first part of this verse contains a great problem: God did not create the day and night, and the sun, moon, and stars to be subjected to man. Man can and does benefit from them but cannot subject them. On the other hand, the other part of the verse says the stars are signs to know God through the mind. Here we can agree and share the verse that says, "The heavens declare the glory of God; the skies proclaim the work of his hands."[4]

Creation: Verse 15

Here we see a repetition of the idea of throwing mountains to stabilize the earth. See notes on sura 15:19.

---

2. Ps. 139:13–16.
3. Gen. 1:28–30.
4. Ps. 19:1.

God Knows Man's Heart: Verses 19–23

Verse 19 says that God knows what you hide or what you reveal and he knows when the heart is full of pride. Here we can share with our Muslim friend that Jesus also knew what was in the hearts of people. Then we can read several incidents of this from the Bible, and even one from the Qur'an.[5] We can cross this bridge by sharing that this is proof of God's essence in Christ and continue by talking about his deity.

Hell: Verse 29

We can see here the picture the Qur'an gives of hell as an eternal place with doors. From this point we can continue by saying that hell is not only the place of the prideful but also the place for all who do not accept Jesus and who are thus the true blasphemers in the view of Christianity. People can believe in God, in angels, and in the Day of Judgment, but if they do not personally believe in the saving work of Jesus, they will be in this place described in verse 29.

Paradise, Garden of Eden: Verse 31

Once again paradise (heaven) is referred to as the Garden of Eden (see notes on sura 13:23), but we need to share with our friend that it is not the Garden of Eden anymore, but a new heaven—not a physical, earthly place. The lack of water in the desert lands inspired Muhammad to always include a statement about "rivers of water" flowing every time paradise is mentioned, as this would appeal greatly to a desert people.

Predestination: Verse 35

Blasphemers are blaming God for predestining them to hell. The Qur'an here says they cannot do that, because God sent messengers. We can see here a great contradiction, because in total the qur'anic teaching is that man is predestined. We can ask our friend about this, perhaps raising awareness in a loving way as to the contradictions of the Qur'an, but also looking for an opportunity to bridge to the topic of free will and man's need to choose.

Veracity of the Bible: Verse 43

God is saying to the blasphemers that he sent messengers who were mere men (not angels), and they should ask the people of the Holy Books (Jews

---

5.   Matt. 9:4; 22:18; Luke 9:47; John 6:15; and sura 3:49.

and Christians) if they do not know this. Here we see how Muhammad is asking the Christians and Jews to prove his apostleship. This proves that the books in Muhammad's time were authentic and the leaders in his time (Christians and Jews) used them to judge his message. This destroys the theory of the corruption of the biblical text, showing that Muhammad still trusted in it.

God Protects His Message: Verse 44

It is good to notice here that the same word, *zikr*, is used for the Qur'an as was used for the *Tawrat* and *Injil* in sura 15:9. That is why any Muslim will be quick to tell you that the Holy Books are three—*Tawrat*, *Injil*, and the Qur'an. These are the books of the only religions (Judaism, Christianity, and Islam) recognized by Islam, while all others are blasphemous. However, if a Muslim is a hardcore fundamentalist, he will refer only to Islam as the pure religion and everything else as blasphemy.

Creation Worships God: Verse 49

Here is a beautiful illustration of all creation bowing before God and worshiping him. Everything in heaven and on earth, even the animals and angels, worship God; nothing is prideful before him. How wonderful to share the picture of the second coming of Jesus when the Bible says every knee shall bow and every tongue confess that he is Lord.[6]

Dualism: Verse 51

The concept of dualism led to the revelation of this verse: "Do not worship two gods, for he is One God." Dualism promoted the presence of two gods, one good and the other evil.

The Purpose of the Qur'an: Verse 64

In this verse the purpose of the Qur'an is given as being to finish disputes and arguments between the people. The Bible, on the other hand, is given to lead mankind to know God. From the account of creation through the teaching on the second coming of Jesus, we are told how God entered history and desired for a relationship with man. An important point needs to be made here. If the Qur'an is given only to finalize disputes between people, when the arguments are finished, we find man still going astray. God's Word

---

6. Phil. 2:9–11.

needs to be more than that. It should lead people in all aspects of life to know him and to prepare them to live in his presence for eternity.[7]

Alcohol: Verse 67

This verse says that God made dates and grapes for the making of alcoholic beverages, which can be sold for money. Most commentators will admit that the Qur'an is referring to alcoholic beverages but that this was revealed before alcohol was forbidden. There is a great debate in the various Islamic schools of thought about making alcoholic drinks from dates, grapes, corn, and other starches. The verse reads that this is a sign from God for the people who have brains to comprehend. We need to share that while wine is mentioned in the Bible, God did not refer to it as a sign for people to believe in him. Christianity encourages self-control and not excessively using any food or drink that robs us of our self-control.[8]

Bees: Verses 68–69

"Bees," from which the name of the whole sura comes, are mentioned for the first time here. God told the bees through inspiration[9] to make homes in the mountains and everywhere. A Muslim should have a big problem if the same word of *inspiration* is used to reveal the Qur'an and to speak to a bee.

Verse 69 carries a lot of scientific contradictions. In reality, bees do not eat fruit but live on the nectar of the flowers. Also, the word *butun* (stomach) is used literally in the previous verses. But in reality the bees bring the honey out of their mouths and not from their stomachs. Toward the end of the verse, it says that the honeybees provide healing for people—meaning healing from sickness and disease. We understand that honey has good nutritional value and has a very small amount of royal jelly, which is the source within honey that provides all the health benefits. Otherwise, honey in itself is basically sugar. This understanding of honey as a healing power, however, has been emphasized so much in Muslim culture that in some countries certain local honeys can be sold as much as $100 per kilo (2.2 pounds).

This can provide a great bridge opportunity as we share that honey in itself has no real healing powers. God made all foods to help man and enabled him to produce medicines from many things. A Muslim may think that honey has "supernatural powers" for healing, but we need to share with

---

7. Luke 24:13–35; Gal. 3; 2 Tim. 3:16.
8. Eph. 5:18; 1 Tim. 3:8; 5:23; Titus 2:3.
9. Yusuf Ali uses the word *taught*, though the correct translation of the word *awha* is "inspired."

our friend that even though we can get healed through the use of physical medicine, we need spiritual medicine to heal our hearts. Honey will not take care of the spiritual dimension.

Parables: Verses 75–76

We find that God is giving parables in these verses. These two parables are hard to understand for a simple reason—there is no wisdom or truth in them. It would be a great idea to compare such parables with those of Jesus, which have clear, intact messages in them. See notes on sura 2:26.

Prophets: Verse 89

God says that he sent a messenger to every nation to be a witness for the nation, and he brought Muhammad as a witness to the Muslims, and he gave them the Qur'an. We need to share with our Muslim friend that God did not send prophets to all nations. In reality, all of God's prophets were Jews. God chose Abraham, and he continued to send the prophets to the nation of Abraham's descendants until he sent Jesus. After Jesus, the Holy Spirit remained to be with the believers, while Jesus went to be at the right hand of God.

Islam also contradicts itself, because in other places it says that Judaism, Christianity, and Islam are the only true religions, which means they alone have the true messengers from God. Yet, this verse says that God sent or will send a messenger for each nation, which would be erroneous if referring to the past. If referring to the future, then how could Muhammad be considered the seal of the prophets?

Holy Spirit: Verse 102

This verse says that the Holy Spirit gave the Qur'an to Muhammad. Most commentators refer to the Holy Spirit as the angel Gabriel.[10] We need to explain that the Holy Spirit is not Gabriel and that the Qur'an can never be from the Holy Spirit, mainly because it denies the deity of Christ, denies that God came in the flesh as Jesus, denies the crucifixion, and reduces Jesus to just a prophet. In the first epistle of John, we learn how to recognize what is from the Holy Spirit.[11]

---

10. Ibn Kathir, *Tafseer al-Qur'an al-Azeem*, 2:538; Ali, *The Holy Qur'an*, 684; Committee of the Qur'an and Sunna, *Al-Muntakhab*, 465.
11. 1 John 4.

Abraham: Verses 120–123

These verses refer to Abraham as a good believer and not like the Jews (maybe referring to those in Muhammad's time). A great parallel can be drawn when we share what Jesus said to the Jews, telling them that if they were truly descendants of Abraham, they would know he was from God.[12] We can use this as a bridge to share with Muslims that Jesus came to his own people (the Jews), and they refused him. Now it is not a certain nation but whoever believes in him that becomes his *tribe* (own people).[13]

Sabbath: Verse 124

The Jews found fault with Muhammad for worshiping on Fridays. He responds by saying that keeping the Sabbath is only for the Jews, even though they themselves do not keep it. We can move from here to refer to the words of Jesus: "The Sabbath was made for man, not man for the Sabbath. So the Son of Man is Lord even of the Sabbath."[14] We can then share with them the conversation between Jesus and the woman at the well.[15] If we look at it from the perspective of our need to be holy in order to be in the presence of God, we can agree that man is never clean enough to stand in his presence (Friday, Saturday, or Sunday); but when our sins are forgiven by accepting Christ's redemptive act on the cross, we become a new creation in Christ and can be holy on all days, including the Sabbath. This leads us to the conclusion that it is not the day but the relationship that leads us to worship him in spirit and truth.

---

12. John 8:12–59.
13. Matt. 21:42–44; Acts 4:11–12; 7; 2 Cor. 4:12–18.
14. Mark 2:27–28.
15. John 4.

Bani Isra-il *or* Al-Israa

The Children of Israel or *Journey of Muhammad Between Mecca and Jerusalem*

ONE YEAR BEFORE THE *HIJRA*

Overview

This sura begins with the revelation of Muhammad's trip between the Ka'ba and the temple in Jerusalem. It continues by sharing about Moses, the Israelites, and the value of the Qur'an for leading people to truth. Sura *Bani Isra-il* also reveals what will happen on the end day. A description is given about the corruption of nations, as well as directions on how the believers should live. Readers learn how God dealt in the past with nonbelievers and how he will deal with those in the present day and after the Day of Judgment. The origin of man and Satan are mentioned as well.

Verses also describe the miracle that is the Qur'an and how no one (either human or jinn) can bring even one verse to match its beauty. We will look at this point in detail in the notes that follow.

Comments and Possible Bridges

Muhammad's Trip to Jerusalem: Verse 1

This verse refers to the trip Muhammad took from Mecca to Jerusalem. Some of the *hadith* say that Muhammad took the *buraq* (an animal bigger than the mule and having two wings in its thighs). This animal's specialty is carrying the prophets. The *buraq* carried him to Jerusalem and also to the heavens, where he saw Abraham, Moses, and Jesus, and led them in prayers. Then Muhammad went back to Mecca. Various *hadith* provide evidence for this physical trip. However, other *hadith* record Aisha saying, "Muhammad's body was always present, but God gave him this trip in the spirit."[1] Thus commentators still continue to argue both views.

Lack of Belief in the Hereafter: Verse 10

The Qur'an says that God saves the greatest torment for those who do not believe in the end day or hereafter. We need to share that people will go to hell, not because they do not believe in the hereafter, but because they do not believe in the saving work of Christ. As to the hereafter, anyone with limited logic will know that life on earth is short and that eternity must exist. Even the ancient Egyptians believed in the afterlife and built great tombs and boats to insure their destination; yet we, the people of the Book and of the Qur'an, know that the gods of the ancient Egyptians did not save them from an eternity in hell.

Scroll of Deeds: Verses 13–14

These verses reveal that every human has a diary hanging around his neck, and on the end day whatever is written on this diary will be known. We can share a great parallel from the Bible when Jesus said, "The good man brings good things out of the good stored up in him, and the evil man brings evil things out of the evil stored up in him. But I tell you that men will have to give account on the day of judgment for every careless word they have spoken. For by your words you will be acquitted, and by your words you will be condemned."[2]

We can also tell our Muslim friend the parable of the talents.[3]

Individual Responsibility: Verse 15

Every person is responsible for himself. This is a fundamental teaching of Islam. That is why it is very hard for Muslims to understand the free gift of salvation through Jesus. If no one else can bear the burdens of another, then

1. Ibn Kathir, *Al Bedaya wa Nahiya*, 3:160.
2. Matt. 12:35–37.
3. Matt. 25:14–30.

how can Jesus bear our sins? We can use this thought to move to the issue of sins as something spiritual and not material that cannot be paid for by works but only through the atoning work of Christ on the cross.

God Forcing People to Sin: Verse 16

In discussing this verse, a great theological dilemma should be pointed out, for the verse says that God is commanding people to sin. The way the Arabic reads (which is not adequately conveyed in the English translation) is that God decides to destroy a people; so he gives a command for them to do something that he knows they will not be able to do. This will force them to do wrong. We need to share with our Muslim friend that God is holy, and he will extend his grace, never allowing us to be tempted beyond what we can bear. He enables us to please him by doing right.

Humility: Verses 37–38

The Qur'an is encouraging people to be humble by telling them that it is considered a sin to walk around filled with joy. For this reason, when we look around us at the faces of Muslims, we find them, for the most part, long and sad. They are afraid to show joy or extra exuberance, and even when they do have joy in their hearts, they fear it is a sin and keep asking God's forgiveness. When they laugh, they feel guilty. We need to share with them that the Bible reveals an opposite view—we need to be joyful always.[4] A humble heart does not mean a long, sad-looking face. We can be humble and yet full of joy.

Seven Heavens: Verse 44

This verse reveals that the seven heavens and the earth and whatever is in them worship God. We can share parallel verses we find in the Bible.[5]

Zabur *(Psalms): Verse 55*

In sharing about how the Lord gave gifts to the prophets, this verse says that David was given the *Zabur* (the Psalms). We can ask our friend if he or she would like to hear what the Psalms say and then read some selected passages.

Cursed Tree: Verse 60

God tells Muhammad that he gave him a vision of the cursed tree, known as the tree of Zaqqum, which grows in hell. Some commentators say that

---

4. Rom. 12:12; 1 Thess. 5:16.
5. Pss. 19:1; 97:6.

hell is fire, and therefore, no wooden tree could grow there. We bridge this by sharing that the only cursed tree mentioned in the Bible is the one Jesus himself cursed.[6] We can then move from the physical tree that was cursed because it did not provide fruit, to the spiritual trees that will be cursed if they do not produce fruit as a result of their relationship with the vine.[7]

Satan's Fall: Verses 61–64

We read here a retelling of the story of Satan's fall. See notes on sura 15:31–35.

Prayer Times: Verses 78–79

Here we find the exhortation to establish regular times for prayers. They include:

- *Fajr*:   Dawn (also the time to read the Qur'an)
- *Zuhr*:   When the sun starts down
- *'Asr*:   Late afternoon
- *Magrib*: At sunset
- *Isha*:   Full darkness

We can relate this to the way we as Christians are exhorted to pray (without ceasing) and what prayer means to us.

Holy Spirit: Verse 85

Mankind is very limited in knowledge, and the spirit is God's business. The meaning of this verse is that we cannot really understand much about God's Spirit. We can share that when a man named Nicodemus asked Jesus about the Spirit of God and how to be born again, Jesus took the time to explain it to him. He did not rebuke his limited understanding but explained to him that the Spirit of God is like the wind. We cannot see it, but we feel what it can do. From there we can continue to build a wonderful bridge to speak to our Muslim friend about the Holy Spirit and his powerful work in our life.

Nothing Like the Qur'an: Verse 88

This verse makes God seem very arrogant in his challenge to mankind and jinn to come together and try to produce anything like the Qur'an.

---

6. Mark 11:12–14, 20.
7. John 15.

Many questions come to mind as we read this verse. Would God really make such a challenge? Would not a challenge such as this reduce the value of his creation? Would the Creator of the universe enter into a challenge with his subjects?

From another perspective, if we look objectively at the writings of people throughout history, we can find some superior to the Qur'an. The poetry written in the Arabian Peninsula prior to Islam is linguistically superior to parts of the Qur'an. We can even find many verses in the Qur'an taken from this pre-Islamic poetry.

Muhammad's Justification as a Prophet: Verses 90–98

These verses tell how the people of Mecca were asking Muhammad to produce some signs in order for them to believe that he was the messenger of God. He gave them nothing and called them blasphemers. God tells him that he himself is enough witness to Muhammad's prophethood. He then proceeds to call all who do not believe in their signs (the Qur'an and the witness of God through Muhammad) blasphemers.

Plagues: Verse 101

The Qur'an says that Moses had nine signs. The Bible calls them plagues, and there were ten of them. We can ask our Muslim friend if he or she would like to know what these signs were. If so, we can lead our friend through a nice Bible study of the ten plagues, with the ultimate bridge being that of the death of the firstborn. The earthly salvation of the Israelites came with a sacrifice; our salvation comes the same way, but it is eternal.

Pharaoh: Verse 103

The Qur'an reads here that God killed Pharaoh and his army by drowning them in the sea. In some other places it says that he was saved. We can lead our friend to read the account from the Bible to get the full picture of what really happened.

Al-Kahf

The Cave

MECCAN

Overview

The sura begins with a warning to the people who say that God has a son. We are then told the story of the people of the cave. A number of people of the Book fled from the Romans to the cave and stayed there asleep for more than three hundred years. God then brought them back to life. The purpose of this story is to show that life is brief and uncertain.

Other topics covered in this sura are heaven, hell, parts of Moses' story, and the story of the two-horned person, which will be explained in detail in the comments below.

Comments and Possible Bridges

Son of God: Verse 4

God is telling Muhammad, "Warn the ones that say that God has a son (physical)." See notes on sura 9:30.

Muhammad Worried About the Nonbelievers: Verses 5–6

God is telling Muhammad that those who do not believe in his message have gone too far in their lying, and he encourages Muhammad not to feel bad because of them. This shows us that Muhammad had really been troubled by Christians and others who did not put their trust in his message. We will see as the suras progress that more and more revelations come in relation to Muhammad's desire to try to prove himself as a prophet.

People of the Cave: Verses 9–26

God continues by giving the account of the people of the cave. The placement of this story just after the above revelation of Muhammad's feelings gives the impression that he wants to reveal a miracle equal to or counter to that of God having a son.

The story recounts that a small group of people went to the cave in order to escape from the heretical society of the time. The cave was a refuge for them from the blasphemers of the town, and God took care of them while they were sleeping in the cave.

Verse 18 gives a description of the sleepers. It says they looked like they were awake, but they were actually in a deep sleep. God turned them to the right side and left side, so that their bodies would not get hurt by sleeping a long time on one side. The second half of the verse says, "If you looked at them, you would be terrorized."

When the people of the cave woke up, they expressed to each other their fear of being stoned if they went into the city. However, God revealed to the people of the city that he had raised them from sleep after a very long period of time. The people of the city then believed in God, and the people of the cave died a natural death shortly thereafter. Then some people of the city proposed to build a mosque over them, while others instead wanted to put them in the cave and seal the entrance. There was a dispute about the number of people in the cave. They were from three to five persons, but for sure they had a dog with them. It was said that they stayed in the cave from 300 to 309 years.

It is good to know the history of this story, though it has many versions. The most common account is that first given by Gregory of Tours (538–594). The group is referred to in Christian tradition as the Seven Sleepers of Ephesus. The myth tells that they were seven Christians who faced persecution during the reign of the Roman emperor Decius around AD 250. When they would not recant their faith, they were sealed alive in a cave and found by a farmer during the reign of Theodosius (379–395). Once the cave was opened, the men came out thinking they had slept only a day, only to find that their world was now Christian and crosses were everywhere. They gave praise to God, told their story to the bishop, and died praising God.[1] It is accepted across the Christian world today that this story is merely a myth and not a true event.

We need to ask our beloved Muslim friend some questions here. What is the wisdom behind this story? Commentators say that it shows that God can raise people from the dead, but were the people dead or just sleeping? The Qur'an does not say they were dead. They were asleep, though looking as if they were awake, with a terrorizing look on their faces. We can share that the only time we know that God put someone to sleep was for an understandable purpose clearly stated in the Bible. We do not know how long he was asleep, but it certainly was not for three hundred years. God put the man to sleep in order to do the greatest operation ever—to create a woman out of his rib.[2]

God Willing: Verses 23–24

If you enter a building and ask a Muslim whether the staircase is to the right or the left, he or she will reply, "*In sha Allah*, right" ("God willing," right). In verse 24, a Muslim is directed not to think for the next moment to come. He has to be so trapped in the present, that to think of the moment to come is blasphemy; so he has to say "God willing." He is never sure. We need to be very careful when asking a Muslim about the weather forecast.

Having a personal relationship with God gives us more trust for tomorrow. This is the essence of faith. In the Bible there is a passage very close to this, but it is used in a completely different way. It urges us to say, "God willing, we will do something."[3] To the best of our understanding, we need to pray for what God has for us in the future, because without a vision, people go astray.[4] God gives us a vision so that we can move forward, and we move forward and plan for tomorrow as if it has already happened by faith. In grasping these concepts, we can understand better the contrasting fatalistic approach with which the Muslim faces life.

Paradise, Garden of Eden: Verse 31

We can identify a Muslim today by looking at the person's wedding band. A Muslim's wedding band will be silver, not gold. A Muslim cannot

---

1. Fortescue, "The Seven Sleepers of Ephesus."
2. Gen. 2:20–25.
3. James 4:13–17.
4. Prov. 11:14; 29:18.

wear gold or silk or drink wine. However, this verse tells us that in heaven, Muslims will have golden bands, clothes made out of green silk, and sit on couches, enjoying life. Why would God forbid good things for us to use here on earth when he gives it to us in heaven? We can share that when we believe in Christ as Savior, God gives us the Holy Spirit as a down payment for eternity, and we start to experience God's kingdom in our hearts prior to death. We have joy, hope, and peace now, and when we go to be in heaven, we will have all these things in abundance. God is not robbing us of peace here in order to give it to us over there; he gives us peace here and provides complete peace in eternity. There is no purpose for denying gold now and allowing it later.

Parable of Two Men: Verses 32–38

The parable of two men presents a wonderful opportunity to parallel it to Jesus' story of the two men who went to the temple to pray. In Jesus' story one man lifted up his hands, claiming all God's goodness in his life. The other one, with a broken heart and not even able to lift his eyes, asked for forgiveness. He was forgiven. The purpose in sharing this parable is to be able to introduce our friend to the one who told the story in the first place and to explain what forgiveness is all about.[5]

Wealth and Sons: Verse 46

The Qur'an points to money and children as the ultimate pleasures in earthly life. We need to share that money can be lost at any moment and children will grow up and eventually die. We should fill our hearts with the joy of a relationship with God, not with the temporary joy money and children bring. While a Muslim will never quote this verse, the way the majority of them live and follow folk Islam reveals that their main goals in life are to gain children (sons) and money.

Prophets: Verse 56

The Qur'an states clearly here that God sent his prophets and messengers for the ultimate purpose of revealing right and wrong and the consequences of each. We can agree with them that this is really what the prophets were all about. But out of all these prophets, there was only one who had the ability not only to warn and give good news but also to be the Savior for mankind.

---

5. Luke 18:9–14.

God's Wisdom: Verses 61–82

We find here a very unusual account of Moses accompanying what the Qur'an calls "a good man," apparently an angel. Moses wants to learn from this man's wisdom, but as he walks with him, the good man does a lot of unusual things and then tells Moses the wisdom behind his actions. In reading these verses, we find many contradictions to God's wisdom. For example, when the man kills a young boy, Moses asks him why. He explains that the boy will grow up to be a bad man and be the reason for his parents losing their faith; but because he killed him, the parents will be given a better boy. We can ask, "Does a believer lose his faith? Can a son be the reason for the parents going astray? Was this the only solution—to kill the boy in order to allow the parents to have another boy?" We should ask such questions for it is very hard to see God's wisdom here.

Some commentators compare the good man in Muhammad's account with Melchizedek, who was the priest of Salem.[6] How this man relates to Moses in the Qur'an, however, is very different from how Melchizedek (Khider or Salah) relates to Abraham in Genesis 14.

Two-Horned Person (Zul-qarnain): Verses 83–101

When the people ask about the two-horned person (*zul-qarnain*), Muhammad is ready to tell the story. Muhammad says this person was a man of great knowledge, and he used his might to go to where the sun sets. There he found that the sun goes down into a hole in the ground filled with water and black mud. He found people there who did not know God, and he witnessed to them. Then he went to where the sun rises and also found people there to preach to about God. Finally, he went to a place between two mountains, where the people were threatened by their enemy. He asked them to collect pieces of iron. He poured over the iron molten brass and asked them to build a big fire. The iron and brass melted to make a very strong dam that no one could penetrate. The dam protected this valley from the evil ones, Gog and Magog.

We cannot move past this account without asking some serious questions. When the sun goes down, does it really go into a hole in the ground? Is there a place where the sun comes out of the earth for rising? As we consider this account, we need to remember what we read before about the qur'anic concept of the earth being a flat plain. It will not be difficult to convince even

---

6. Elass, *Understanding the Koran*, 117–18; Ali, *The Holy Qur'an*, 748.

the least educated person that the earth is like a ball that rotates on its own axis, which explains sunrise and sunset. In light of this truth, we can then truly evaluate the Qur'an's account.

Other things that catch our attention are the two names, Gog and Magog, and the building of the huge dam of iron and brass. How much fire and intense heat would be needed to melt a mountain of stacked iron? It is impossible. The purpose in building the huge dam is in order to stop Gog and Magog. We can bring Muslims to the book of Revelation, where the Bible talks about the battle (either in the spiritual or physical realm, depending on the school of interpretation one follows), where no such dam, even if built from steel, could stop the ultimate battle between good and evil.[7]

---

7.   Rev. 20.

Maryam

Mary

SEVEN YEARS BEFORE THE *HIJRA*

Overview

The name of the sura, Mary, refers to the mother of Jesus. It reveals the story of the birth of John the Baptist (*Yahya*) to Elizabeth and Zechariah (*Zakariya*) and the story of Mary and how she heard about Jesus. It also refers to the Old Testament character Abraham asking his father to stop worshiping idols and to worship the only one God. This sura contains the genealogy of Abraham, Ishmael, and Isaac, and the story of Idris. Reference is made to heaven and hell, and the sura ends with verses about blasphemers who say God has a son.

Comments and Possible Bridges

John the Baptist: Verses 2–14

The account of John the Baptist (*Yahya*) is close to that of the Bible. There are some differences, however, such as when Zechariah asked God for a sign. In the qur'anic version, the Lord makes him dumb for three nights (in the Bible he is dumb until John is born). We can share with our Muslim friend that this dumbness was not a sign but because Zechariah did not believe what God was telling him.

While the Qur'an tells us that John the Baptist was a very unusual person, not much more information is given about him. We can therefore use the opportunity to introduce our friend to the account of John the Baptist as given in the Bible.

Peace on Him: Verses 14–15; 32–33

Verses 14 and 15 parallel verses 32 and 33. The first two verses refer to John the Baptist, while the second two refer to Jesus. Some Muslim commentators, like Ibn Kathir, quote from the *Hadith* a dialogue between Jesus and John the Baptist. Jesus asks John the Baptist to intercede to God for him. Then John the Baptist says something very similar to what we find in the Bible: "No, Jesus you are ahead of me." This *hadith* also says that John the Baptist has no sin.[1] This presents a great opportunity to share what Jesus said about John the Baptist: "I tell you the truth: Among those born of women there has not risen anyone greater than John the Baptist; yet he who is least in the kingdom of heaven is greater than he."[2] This shows that although he was great, John the Baptist was like other men and had a sinful nature.

We then need to share with our Muslim friend the true dialogue that took place between Jesus and John, when Jesus asked John to baptize him.[3] It is important to say that Jesus asked John to do this, not because John was greater than Jesus, but because Jesus wanted to complete all righteousness and to be an example for mankind.

Revelation of Jesus' Birth to Mary: Verses 17–20

Verse 17 is one of the most important verses in this sura. The simple approach for commentators of this verse is to take the spirit here as God's Spirit, which is Gabriel, and affirm that he appeared to Mary exactly like a man.[4] Another view comes from the *Hadith*, as given by Ibn Ka'ab, which says that the spirit of Jesus is one of the spirits God used in making an oath in Adam's time. This is the spirit that appeared to Mary as a complete man. This means that Jesus' spirit appeared to Mary, and he dwelled inside of her.[5] In general, most Muslim scholars consider the angel Gabriel and the Holy Spirit

---

1.   Ibn Kathir, *Tafseer al-Qur'an al-Azeem*, 3:108.
2.   Matt. 11:11.
3.   Matt. 3:13–17.
4.   Yusuf Ali translates *ruhana* (our spirit) as "our angel," which is not a correct literal translation.
5.   Ibn Kathir, *Tafseer al-Qur'an al-Azeem*, 3:109.

as one. Whatever the Islamic interpretation might be, we need to share the biblical truth—the Spirit of God came upon Mary and she became with child.[6]

The dialogue between Mary and the angel is very close to the account we have in the Bible, especially from verse 20: "How can I become pregnant and I have never been touched by a man?"[7] We can take this parallel and read the full account from the Bible to compare.

Jesus as Pure: Verse 19

The word zakiyan, which is a title of Jesus, is interpreted by commentators as meaning "pure." This is the closest the Qur'an comes to explaining or admitting that Jesus was without sin.

Jesus' Birth: Verses 23–26

These verses say that Mary lost control during childbirth and asked to die at the moment of delivery. We have to share with our friend that Mary never regretted having Jesus, nor did she give birth under a tree, but in a stable.

Jesus Spoke as a Baby: Verses 29–33

These verses tell how Jesus spoke as a baby in order to defend his mother. All the miracles in the Bible are to reveal the deity of Christ or are for the welfare of mankind. Jesus' speaking while a baby appears more like magic than a miracle that demonstrates his deity. If he spoke only this one time and did not speak again until he was an adult, the miracle has no purpose. We need to explain here that Jesus lived a very normal life till the age of thirty; and when the time came, he revealed his deity through his miracles and in the transfiguration. It is not important for an infant to speak, but it is important that we become like an infant, desiring for God speak to us.

Jesus' Death and Resurrection: Verse 33

This is one of only two verses in the Qur'an that refer to the death of Jesus.[8] Many Christians use this verse as qur'anic evidence for the death and resurrection of Jesus. We need to be careful in doing this in light of the verses previously mentioned (14–15), which refer to John the Baptist in the same way.

---

6. Luke 1:35.
7. See Luke 1:34.
8. See also sura 4:157.

Son of God: Verse 35

We see repeatedly that the Qur'an denies the sonship of Jesus. It says that it would not suit God, who is the Creator of all things, to have a son, since all he has to do is to say "Be" and creation takes place. However, we could look at this from another angle. If all God has to do is say "Be" for something to happen, then it proves that he would not have to have had sexual relations with Mary in order to have Jesus.

Abraham: Verse 41–50

Here Abraham is encouraging his father to stop worshiping Satan. In guiding our Muslim friend through the biblical text, we can share that though at one time Terah did worship idols,[9] he obviously came to belief in God[10] and played a role in God's plan for Abraham to become the father of his chosen nation.[11]

Prophets: Verse 58

God gives an account of many prophets: the sons of Adam, the sons of Noah, and the sons of Abraham and Israel. When they are told verses from the Qur'an (the signs most gracious), they bow down in worship, crying. A question arises here: How can these people hear the Qur'an? They died many, many years before the Qur'an. For a Muslim, the highest place has been given to Muhammad, but we can encourage them to think about this line of amazing prophets. Can Muhammad really measure up to them?

Mediators to God: Verses 81–90

These verses say that the blasphemers took many idols as mediators to God. Verse 87 reveals that no one has the power of intercession (mediating) except the one who made a covenant with God. Verse 88 then says, "Then the blasphemers (Christians) say God has a son." Muhammad denies this strongly, saying that such a proclamation is so wrong or horrible that it could tear the heavens and break the mountains.

These verses can be used to lead our Muslim friend to understand that Jesus is the only one who has the power to be our mediator with God. He is the only one, as verse 87 says, who has made a covenant with God, because

---

9.   Josh. 24:2.
10.   Gen. 31:53.
11.   Gen. 11:24–32.

he is one with God. It is the same concept that we have as Christians in marriage. When a man and woman marry, they make a covenant to stay together forever. Yes, Christians say that Jesus is the Son of God, and, yes, this truth is so powerful that it tore the heavens apart, and it is so true that the mountains were broken and the graves opened when he died. Through these verses, a Muslim is so close to the truth, yet so far away. Only the power of the Holy Spirit at work while we are sharing with our Muslim friend can make the difference.

Qur'an, Easy for Arabic Speakers: Verse 97

God says, "We made the Qur'an easy in thine own tongue." We can say it is not easy either for a Muslim or for a Christian, Arabic speaker or not, because not only is the language of the Qur'an difficult to understand but also complete details of accounts are not revealed in one passage. The settings of where these verses came upon Muhammad are not there, and so we have to use another book, which gives the reasons for the revelation. We can also find it difficult because the accounts of personalities, stories, and teachings are not given together or systematically. This is a good opportunity to lovingly share the differences we see between the Qur'an and the Bible in the way the material is presented and in the language that is used. We could even give our Muslim friends a copy of the Bible and let them discover for themselves the differences and decide which is easier to understand.

Ta-Ha

Mystic Letters, Ta *and* Ha

Overview

Though the true understanding of these letters is unknown, there is an interpretation of them as meaning "O man!" One *hadith* records Muhammad as saying that God read suras *Ta-Ha* and *Ya-Seen* (sura 36) a thousand years before the creation of Adam. The sura elevates the Qur'an to the same status of the one who gave it. This means that the Qur'an is equal to God.

Within this sura, we read the account of Moses and how he asked for Aaron (*Haron*) to be his helper. It also tells about Pharaoh and his magicians, who became believers in God and thus received Pharaoh's torment. *Ta-Ha* records that Pharaoh died in the sea after it had been split apart. When Moses goes up the mountain to talk to God, the Samaritans lured the Israelites to make the golden calf.

Comments and Possible Bridges

Human Characteristics of God: Verse 5

As with other verses, this reads that God is "sitting on the throne." See notes on suras 5:64; 7:54; and 48:10.

Moses: Verses 10–36

Moses sees the fire and starts wondering about it. When he approaches it, he hears a voice calling him (v. 11). God tells him to take off his sandals. "I choose you, so listen," God says. We read that God gives Moses all the instructions for what he should do, even the miracles he is to perform before Pharaoh; then he tells Moses to go to Pharaoh. The first reaction we see from Moses toward God is in verse 25. Moses asks God to take anger from him, to help him do his tasks, and to make his tongue able to speak so that the people may understand. He also asks God to give him Aaron as his helper. In verse 36, we read that God guaranteed Moses all that he asked.

We need to share with our Muslim friend the complete account of the encounter between Moses and God, and how at first Moses refused to go and lead the Israelites out of Egypt. He said the people would not listen to him because he was not able to speak well. So it was God who said he would put Aaron with him to be his spokesman. It will be an eye-opener for a Muslim to see the dialogue between God and Moses and to compare the two accounts verse by verse. The account in the Qur'an is very similar, but it is for the most part only a one-sided conversation.

Moses' Birth: Verses 37–40

The story here goes back to tell how Moses was born and saved as a child. We can compare again what we have in the Bible to the Qur'an, taking note of the Bible's clearer, linear approach to the story of Moses.

Made to Be God's: Verse 41

Here God says, "I made you for myself." We can tell our friend, "This verse is not only for Moses, but for you too—God made you to be his." Psalm 139 will show our friend how precious we are in God's sight and how he planned us to be in this world. These verses tell how he loves us so much that he saves us through his Son so that we might live for him always:

> But because of his great love for us, God, who is rich in mercy, made us alive with Christ even when we were dead in transgressions—it is by grace you have been saved. And God raised us up with Christ and seated us with him in the heavenly realms in Christ Jesus, in order that in the coming ages he might show the incomparable riches of his grace, expressed in his kindness to us in Christ Jesus. For it is by grace you have

been saved, through faith—and this not from yourselves, it is the gift of God—not by works, so that no one can boast. For we are God's workmanship, created in Christ Jesus to do good works, which God prepared in advance for us to do.[1]

Pharaoh: Verses 57–71

Moses was in the presence of Pharaoh. Pharaoh's magicians threw down their sticks and ropes, and Moses imagined that these sticks and ropes had become snakes, and he became afraid. God told Moses to throw down his stick, so he did. Moses' stick became a big snake and ate all the other snakes. The magicians believed in Moses and his God. Pharaoh in anger threatened to cut off their hands and feet and crucify them on a date palm tree. (It is important to notice that all the trees in the Qur'an are date palm trees.) Even so, the magicians chose to believe in the God of Moses.

Here we just need to expose our Muslim friend to the real story of Moses. Moses did not merely do this one sign but many others as well; but according to the Qur'an, this is the only sign given to Pharaoh. Nor do we read in the Bible that Pharaoh's magicians came to believe in God.

Moses: Verses 77–80

The story jumps from the encounter with the magicians to the exodus. God tells Moses to take the people at night and cross the sea, where he will make a way in the water. All other details known to us from the Bible are not mentioned. We can easily use this as an opportunity to share all that took place from the time Moses began talking with Pharaoh to the time Moses and the people went through the sea. Knowing they were several million Israelites, it will become logical that it could not happen within such a short span of time.

Moses and the Golden Calf: Verses 85–97

These verses claim that the Samaritans led the Israelites astray while Moses was on the mountain. They blame the Samaritans for asking the Israelites to give up their ornaments, which they threw on the fire, out of which came the body of a calf. It was the Samaritans, not Aaron, who told them the calf was their god.

Moses asks Aaron about where he was during this time, and Aaron tells him, "I cannot push the people or they will scatter." So Moses punishes

_____

1. Eph. 2:4–10.

the Samaritans by casting them out of the camp. We can ask our friend what he or she knows of the Samaritan people, and then we can share the information we have, which is that these people appear only very late in the time of the kings of Judah (long after Moses) and were located in Palestine, not the Sinai.

We also can say that we know a story about a Samaritan who was called the Good Samaritan. Our friend most likely will ask, "What is the story of that Samaritan?" Then we can share the story in full.

The Qur'an refrains from blaming Aaron as the one who made the golden calf, because in general it does not point out the sins or mistakes of prophets. We can share that the Bible takes time to show the prophets as normal people, who did things beyond human ability. The Bible shows God's power through his prophets but also shows how degradation can take place in a man's life (even a prophet's) when he is away from God. We can give as an example David's sin with Bathsheba.

Adam: Verse 115

God created Adam in a perfect state, but in this verse, it says that when God trusted or made a covenant with Adam, Adam forgot and disobeyed. Commentators say that Adam was not firm (in his resolve). This speaks against God himself, because when God created Adam, Adam was firm, strong, and able to say yes or no. It was out of his free will that he chose to sin, because God did not make man a robot but a person of choice.

Tree of Eternity: Verses 120–122

Satan is asking Adam to eat from the Tree of Eternity or Immortality. The Bible says it was the Tree of the Knowledge of Good and Evil, and we can use this point to compare the two stories. Adam and Eve did eat from the Tree of the Knowledge of Good and Evil, and, as the Qur'an also says, when they ate, they recognized they were naked and started to cover themselves with the leaves of the garden.

In the Bible the Tree of Life is different from the Tree of the Knowledge of Good and Evil. Adam ate from the latter and eventually died—he was mortal. If he had eaten from, or continued to eat from the Tree of Life, he would not have died. This is why God sent Adam and Eve out of the garden, so that they would not eat from this tree and live forever in their new sinful state.

We do not read in the qur'anic account, as we do in the Bible, that God came to the garden asking, "Where are you, Adam?" Once Adam and Eve ate, they felt shame and covered themselves and tried to hide from God. In the biblical account, when God came to find them, he asked where Adam was. Adam said, "I heard you in the garden, and I was afraid because I was naked; so I hid."[2] God's question did not mean he did not know where Adam was; but sometimes God asks questions to give us a chance to confess our sins and deal with them openly. This is not mentioned in the Qur'an, because we see in verse 122 that it merely says that God chose him; meaning he showed him mercy and guidance without asking for a confession of sin. We can build a great bridge here by saying that when we commit sin, forgiveness can never come unless the price is paid for that sin. That is why the biblical account tells that the Savior will come from Eve.[3]

2.   Gen. 3:10.
3.   Gen. 3:15.

Al-Anbiyaa

The Prophets

MIDDLE MECCAN

Overview

The sura begins by saying that the end days are soon and the blasphemers are not taking this into consideration. They are claiming that Muhammad is not a prophet, because a prophet should not be human. They are also saying that the Qur'an is just magic, poetry, or crazy dreams. God's punishment is revealed to people who make such accusations. The sura tells of the glory of God in creating the heavens and earth. It reveals what will happen to people on the *end day*. As with other suras, several stories are included about personalities such as Moses, Aaron and Pharaoh, Abraham and Lot, Noah, Solomon, David, Job, Ishmael, Idris, Jonah, Zechariah, Mary, and Jesus. It also talks about Gog and Magog.

Comments and Possible Bridges

God Protects His Message: Verse 7

We see the Qur'an here clearly uses the word *zikr* for the books of the Old and New Testaments. The Qur'an in sura *al-Hijr*[1] said that God is the one who

---

1. Sura 15:9.

sent down the *zikr* (Holy Books or message), and he is the preserver of them. Thus, this verse means that the Bible is authentic and cannot be changed.

How to Judge Prophets: Verse 25

We need to share with our Muslim friend that not all prophets are true prophets. We can agree that a true prophet will say God is one, but this is not the only factor in knowing whether one is from God or not. We can use this to talk about the false prophets in the Bible, such as the prophets of Baal.

Creation: Verse 33

The use of "swim" in this verse in reference to the sun and moon obviously presents a scientific difficulty. The meaning of the word denotes a certain body floating or moving within another medium. We can say the airplane swims in the air, or the ship swims in the sea, but we cannot say that something swims in a vacuum. God created the sun and moon, and they are moving in a vacuum. If the planets are really "swimming" at the very high speeds they are moving, friction would burn them up. We can share with our Muslim friend that the true wonder of God's mighty creation is the fact that he created a vacuum around the celestials.

Every Soul Will Taste Death: Verse 35

This verse says that every soul will taste death. We can catch our friend's attention by saying that there are some people who never died, and then we can tell him about Elijah and Enoch, who walked with God. Once we share their stories, we can then explain that it is true that death comes to man, but only because of one thing—sin. This will allow us to share about this problem's solution.[2]

Scales: Verse 47

The Qur'an describes how judgment will take place on the *end day* and how accurate God is in his judgment as people's deeds are put on a scale that can measure the weight of a mustard seed. Most commentators will use this to show how amazing the Qur'an is, because the mustard seed is about 1/1000 of a gram. We know about the mustard seed from the Bible. If there is anything amazing about this issue, then the credit should go to the Bible, not the Qur'an, because the Bible mentioned it first.

This would be a good place to share that it is not the one mustard seed of difference that will tip the scale, but as Jesus said, it only takes one "mustard

---

2.   Rom. 6:23.

seed" of sin to tip the whole scale to hell. With one small hateful word ("fool") toward our brother, we are deserving of damnation.[3] We can never bring balance to the scales by our good works; a price has to be paid for our sin. Thankfully it has been paid through Jesus.

In the meantime, the mustard seed also is used in relation to faith. It represents not the amount of works, but the amount of faith that is needed.[4]

Furqan: Verse 48

In this verse we find the word *furqan* used in reference to "the books given to Moses." However, this word is used to also refer to the Qur'an. We can bring our Muslim friend to the understanding that the books of Moses are at the same level, because the meaning of the word *furqan* is "measure" or "canon." We can share many things that are found in Moses' books that serve as a canon for what Muslims practice today, such as: do not kill, do not steal, and do not covet a woman. This could prove to be a revelation to our friend.

Abraham: Verses 51–70

Abraham went to the temple, and there were so many idols that he broke them all and left the biggest. When his people asked him if he broke them, he lied (v. 63) and said no. He then told them to ask the big idol, which he had left intact. He said if it really were a god, it would answer them. This made them understand that idols are just stone and cannot talk. The people asked Abraham's forgiveness.

We serve a holy God, and we need to use holy means when leading others to him. The end does not justify the means. Abraham here is giving correct teaching, but in the context he is also lying. This account is not biblical, so we can move from it to read the true story of Abraham in the Old Testament.

Solomon's Wisdom: Verse 78

This is a classic example of not being able to understand a verse without referring to the *Hadith* in order to get its background. We can ask our Muslim friend, "Is the Qur'an the complete Word of God? If so, why do we have to refer so often to the *Hadith* in order to understand it? Can God not make his Word clear to us?"

The story behind verse 78 is that there was a dispute that took place between two people. One had some sheep, which ate the vineyard of the

3. Matt. 5:22.
4. Matt. 17:20; Luke 17:6.

other at night. David said, "Give the sheep to the landowner as a payment for the damage." Solomon said, "Give the sheep only temporarily to the man until his fields grow back to their original state." The point of this is to show how wise Solomon was. While we can agree that Solomon was wise, we should make clear that Solomon did not interfere in the king's rule before he himself was anointed as king. This would not have been a wise thing for the king's son to do. Also, the Bible tells us that Solomon did not ask for wisdom until he had been made king,[5] and the first opportunity to employ his God-given wisdom came when the two women brought to him the child they both claimed as their own.[6]

David Singing Praise to God: Verse 79

The commentators say that David had a wonderful, beautiful voice. When he sang, the birds stood still in the air and echoed his songs, and the mountains sang back to him his songs. What a wonderful opportunity this gives to talk about Israel's singer of songs[7] and share some of his psalms with our friend. The poetry of David will be very interesting and attractive to a Muslim. It will be good to show them the great variety of issues addressed and emotions shown through the psalms of David.

Solomon and Demons: Verse 82

The understanding of this verse is that God provided some demons (evil ones) to work for Solomon, to go to the depths of the sea, to bring him pearls, and to perform other unusual work that no human could do. As they worked, God protected them. We can ask some questions here: Does God really protect demons? Do we really deal with jinn or not? What happened to the jinn? Where are they now? Are they mortal? The most important thing we can share with our friend is that the Bible warns us not to get mixed up with the world of the spirits.[8]

Jonah: Verses 87–88

Jonah (*Zun-nun*) called to God from the belly of the fish, and God saved him. In the next verse, we read that God saved not only him but also the

---

5. 1 Kings 3:7–15.
6. 1 Kings 3:16–28.
7. 2 Sam. 23:1.
8. Luke 10:17–20; 1 Cor. 10:18–22; 1 Tim. 4:1–5.

believers. This is the end of the story here, but we can ask, "Who are the believers?" Then we can share the rest of the story of Nineveh.

Jesus, a Sign for All Peoples: Verse 91

We can see here a glimpse of how the Qur'an explains the birth of Jesus in very physical terms. This verse literally reads that Mary protected her vagina. These are very explicit words for us.

The verse then reads that God would make her and her son a sign. We can ask our friend, "What does it mean that Jesus is a sign? Of what is he a sign? Is he a spiritual or physical sign?" We can lead our friend to understand the deity of Jesus by showing the signs throughout the Bible that pointed to him. He is the torch between the pieces of Abraham's sacrifice, when he made a covenant with God. He is the one who looked like the Son of God in the furnace with Shadrach, Meshach, and Abednego.

The Good Shall Inherit the Earth: Verse 105

This verse makes an easy parallel to the Old Testament, as we show our Muslim friend the verse that reads: "The righteous will inherit the land and dwell in it forever."[9] We can then move to what Jesus says about inheritance. It is not the land or earth that is of ultimate importance to him, but the kingdom or eternal life.[10] For what good does it do to inherit things on this earth and lose one's soul?[11]

---

9. Ps. 37:29.
10. Matt. 19:29.
11. Matt. 6:19–20; Mark 8:34–37; Luke 12:16–21.

Al-Hajj

The Pilgrimage

LATE MECCAN OR MEDINAN

Overview

A warning about the terrible Day of Judgment begins this sura. The creation of man also is described here. The Qur'an says that God gives Muslims the right to kill. God takes time to comfort Muhammad because of the persecution he is experiencing at the hand of the unbelievers. Then God goes on to mock the unbelievers, revealing his majesty and challenging them to create even a fly. The sura discusses alms, worship, and the holy war and ends with the need to be dependent on God because he is the best supporter.

Comments and Possible Bridges

Creation of Man: Verse 5

The Qur'an explains how a person develops. We do not want to argue with our Muslim friend about the scientific inaccuracies here, like the use of the word *nutfa*, which means a clot of blood. Once the blood clots, the structure of the blood changes, and it is not in the liquid form anymore and cannot sustain life, contrary to what the Qur'an teaches here. Instead of disputing such details, we can simply agree with them that God knows what is in the womb of the mother. Then we can share with them from the book of Psalms what David wrote about how God made him.[1]

Weak in Faith: Verse 11

This verse talks about those who do not have strong faith. We can share what the epistle of James says: "If any of you lacks wisdom, he should ask God, who gives generously to all without finding fault, and it will be given to him. But when he asks, he must believe and not doubt, because he who doubts is like a wave of the sea, blown and tossed by the wind. That man should not think he will receive anything from the Lord; he is a double-minded man, unstable in all he does."[2]

The Qur'an says here that some people worship God "on the letter."[3] We can share the verse that says, "The letter kills, but the Spirit gives life."[4] The Spirit of God lets us gain both the earthly life and eternity to come.

Creation Worships God: Verse 18

We can see through this verse the whole of creation worshiping God and bowing down before him in heaven. We can share that in the heavenly Holy of Holies, the seraphim are covering their eyes and legs, and flying in his presence saying, "Holy, holy, holy."[5] The sunrise and sunset declare God's glory. The moon and the stars reveal to us the mighty Creator. The mountains, trees, and animals can show us how wise a creator he is; yet, God's greatest joy is, as Jesus said, when a person willingly comes to worship him in the spirit.[6]

Hell: Verses 19–21

These verses present a very graphic picture of hell and its torment of those who reject the Lord.

Hajj: Verses 26–28

The concept of the pilgrimage is taken all the way back to Abraham. We shared before the impossibility of Abraham making it all the way to Mecca.

---

1. Ps. 139.
2. James 1:5–8.
3. Yusuf Ali translates it "on the verge."
4. 2 Cor. 3:6.
5. Cf. Isa. 6:1–3.
6. John 4:24.

However, the question we can ask is this: Do we really need to go to Mecca to worship God? Is God limited and bound to a certain place? Do we really need to look in the direction of Mecca when we bow down to pray to God, or can we, deep in our hearts, submit to God anywhere we are? Does God dwell in Mecca or in heaven? If he is in heaven, why do we need to bow toward Mecca?

One of the reasons for the pilgrimage is revealed in verse 28. It is to remember God through these days, to eat of the sacrificed animal, and to feed the poor. Even though the full details of how to perform the pilgrimage are not given in the Qur'an, the basic practices include the following:

- After entering the state of *ihram* (purity), Muslim pilgrims walk around the Ka'ba seven times while reciting the *talbiya*. They then kiss or touch the Black Stone of the Ka'ba, pray twice toward the Station of Abraham and the Ka'ba, and run seven times between the small mountains of Safa and Marwa.
- The second stage takes place between the eighth and twelfth days of the Hajj. Pilgrims stay at Mina or Arafat and on the ninth day, perform the ritual of *wuquf* (standing) on the hill of *al-Rahma* (mercy).
- The tenth day is the *Eid al-Adha* (the Feast of Sacrifice), which is a major holiday for Muslims. Animals are sacrificed in Mina, and then pilgrims throw seven small stones at each of three pillars on three consecutive days. Afterward they return to Mecca, once again performing the *tawaf* (circumambulation of the Ka'ba). Their heads are shaved or trimmed to mark the end of the stage of purity.[7]

Piety Reaches God: Verse 37

This verse presents a great parallel to what we have in the Bible and a wonderful opportunity to talk about sacrifice and what God requires from us. This verse says that it is not the meat or blood that reaches God but the believer's piety. We can quote to our Muslim friends the following from the Bible: "I desire mercy, not sacrifice, and acknowledgment of God rather than burnt offerings."[8]

A Day Is Like a Thousand Years: Verse 47

The concept here is that God is in charge of time. It reads that a day with God is like a thousand years. He makes this comment, however, as

7. "Hajj: Pilgrimage to Mecca."
8. Hos. 6:6.

a rejection of the blasphemers' attempts to make Muhammad quicken the judgment of God. We can draw a parallel from the Bible, which says, "But do not forget this one thing, dear friends: With the Lord a day is like a thousand years, and a thousand years are like a day. The Lord is not slow in keeping his promise, as some understand slowness. He is patient with you, not wanting anyone to perish, but everyone to come to repentance."[9]

Instead of referring to God taking as much time as he wants to bring the judgment, the Bible here is illustrating God's mercy and patience with mankind and his desire to see all people come to him in repentance.

How to Judge Prophets: Verse 52

God offers comfort to Muhammad by saying that Satan tried to lure away all the prophets who came before him, but the Lord protected them all. We need to show our Muslim friend that many prophets in the Old Testament suffered, were rejected, tortured, and in the end killed. This does not mean that God could not protect them but that he allowed their suffering in order to get his message across to the people. Success, health, and wealth are not the measure of God's call on a person; rather the real measure is the prophet's faithfulness in giving out God's message.

Consequences for Rejecting the Qur'an: Verse 57

The meaning of this verse is something that is repeated many times in the Qur'an. Basically, anyone who does not believe in the Qur'an and who says the Qur'an is not from God goes to hell and will be greatly tormented.

Qur'an Makes Previous Books Obsolete: Verses 67–69

God has provided legislation for every nation before Muhammad, and he tells Muhammad that his words make obsolete those that came previously. In the next verses, he tells Muhammad not to argue with the blasphemers. The question is: How could God give directions to previous prophets that contradict those he gave to Muhammad and still be considered the same God? This should be a revelation to our Muslim friend to think about what is from God and what is not. We cannot wait until the end day, as verse 69 says, to figure out what is from God and what is not. That will be too late, for the books will be closed for each human being, and every soul will stand before God to give an account.

---

9.   2 Peter 3:8–9.

Muslims Named by Abraham: Verse 78

This verse says that Abraham named the believers Muslims and began the religion. Abraham, who came more than 2,600 years before Muhammad, could never have been a Muslim; and if somehow he could have been a Muslim, he would have done things consistent with modern-day Islam.

Al-Mu-minun

The Believers

LATE MECCAN

Overview

The sura begins with encouragement or blessing for the believers and a description of their qualities. It talks about the creation of man and then records some of the stories of the prophets, though very briefly and with much less information than found in previous suras. The stance of the unbelievers against the Prophet is touched upon, while again more details are found in earlier suras. It provides evidence of the deity of God, and speaks of the end day and the glory of God.

Comments and Possible Bridges

Qualities of Believers: Verses 1–9

These verses speak in general about the qualities of the believers. We can use this as a bridge with our Muslim friend when we share how the Bible says we are to live as followers of Jesus.[1] We can compare issues like chastity and prayer.

---

1. Look at passages such as Rom. 12 and Col. 3.

Inheritance: Verses 10–11

These verses say that these believers will be the heirs. We can use this to discuss the topic of our inheritance as believers in Christ.[2] The inheritance the Qur'an speaks of in these verses is paradise. We must share that only through Christ can we have this inheritance. It cannot be achieved through Muslim *tawhid*, because Islam says everyone is responsible for himself. Therefore, a person cannot inherit something from anyone else. The Bible agrees, and that is why in Christ only will the inheritance truly be realized.

Creation of Man: Verses 13–14

These verses continue the development of man's creation, adding bones to the equation.

Noah: Verses 27–28

These two verses talk about Noah's ark. We can ask our Muslim friends if they would like to know the rest of the story, as it is given only briefly here; then we can take them through a wonderful Bible study, giving them the complete story. If they do not agree to this, we can simply ask if they know there is a problem in the story here. In verse 27, after Noah made the ark and after the water started coming down, Noah began to get the animals in. We can then ask, "Can you imagine getting thousands of animals into this huge ark while it is raining?" We can share that the Bible says that *after* Noah got all the animals in, the rain began.[3]

No Burden More Than We Can Bear: Verse 62

We can quote the parallel verse for this from the Bible, which says, "No temptation has seized you except what is common to man. And God is faithful; he will not let you be tempted beyond what you can bear. But when you are tempted, he will also provide a way out so that you can stand up under it."[4]

Scales: Verses 102–103

These verses say that those whose good works are heavy on the scale will go to heaven. Those whose scale is light with good works will go to hell. We

---

2. Gal. 3:18–29; Eph. 1:13–14; 1 Peter 1:3–9.
3. Gen. 7:9–10.
4. 1 Cor. 10:13.

can take this subject and talk about works without faith being like the dust on the scale.[5] All mankind's good works will not even tip the scale. After faith in Christ, however, works make quite a difference. Our works will be tested by fire. Some works will have no value; others will have great value. But without salvation, no matter how many good works we have, we will never move the "scale."

Muhammad Asks for Forgiveness: Verse 118

This is one of many places in the Qur'an where we see Muhammad, the head of the Muslim faith, asking for forgiveness. Jesus never asked forgiveness for himself, but he himself provided forgiveness for many sinners.[6] We can ask our Muslim friend, "Which one will you follow—a prophet who admitted in many verses in the Qur'an that he was a sinner, or Christ, who forgave the sins of all who asked?"

---

5. Isa. 40:15.
6. Mark 2:1–12.

Al-Nur

Light

MEDINAN

Overview

Though this sura is called "Light," that theme is reflected in only a couple of verses, as the majority of verses speak about sexual conduct. These verses came to the Prophet as a reaction to accusations made against Aisha, one of his wives, for her misconduct during their return from a battle (she often accompanied him). Aisha was missed at some point during the trip back and accused of adultery. This is why most of the verses speak harshly not only about those who commit adultery but also about those who gossip about it. The sura also talks about those who falsely accuse a woman of adultery. Verses give instructions about how a male should enter a home that has women in it and who has the right to see the ornament of a woman. Only certain people can be trusted around a man's women: the blind, children who have not yet reached puberty, and very close relations. This basically implies that anyone who has any sexual desire should not be allowed to see the women of the household.

Comments and Possible Bridges

Adultery: Verse 2

The Qur'an orders punishment for those who commit adultery (male and female) by the application of a hundred lashes. We need to point out that this contradicts another verse in the Qur'an, which gives the punishment as death for the woman only.[1] A question can then be asked: Do God's standards change and change that quickly (within the thirty years of Muhammad's revelation)? God's Word should be consistent.

We can build a bridge on this subject by sharing that in the Bible, one of the Ten Commandments God gave to the people of Israel through Moses was that they should not commit adultery. God's standard from the beginning was one man for one woman; thus the punishment for adultery was death for both the man and the woman caught in adultery.[2] In moving over the bridge to Jesus, we should share how Jesus took the issue even further. He agreed that man should not commit adultery, but he went on to say that if a man looks at a woman with lust in his eyes, he has already committed adultery in his heart.[3] Jesus required an even higher morality for those who choose to follow him.

Another way to relate this to Jesus is in telling the story from John 8 of the woman caught in adultery. No matter how big the crime is, if we confess our sin, in Christ we will be instantly forgiven. Jesus did not punish the woman with lashes. He simply told her not to sin again and set her free. The sin of adultery is not only against ourselves and others; it is also against God. For God, all that is required is repentance. Lashes is not the solution.

Witnesses for Adultery: Verse 4

The Qur'an requires four witnesses in order to accuse a woman of committing adultery. If the accuser cannot provide such witnesses, the one who brought the charges will be punished with eighty lashes and will never be trusted again. But how can one bring four eyewitnesses against a woman for committing adultery? Adultery is usually committed in secret, but if there are eight eyes watching the act, then no witnesses will be needed, because it will be a public display.

However, adultery is a two-sided issue: social and spiritual. If the man and woman never confess to committing adultery, punishing them will bring more harm to the structure of the society than good. On the spiritual side, the only requirement is to ask forgiveness from God and from the ones against whom the act was committed. From the social side, if the adultery has been proven, the law needs to take effect. This may include the right to divorce.

---

1. See sura 4:15.
2. Lev. 20:10.
3. Matt. 5:27–28.

Adultery: Verses 6–8

These verses deal with a husband or wife accusing his or her spouse of adultery without any evidence to prove the case. Thus they simply swear against each other without ever getting to the bottom of the issue. We need to explain that the issue is not legalistic as much as it is spiritual. We can also use this opportunity to share about the differences between Christian marriage and Muslim marriage (covenant versus contract). For Christians adultery breaks a spiritual covenant. The parties will feel guilty and will be burdened spiritually, and they have to deal with the sin on a personal level with God.

Punishment for Slander of Chaste Women: Verse 23

This is a very strong verse. God curses, in this life and in the life after death, those who slander chaste women. This could be as a result of the Prophet's strong feelings for Aisha. We know that he loved her very much.

Sexual Conduct: Verses 27–34

Muslims are encouraged to conduct themselves in a proper way sexually. Here are guidelines for protecting their chastity and for sexual relations. We can build a bridge here by sharing the commands God gave through Moses regarding the same issues.[4] We can then move to the New Testament teaching, ultimately quoting the apostle Paul's words to the church in Corinth: "Flee from sexual immorality. All other sins a man commits are outside his body, but he who sins sexually sins against his own body. Do you not know that your body is a temple of the Holy Spirit, who is in you, whom you have received from God? You are not your own; you were bought at a price. Therefore honor God with your body."[5]

Parable of the Light: Verse 35

In reading this verse we realize how impressed Muhammad was with the sight Moses saw on the mountain (the burning bush), for he tried to equal it with his own parable. As for this parable, we can point out to our friend that it is not clear whether the tree was an olive tree or not, because the Qur'an reads that Muhammad was not sure because it was neither eastern nor western but looked like glass from another planet. We can bridge this by

---

4.   Lev. 18.
5.   1 Cor. 6:18–20.

sharing the account of another amazing tree (the burning bush), and how God spoke to Moses and gave him a vision of what he was to do.

Obey God and Muhammad: Verses 52–54

The Qur'an says we must obey God and Muhammad. However, those around the Prophet never heard God directly. All they heard was Muhammad telling them what he said God revealed. But how could a Muslim be sure that this was really God's voice? In almost every sura of the Qur'an, Muhammad gave "evidence" that the Qur'an was the Word of God and that he was God's prophet. Yet, all the evidence delivered was such that anyone could produce. When God spoke to Jesus and the prophets of the Old Testament, others heard and saw. When the ascended Jesus appeared to Paul, Paul's companions saw the light. John said, "That which was from the beginning, which we have heard, which we have seen with our eyes, which we have looked at and our hands have touched—this we proclaim concerning the Word of life. The life appeared; we have seen it and testify to it, and we proclaim to you the eternal life, which was with the Father and has appeared to us. We proclaim to you what we have seen and heard, so that you also may have fellowship with us."[6] Our question must be: How can we accept only one person's testimony about everything—creation, man's destiny, and the way of life? This would be a great risk and probably fatal.

Clothing Instructions: Verse 58

Instructions are given concerning conduct between males and females within the same family. At certain times, when people are in their sleeping dresses, which may reveal certain parts of their bodies, they must receive permission before entering into the presence of the opposite sex, to make sure they are covered. At other times of the day, they do not have to seek permission, because they will be in their daily clothes. Many directions are given as to how to cover oneself and to avoid looking at and touching members of the opposite sex. While we can agree that proper family relations are needed, we should share with our Muslim friend that it is not the person or their way of dress that is the source of sin; the source of sin is in our own eyes and hearts. If our eyes are pure, our whole body will be pure. If our heart is pure, we will not commit such acts. God's Word gives much insight into this concept. David wrote, "I will walk in my house with blameless

---

6.   1 John 1:1–3.

heart. I will set before my eyes no vile thing."[7] Jesus said, "Your eye is the lamp of your body. When your eyes are good, your whole body also is full of light. But when they are bad, your body also is full of darkness. See to it, then, that the light within you is not darkness. Therefore, if your whole body is full of light, and no part of it dark, it will be completely lighted, as when the light of a lamp shines on you."[8] "To the pure, all things are pure, but to those who are corrupted and do not believe, nothing is pure. In fact, both their minds and consciences are corrupted. They claim to know God, but by their actions they deny him. They are detestable, disobedient and unfit for doing anything good."[9]

Muhammad's Elevation as Prophet: Verses 62–63

These verses continue the effort to elevate Muhammad higher than ordinary people by saying that a person cannot leave the room while Muhammad is talking to them. They must wait on him until he finishes. We can share that Jesus said, "Instead, whoever wants to become great among you must be your servant, and whoever wants to be first must be your slave—just as the Son of Man did not come to be served, but to serve, and to give his life as a ransom for many."[10] Even though he was God, in the flesh Jesus took the shape of the lowest servant. He was humble and meek, and we should be like him.

---

7.   Ps. 101:2–3.
8.   Luke 11:34–36.
9.   Titus 1:15–16.
10.   Matt. 20:26–28.

Al-Furqan

The Criterion

EARLY MECCAN

Overview

The beginning of the sura speaks of the importance of the Qur'an. God defends the Qur'an against blasphemers who accuse Muhammad of being just a man. The challenge they bring is that if the Qur'an is truly from God, angels would be bringing the message to them. So God gives Muhammad examples to share with them about the prophets, as well as other verses about his own majesty and might. At the end of the sura, a picture is given of the good Muslim believers who deserve to be in paradise.

Comments and Possible Bridges

Furqan: *Verse 1*

This verse gives the reason why God gave the *Furqan* (Criterion), which is another word used for the Qur'an. It is to be a warning for mankind. We can share with our Muslim friend that God's Word needs to be more than just a warning. If we only warn people about sin, they will be aware of it but will not have the power to avoid it. The Qur'an works like a red light, telling people what is right and wrong (according to Islam). But mankind needs more than just a red light; man needs the breaks to stop the car. Otherwise, his soul will face eternal destruction, for the red light itself will not stop him. The Bible is different—God warns people about sin, but he also shows them how to get the power to stop the sin in their life.

God Has No Son: Verses 2–3

These verses constitute a clear rejection of the deity of Christ and reveal the reasons behind it. They tell us that non-Muslims made gods out of people and idols, which have no power over life and death. This could be a reaction to accusations from the same people that Muhammad was just a man (see v. 7). Therefore, Jesus too is reduced to simply a mere man, with no power over life or death.

We can share with our friend that the Qur'an reveals that Jesus raised the dead, ordered a tree to die, and at the end of the days will come and have the ultimate authority over eternal life in heaven or hell. Therefore, the comparison here between Muhammad and Jesus cannot be made. Yet, we can suggest that our friend compare Jesus, as the Word of God, with the Qur'an itself.

Muhammad's Justification as a Prophet: Verse 20

God continues with his defense of Muhammad in answer to the accusations by saying that all the prophets were like him, eating and walking in the markets.

End Day: Verses 23–30

Muhammad begins talking about eschatology and how the end day will be very difficult for the nonbelievers. An important question here is: How can we be sure the Prophet's eschatology is correct? We would not want to risk our entire life on earth waiting till that day to see if Muhammad is telling the truth or not. Eternity is too big an issue to depend on just one man's word. We need to show that when Jesus talked about eschatology and what will happen, he provided a way for us to be sure that his words were true. He planted the everlasting kingdom within our hearts on the day that we trusted in him. He did not just promise something in the future but looked at those around him, touched them, and said, "The kingdom of God is within you."[1] When a person believes in the atoning work of Christ, there is a change that takes place in that person's heart, allowing him to know, beyond all doubts, his eternal destiny. This initial act is then followed by

---

1. Luke 17:21.

changes in his day-to-day life, which shows tangibly the spiritual change that has taken place in his heart.

Revelation of the Qur'an: Verse 32

The blasphemers ask the Prophet why the Qur'an was not given in one setting. God tells Muhammad to reply that it was revealed in segments in order to strengthen Muhammad's heart. It was given verse by verse, with a musical quality (like singing a hymn). Poetry in the Arabic world of the time carried great strength through its rhythmic language. A poet could be extremely powerful and even paid by kings and queens to write and recite his poems because of the power of the words. When we look at the Qur'an, we can see that it is written with this same poetic or musical style. It therefore has a huge impact on Arab minds and Muslim hearts. It is much like a song is to us that we cannot get out of our minds. This is the reason that in the early days, it was forbidden to translate the Qur'an. When the text of the Qur'an loses its melodic flow, it loses much of its effect and thus power over the hearer.

Another reason the blasphemers were asking why the Qur'an did not come down in one setting is because of the way God's revelation to Muhammad seemed to come as he went through particular experiences in life. For example, the previous sura gives considerable space to justifying the disappearance of Aisha from the caravan and to speaking against the accusations directed at her. Muhammad's marriage to the wife of his adopted son is another example.[2] God took a lot of time to deal with such issues in the Qur'an, which helps us understand why the non-Muslims questioned the timing of the revelation of the Qur'an to Muhammad.

However, if we want to build a bridge here, we can share that we do believe that God's revelation is progressive. If we look at the Bible, for example, it is clear it did not all come in one setting. Sometimes God's Word was given to tell about something about the future. In several places we can see that God used the prophets themselves as examples of the revelation, as with Hosea and Isaiah. God's revelation in these cases was not a reaction to something happening in their lives but pointed to events that would happen in the future and usually in relation to the whole nation.

Muhammad Compared to Other Prophets: Verses 35–42

These verses compare Muhammad to prophets such as Moses, Noah, and 'Ad in the way people took a stand against them and were punished by

---

2. Sura 33.

God as a result. Indirectly, Muhammad is telling the people, "If you take a stand against me, God will do to you as he did with those who opposed the prophets before me." Here is the question that needs to be asked: How can Muhammad measure up to those prophets? We can make a comparison by studying the biblical prophets' lives with our friend. What each one did and what each one wrote will bring a lot of truth to light.

Shadow Stands Still: Verse 45

With the understanding of the celestial bodies today, we can easily dispute this verse. Why would God ever make a shadow stand still? The way that he has created the universe requires that the solar system be in motion, which means that shadows will change from morning to evening. To keep the universe running, shadows must be changing all the time. In relation to this verse, most of the commentators say that God could stop the shadow, prohibiting mankind from going through life for the day.

This verse does not have the same meaning as the accounts in the Bible when God made the sun to stop or the shadow to go back ten steps.[3] In the Qur'an the purpose is only to show the power or ability of God to do this. In the biblical accounts, it was done as a sign for King Hezekiah and to allow Joshua's troops to defeat their enemy. We can use these events as a bridge to show that indeed God does have the power to control the sun and shadows, but he would not do it without a purpose, for he knows it would be against his own created order.

Sweet and Salt Waters: Verse 53

We can use the picture in this verse to refer to verses found in the book of James: "With the tongue we praise our Lord and Father, and with it we curse men, who have been made in God's likeness. Out of the same mouth come praise and cursing. My brothers, this should not be. Can both fresh water and salt water flow from the same spring? My brothers, can a fig tree bear olives, or a grapevine bear figs? Neither can a salt spring produce fresh water."[4]

The two springs are the two things that could come out of our mouth—either good, sweet words or harsh, hurting words. We can share that it is God who has put a divider between the two, and he is Jesus. Jesus is the real stone (or cornerstone) who enables us to speak in a way that is pleasing to God.

---

3.   Josh. 10; 2 Kings 20; Isa. 38.
4.   James 3:9–12.

Creation: Verses 54–60

These verses show almighty God as Creator. We can use these verses to connect with the biblical descriptions of the Creator in the book of Psalms.[5]

---

5.   E.g., Pss. 89, 139, 148.

Al-Shu'araa

The Poets

MIDDLE MECCAN

Overview

The sura begins by telling about the greatness of the Qur'an. It then threatens the non-Muslims for their denial of God's power. In an effort to comfort the Prophet, when his people called him a liar, accounts are shared of the prophets Moses and Aaron, when Pharaoh called them liars. Other prophets also are referred to, including Abraham, Noah, 'Ad, Lot, Salih, and Shu'aib. The sura ends with a denial that Muhammad is just a poet and that the Qur'an is no more than simple poetry.

No new material is given in the accounts of the prophets mentioned in this sura. The point is to say that all these prophets were harassed and rejected by those to whom they were giving their message, and thus Muhammad is not experiencing anything less than the prophets before him experienced. This is, therefore, an attempt to give credence to his message.

Comments and Possible Bridges

Moses: Verses 18–21

We find in these verses that Pharaoh is accusing Moses of a deed he did in the past. Moses tells Pharaoh that he did it when he was not a believer and then fled. We need to share with our friend the meaning of these verses, because the Qur'an, up to this point, has not provided a full account of Moses' killing of the Egyptian to defend his people.[1] Moses did this because of his jealousy for God's people. Through the reading of the biblical account, we can also show that Pharaoh never brought up this incident when Moses confronted him and demanded the release of the Hebrews.

Pharaoh: Verses 23–34

We see here an echo of the response of Pharaoh to Moses as found in the Bible: "Who is the LORD, that I should obey him and let Israel go? I do not know the LORD and I will not let Israel go."[2] This shows clearly that Pharaoh refused God, which is an important note, because the Qur'an indicates previously that he did not.[3] These verses also show that Pharaoh called Moses crazy and a magician and threatened to put him in jail for considering anyone god but Pharaoh himself.

Pharaoh's Magicians Believe: Verses 47–52

These verses tell us that upon seeing Moses' staff turned to a snake that ate the snakes of the magicians of Pharaoh, those magicians believed so strongly in the God of Moses and Aaron that they were willing to endure the wrath of Pharaoh in having their hands and feet cut off.[4] We can agree that the magicians eventually did come to recognize the power of God, though the Bible does not say that they put their faith in him. As we share from the biblical account, we can see that the magicians did not really recognize the power of God until the plague of gnats, when they were no longer able to copy the signs of God.[5]

Moses Leads the People Across the Sea: Verses 53–69

This is a repetition of the account given previously of Moses taking the people out by night and crossing the sea with them.[6]

---

1. We do find it later in sura 28:15–21.
2. Exod. 5:2.
3. Sura 10:90.
4. See also sura 20:70–71.
5. Exod. 8:19.
6. Sura 2:49–50.

Abraham: Verses 70–104

This is the account of Abraham and includes much of the same material seen previously.

Noah: Verses 105–122

See notes on suras 10:71–73 and 23:27–28 for explanations in relation to the account of Noah.

'Ad People: Verses 123–140

This is an account of the 'Ad people and the prophet Hud, who was rejected. There is no biblical correlation to this story.

Salih: Verses 141–159

The Thamud tribe refuses the message of Salih, who claimed God is one. See notes on sura 11:61–68.

Lot: Verses 160–175

This is another account of the people of Sodom and Gomorrah and their rejection of Lot. God saved Lot from destruction when he brought his wrath on the cities.

Shu'aib: Verses 176–191

The Companions of the Wood rejected the apostles, but Shu'aib testified for the Lord.

Revelation of the Qur'an: Verses 192–227

These verses tell how the Qur'an was revealed to the Prophet. It says that the faithful spirit (Gabriel, according to commentators) gave the account so that Muhammad's heart would be comforted and that he revealed it in the Arabic language. We can point out here that there are many words within the Qur'an that are not of Arabic origin.[7] These verses provide another justification, according to some Muslim theologians, for the prohibition on translating the Qur'an.

---

7.   Gilchrist, *The Qur'an.*

Al-Naml

The Ants

MIDDLE MECCAN

Overview

The beginning of the sura, as usual, reinforces the importance of the Qur'an. Following this are some accounts of Moses and David and of Solomon's inheriting David's kingdom. Further stories are shared of how Solomon used humans and jinn to serve him and how he understood the talk of the animals. The hoopoe bird brings Solomon the story of Bilqis (Queen of Sheba), and they meet. This sura also speaks about Salih, Lot, and the importance of the Qur'an in God's call. It continues by describing how the non-Muslims try to contradict the verses Muhammad brought. The universe, creation, and mountains are not as permanent as God's Word.

Comments or Possible Bridges

Condemnation for Unbelief: Verses 1–5

These verses begin by praising the Qur'an and then continue with a warning to the non-Muslims that they will go to hell if they do not accept the Qur'an.

Moses and the Fire: Verses 7–8

We see more of the account of Moses that has not yet been mentioned in the Qur'an. It is important to remember that the revelation of the Qur'an did not come to Muhammad in one setting, but in segments. It is for this reason that stories of the prophets are disjointed and incomplete.

Moses saw a fire in the desert (the burning bush), so he told his people, "Let me go and ask if I can see the direction for the road (thinking it was a fire for another camp), or I will bring you some fire, so we can build a fire here and get some warmth." From here we can share with our friend the correct account, that from a distance Moses saw the bush, and then as he got closer, God spoke to him. It was after this encounter that he went back to his father-in-law and told him he wanted to return to Egypt. Through this story we can talk about the progressive revelation of God when he calls us. The account in the Qur'an does not provide that insight into God's call of Moses.

Solomon Talks to Animals and Commands Jinn: Verses 16–18

Solomon inherits David's kingdom and tells the people that he can talk to birds. We need to explain to our Muslim friend that no account was ever given about people talking to animals (except when God opened the mouth of the donkey to talk to Balaam, but that was God allowing the animal to speak, not a person understanding the speech of animals). The animal kingdom behaves on instincts God built inside them. Animals and birds have no logic, and they cannot have a discussion with a human. It is good to say here that man alone was created by God to speak with understanding and to have an intelligent, free discussion with another person. He not only talks but also is able to think and reason with his mind. Talking to an animal shows we are trying to lower God's spirit in us to that of animals, and that is blasphemy.

These odd ideas about Solomon's communicating with animals could have come from two passages in the Bible. The Bible reveals that Solomon's wisdom was so great that he taught many people about animals and birds.[1] Then in the book of Proverbs we find an example of King Solomon's knowledge of ants: "Go to the ant, you sluggard; consider its ways and be wise! It has no commander, no overseer or ruler, yet it stores its provisions in summer and gathers its food at harvest."[2] Though Solomon had great knowledge of the animal kingdom, this does not mean that he was capable of understanding their speech or having conversations with them.

---

1. 1 Kings 4:33.
2. Prov. 6:6–8.

Verse 17 tells how Solomon prepared his army of workers from jinn (demons), men, and birds. We can refer to earlier explanations of jinn as we explain to our friend that a king chosen by God and to whom had been given so much wisdom would never resort to seeking demonic help to reign. In doing so, he would be rejecting the leadership of God in his life and be quickly rejected as king.

Al-Qasas

The Narration, or the Stories

LATE MECCAN

Overview

This sura provides more of the story of Moses, saying that he was born in a time when Pharaoh was killing the children of Israel, because Pharaoh was afraid that a prophet would come and overthrow him. It tells of God speaking to Moses and choosing him to carry his message. We also read again of the encounter between Moses and the magicians of Pharaoh and of how God drowned Pharaoh and his soldiers and saved Moses and his people. This sura also gives the account of Moses and Aaron with the golden calf. The title of the sura (Narratives or Stories) is a result of all of these various accounts.

Comments and Possible Bridges

Pharaoh's Oppression of the Israelites: Verses 4–5

These verses give a very short and incomplete account of the fact that Pharaoh used to oppress the Israelites and kill their boy babies. God's purpose, however, was to be gracious to them and lift them up. We can share with our friend that the Bible gives more details of Pharaoh's acts against the Israelites and how God heard their cries for help.[1]

---

1. Exod. 1–2.

Moses' Birth: Verses 7–14

God told Moses' mother to breastfeed the child (do not let him be killed) and then throw him into the water. Pharaoh's wife found him and took him as her son. Moses' sister watched him in the water. The Qur'an gives a very good reason why Moses came to be raised by his real mother. God made Moses not to suckle from Pharaoh's women, so Moses' sister told them about a woman who could take care of him (his mother). When he came of age, he was raised in Pharaoh's palace. We can compare this account to that in the Bible and discuss the similarities and differences.

Moses Kills the Egyptian: Verses 15–21

These verses give the account of Moses' killing of the Egyptian. Moses killed him with his fists and then regretted his actions and blamed Satan for it. However, in verse 16, which is a pivotal verse in Muslim theology, Moses asks God's forgiveness. God forgives him, because he is the Most Forgiving.

This verse and others of the same nature are important to bring up in our discussions with Muslims. We should emphasize that God cannot just forgive when we ask to be forgiven, because his justice would never be satisfied. Ultimately, payment must be made, and was made in Christ. In this account, Moses did kill the Egyptian as the Bible teaches us, but we do not see in the Bible that he asked forgiveness for what he did. He was jealous for God's people, so he did not regret killing the Egyptian. He knew the consequences of his act, which he dealt with by escaping from Pharaoh and fleeing to Midian.[2]

Moses Works for His Bride: Verses 27–28

Moses has to work eight to ten years in order to wed the daughter of a man in Midian (Jethro). Though this is not in the Bible, we can expect that the idea came from that of Jacob's story.

Moses and the Fire: Verses 29–30

Moses saw a fire from a distance and told his people that he would get them some news or fire for cooking. He then heard a voice from the right side of a nearby tree, talking to him and identifying himself as God. In several ways this is very similar to the account in the Bible. The Bible, however, does not mention the tree, and neither does the Qur'an in the earlier account.[3]

---

2. Exod. 2:11–15.
3. Sura 27:7–8.

Pharaoh Builds a Tower: Verses 38–40

We see here confusion between the account of Pharaoh telling Moses there is no God and that of the Tower of Babel, when the people were trying to make a name for themselves.[4] Pharaoh tells his minister Haman (perhaps another confusion from the story of Esther) to use fired bricks to build a tower for him to look for the God of Moses. We need to bring our Muslim friend's attention to the similarity in the accounts, as Pharaoh is here refusing God's direct command through Moses. In pride, the people of Babel built a tower in defiance of God. The punishment for those who built the tower was that God confused their language. God punished Pharaoh differently, as the story quickly ends by revealing that God threw Pharaoh and his soldiers into the sea. The word for *water* in verse 40 is the same word used in verse 7 in relation to Moses. The most common translation is "sea," but we need to share with our friend that Moses was not thrown into the sea, but into the river Nile.

Qur'an, Repetition of Stories of Old: Verses 43–47

God says to Muhammad, "You were not there when we gave Moses all the account we gave him. Even though you were not there when we gave Moses all these accounts, I am so merciful toward you, Muhammad, that I have revealed to you all these things." (This is a paraphrase.)

We must ask ourselves if God's being merciful to Muhammad is a good reason for God to repeat the same account many times with some differences here and there. Also, what is the wisdom behind repeating all these stories to Muhammad, when they already existed in the *Tawrat* (Torah)? The Bible does not repeat stories over and over as does the Qur'an. Outside of 1 and 2 Chronicles, which overlap the books of Samuel and Kings, the only place we have some repetition is in the four Gospels. However, the purpose of this repetition is different. The provision of four different accounts (from four different persons) of Christ's time on earth gives convincing evidence of the facts and also speaks to different audiences in ways that will specifically reach them.

God Does Not Love the Joyful Ones: Verses 76–82

God blessed Korah (Qarun) with money (he was rich), and he took a stand against Moses; God, therefore, put him inside the earth.[5] A very sad statement is found in verse 76: "God does not love the joyful."[6] Also, verse

---

4. Gen. 11.
5. Cf. Num. 16:1–35.
6. Yusuf Ali's translation is not literal.

77 says that God does not love the troublemakers. Commentators will try to explain "God does not love the joyful (happy ones)" by saying that they were bragging about their wealth, but the statement is very clear that God does not like those who are full of joy. We can share with our Muslim friend that God's ultimate satisfaction is when man is joyful. When a father sees his children full of joy, it brings joy to his heart. When a father sees his kids crying and sad, it reflects in his own heart. A Muslim will reject the parallelism of God and father, but we can assure our friend that even the great will rejoice with the lesser when the lesser one is happy.

If we want to relate this verse to money, we can build a bridge to the verse that reads, "No servant can serve two masters. Either he will hate the one and love the other, or he will be devoted to the one and despise the other. You cannot serve both God and Money."[7] We can also go back to the biblical account of Korah and explain the true reason for God's anger, which had nothing to do with money or joy.

7.   Luke 16:13.

Al-'Ankabut

The Spider

LATE MECCAN

Overview

The sura starts with the trials that test the faith of believers. Suffering helps people to keep their faith. The Qur'an directs people (Muslims) to take care of their parents and to keep the brotherhood of the faith. It shows that there are different kinds of believers—the ones who give lip service and those who are true believers. Accounts are shared of Noah and the struggle he faced with his people and of Abraham's call. These are given to illustrate how Muhammad is like the other prophets in his suffering.

The story of Lot and how God sent angels to destroy his city is recounted. All Lot's people were saved except his wife. Salih, Hud, 'Ad, Pharaoh, Haman, and the arrogance of Qarun (Korah) also are mentioned. The sura gets its title from the passage that tells of blasphemers who worshipped idols. Their lives are as fragile as a spider's web.

God tells Muhammad not to argue with the people of the Book (Christians and Jews) until he has better reasoning. He states that the punishment of non-Muslims who ask Muhammad for physical miracles will be the same as those who opposed Moses. Eternal life is described, with preference in heaven given to those who endure the holy war (jihad).

Comments and Possible Bridges

God Tests the Believers: Verses 2–3

These verses reveal that God tempted all previous nations in order to show who was good and who was bad. The word the Qur'an uses here for God's "testing" actually means "tempting." We need to explain to our friend that God does not tempt people.[1] In fact, "the tempter" is actually one of Satan's titles.[2] God, however, tests believers or puts them through trials so that they may grow stronger.[3]

God Does Not Need: Verse 6

This verse teaches that since God is so highly exalted, he will not really be affected by man's submission. We need to share the essence of God with our friend. God will be affected in his relationship with man. God loves man and enjoys time with him. The relationship between God and man does not change the quantitative essence of God. He is perfect, he is ultimately rich in knowledge, and he is not in need, but a relationship with man affects his emotional attributes (i.e., it makes him happy). Whether a king is happy or sad does not affect his position, only his emotional status. He is still a king. This explanation might impact the heart of our Muslim friend and help him to understand the God/man relationship.

Noah: Verses 14–15

The best reading for this verse is that Noah lived with this people 950 years. We can share with our friend that the Bible tells us more specifically that Noah was 600 years old when the flood started. He then lived another 350 years after that, so that the total life of Noah was 950 years,[4] as in the Qur'an. The only people saved from the flood were Noah, his sons, their wives, and Noah's own wife. No other friends were saved, as the Qur'an suggests.

Lot Believes Abraham's Preaching: Verse 26

This verse is the only new item in the account of Abraham (which starts in verse 16). The Qur'an says that Lot believed in the preaching of Abraham and was willing to leave home for his sake.

---

1. James 1:13.
2. Matt. 4:3; cf. Rev. 12:9.
3. Exod. 16:4; Prov. 17:3; 1 Thess. 2:4.
4. Gen. 9:28–29.

Chosen Prophets: Verse 27

God here tells Muhammad that he gave only Abraham, Isaac, Jacob, and their offspring the prophecy and the books. We can share with our Muslim friend how true this statement is. All the prophets were Hebrews, and the only God-given books (or Scriptures) were given through the line of Abraham, Isaac, and Jacob.

Lot: Verses 28–34

There is no new information in this account of Lot. God saved Lot before destroying the city.

Spider: Verse 41

The sura receives its name from this verse. It is an allegory or parable for the people who have idols instead of God. They are like the spider that builds a home (web), which is very fragile. We can share with our friend the parable about homes that Jesus told in the *Injil*. These two homes are representative of those who either obey or disobey the words of Christ.[5]

One God: Verse 46

This verse reminds Muslims not to argue with Jews and Christians but to work to reason together. The statement "Our God and your God is One; and it is to him we are submitted" is worth noting. From this we can tell our Muslim friend, "You Muslims believe in our God, because we are Christians and our God is the same." What a great opportunity this is to say, "Because you believe in our God, let me tell you something about him." It is amazing to realize that they bow to our God, though we do not bow to theirs.

Though commentators say that this verse was abrogated,[6] the Qur'an never indicates which verses abrogated which. However, the majority of Muslims are not aware of what abrogates what, so we can still use this verse to build our bridge.

---

5.   Matt. 7:24–27.
6.   Gabriel, *Jesus and Muhammad*, 124. Abrogated by verses 8:39, 65.

Al-Rum

The Roman Empire

SIX OR SEVEN YEARS BEFORE THE *HIJRA* (AD 615–616)

Overview

The sura begins with a mention of the defeat of the Romans and God's promise for the believers to overcome the Persians. Time is then given for meditation on God's creation. Several verses explain the condition of people on the end day. The believers will always be worshiping God, morning and evening. The sura gives examples to show how blasphemers are the losers. The sura then goes on to talk about the prohibition of taking interest, the giving of alms, and taking care of one's relatives. Some verses illustrate man's development from youth to old age. The sura ends with verses that refer to the day of resurrection, as well as a verse that encourages Muhammad to be steadfast in the truth and patient in suffering.

The sura gets its name from the defeat of Rome. The Qur'an then says Rome will rise up again and defeat the Persians. This is considered one of the miracles of the Qur'an—the prophecy of the defeat of the Persian Empire. If it is considered a miracle, it is not defined as to when or how.

Comments and Possible Bridges

Creation: Verses 20–22

According to these verses, the main reason for God's creation of male and female is the mercy of God. They also were created, as was the universe, to reflect God's power. The Qur'an says he created the heavens and earth and made people speak different languages and to be different colors. This could be a great opportunity to share with our Muslim friend that the main reason God created humans as both male and female was to reflect his image, not because of his mercy. As we talk about God's image, we have the chance to read about the "motherly" or "female" characteristics in God.[1]

God created the heavens and earth, not to show his might and power as much as to prepare a place in which man could live. Also, it is important to point out that when God created man, only one language was spoken. When man began to build the Tower of Babel, God caused people to speak different languages in order to give humanity time for repentance and a chance to come back to him.[2]

Signs or Miracles: Verses 21–25

If we want to look at these things merely as signs, we can build a bridge by bringing our friend to the Bible, where we read that "the heavens declare the glory of God."[3] However, if, for instance, we read verse 23 as a miracle, then it says that the miracle of God is that we sleep at night and wake up at day. This is not a miracle but the normal rhythm of life that God designed for man. It is a good place here to share with our friend the meaning of the word *miracle*. A miracle is when God overrules his created order to bring something unusual.

Change: Verse 30

The Qur'an says there is no change in God's creation, and it relates this to the idea that man should not change his faith or religion. However, we need to share with our Muslim friend that when we come to believe in Jesus as Savior, we are immediately changed (re-created), and we continue to change to be like Christ.[4] "Therefore, if anyone is in Christ, he is a new creation; the old has gone, the new has come!"[5]

Interest: Verse 39

The Qur'an strictly forbids charging interest; therefore, some banks in the Muslim world do not call it interest but charge large fees for their services.

---

1. Gen. 1:27; Isa. 49:15; 66:13; Matt. 23:37.
2. Gen. 11:1–9.
3. Ps. 19:1.
4. Matt. 18:2–3; Eph. 4:22–24; Col. 3:9–10; Rev. 21:5.
5. 2 Cor. 5:17.

Here we need to share the parable of the talents,[6] which shows the making of interest as a good thing, not a bad thing. We also can point out the countries that have built strong economies while permitting fair interest rates, in contrast to those that apply this Islamic *sharia* and suffer.

Corruption: Verse 41

This verse is clear in saying that corruption is everywhere, in the sea and on land, and it brings destruction. God allows this in order for men to turn back from their bad deeds. This creates an opportunity to share the effect of sin, not only in relation to sinners, but in relation to culture and society as well.

God Does Not Love the Blasphemers: Verse 45

In the Qur'an we find God practicing a different kind of love than what we see in the Bible. Here God's love is very conditional. He will reward well the one who has good deeds, but he does not love blasphemers. With our Muslim friend, we need to share that God loves the sinners as well as the righteous. What he hates is sin.[7]

Winds: Verse 46

We can use this verse about the sign of the winds as a bridge to sharing with our Muslim friend the miracle Jesus performed by calming the winds on the sea.[8] This miracle shows how Jesus has the very quality of God of which this verse in the Qur'an speaks.

Raising the Dead: Verse 50

Man is told to contemplate the might of God, who sends rain and brings to the land different forms of life. The verse also says that the same God will raise the dead, for he can do all things. We can tell our Muslim friend that, yes, God already has performed the acts written about in this verse through Jesus, when he raised the dead. It will be hard for a Muslim to grasp such a concept, even though this truth (that Jesus raised the dead) is mentioned many times in the Qur'an. The problem is not in the mind but in the will. Therefore, we have to be praying for the work of the Holy Spirit in our friend's heart as we are sharing such truth.

---

6. Matt. 25:14–30.
7. Prov. 15:9; John 3:16; 1 John 4:7–12.
8. Matt. 8:23–27.

God Comforts Muhammad: Verses 52–53

God is giving comfort to Muhammad, because the people did not listen to him. He offers comfort by saying that the dead and deaf will not listen; he should not be sad, because basically these people are not meant to believe. We can point out that when a person is sharing the true Word of God, the dead and deaf can hear. We know from the *Injil* that when Jesus spoke, the dead heard him and came back to life. He also made the deaf to hear. This was true of those who were physically deaf as well as those who were spiritually deaf. In referring to verse 53, we can make another great parallel to the times Jesus opened the eyes of the blind as found in the Bible.

God Seals the Heart: Verse 59

This is the second reference we have seen in the Qur'an to God sealing the hearts of unbelievers.[9] We can talk about the seal that will be on the heart of the believers. Whoever believes in Jesus will have the Holy Spirit as the seal of salvation.[10]

---

9. Sura 6:46.

10. Eph. 1:13.

Luqman

The Wise

LATE MECCAN

Overview

The sura starts by describing the good tithers and the end day and by promising the believers paradise. It talks about God's creation and his deity. Then the sura moves to tell about the directions of Luqman to his son and how he should be good to his parents. It talks about the blasphemers and the stand they took against Muhammad and advises the Prophet not to be sad because of them. The central theme is the good news of paradise for believers and the glory of God.

This sura is called by the name *Luqman*, though there is confusion about his actual identity. Was he Luqman the son of 'Ad or another Luqman, who was a philosopher and author? No one really knows.

Comments and Possible Bridges

Characteristics of a Good Believer: Verse 4

The standards of a good believer are regular prayers, the giving of alms, and belief in the afterlife. We need to share with our Muslim friend that a good believer is one who has made a decision to have a personal relationship with God through the atoning work of Jesus. If a person does not do that—

even if he does all that is mentioned in this verse—he cannot be considered a good believer or even a believer at all.[1]

Luqman: Verses 12–19

Verse 12 says that God gave Luqman wisdom. From that great wisdom, Luqman told his son, "Do not have other gods." We can use this as a bridge to share about the wisdom Solomon had and then tie it to how the Lord gives wisdom to all who ask: "If any of you lacks wisdom, he should ask God, who gives generously to all without finding fault, and it will be given to him."[2] We can describe what godly wisdom will look like by referring to the third chapter of James.[3]

Luqman goes on to talk about the importance of children showing gratitude for their parents, because parents have worked hard to care for them. Their mothers bear them and breastfeed them for two years. We can build a bridge by relating the verse from the Ten Commandments, which says, "Honor your father and your mother, so that you may live long in the land the LORD your God is giving you."[4] We can point out that this is the first commandment with a promise.[5]

When Luqman talks against swelling one's cheek in pride, we can relate this to how the Bible speaks of the cheek and tells us that if someone slaps the right, we should give him the left as well.[6] This is the greatest act of humility.

God's Word Is Never Exhausted: Verse 27

If all the trees of the earth became pens and all the water of the sea became ink, they would all be finished writing before the Word of God would be exhausted. Here we can share what John wrote about Jesus: "Jesus did many other things as well. If every one of them were written down, I suppose that even the whole world would not have room for the books that would be written."[7]

---

1. Rom. 10:1–13; Heb. 11:6; 12:1–3.
2. James 1:5.
3. James 3:13–18.
4. Exod. 20:12.
5. Eph. 6:1–3.
6. Matt. 5:38–42.
7. John 21:25.

This parallel allows us to show our Muslim friend, not only that we agree that God's Word will not be exhausted, but also that the Word of God is Jesus.[8]

---

8.   John 1:1, 14.

Al-Sajda

Adoration, or Bowing Down

MIDDLE MECCAN

Overview

This sura focuses on the creation of man and warns the ones who denied Muhammad as a prophet by reminding them of those who were destroyed before them.

Comments and Possible Bridges

No Doubt in the Qur'an: Verse 2

Here Muhammad is saying that this book is from God; there is no doubt in it. Most of the proofs Muhammad brought for his revelation seek to reveal the power of God through nature or by warning the people that if they do not listen to him, God will abuse them as he did the ones who did not listen to prophets in the past. The greatest miracle that proves God's revelation is the Qur'an itself. Now if the Qur'an testifies for Muhammad, who will testify for the Qur'an?

A Day Is Like a Thousand Years: Verse 5

This verse gives the understanding that a day in God's sight is like a thousand years. We can find a parallel to this in the Psalms.[1]

---

1.   Ps. 90:4.

Creation of Man: Verse 9

We can see in this sura that the creation of Adam is very close to what we have in the Bible—God made him out of clay and breathed into him from his own spirit. We can move from talking of man's creation to sharing about what happened to God's spirit in man when he committed sin.

God Could Send All to Hell: Verse 13

This is a dangerous verse, as we see God bragging to mankind, "If I so desire, I could put all mankind, even the ones already in heaven into hell." How completely different this God is from the God we know from the Bible, who made hell only for Satan and his cohorts. We also know through the Bible that God does not desire for any to be lost, but for all to come to salvation through Christ.[2]

Consequences for Rejecting the Qur'an: Verse 23

In this brief reference to Moses, the Qur'an again makes a comparison between those who refused to listen to the prophets and those who reject the revelation of Muhammad. God will do to those who reject Muhammad as he did to those who rejected the prophets in the past. We see this pattern time after time in the Qur'an, as God tells the people, "Either listen to Muhammad and to his message, or I will smite you as I did all those who did not listen to the previous prophets." Accounts are then given of prophets from Adam to Jesus, including others who are not found in the Bible and cannot be traced historically.

---

2.   1 Tim. 2:3–4.

Al-Ahzab

The Confederates, or Parties

AH 5 AND AH 7

Overview

The sura starts with God giving directions to people to obey and respect Muhammad and his wives and Muhammad reminding them of the triumph in the battle. God also gives directions to Muhammad's wives as to how they are to behave. Permission is given to Muhammad to marry the wife of his adopted son. God then gives rules for divorce.

An important note about this sura is that in it God gives the Prophet Muhammad the right to marry (sexually) any woman who offers herself to him. It also gives directions on how to enter the Prophet's house, basically telling believers not to talk directly to his wives, who must remain behind the *hijab*.

Comments and Possible Bridges

Blasphemers: Verse 1

God is telling Muhammad to obey him and not obey the blasphemers (i.e., those who take a stand that differs from Muhammad's). This gives the impression that anyone who does not agree with Muhammad is a blasphemer. We need to share with our Muslim friend that this way of thinking will discourage dialogue. In contrast, we can encourage our friend to have a dialogue with us and to not call anyone who opposes Islamic thought a blasphemer, which only builds walls between people and discourages non-Muslims from even considering the Islamic faith.

Adoption: Verses 4–5

Muhammad is building the stage for the recanting of his adoption of Zaid. It starts very smartly with a wonderful statement: "God did not create two hearts for a man." Most commentators say this verse has been taken from older writers and means that a person should not be hypocritical. Muhammad, however, is using it in the physical sense. He then says that even though you tell your wife, "you are good, like my mother," it will not make her your mother. Certainly here we are playing with the abstract and concrete. Muhammad's examples are abstract, but marrying the wife of one's adopted son, which he is seeking to justify, is concrete. He concludes by saying, "Just because I said to Zaid, 'You are my son,' it does not make him my physical son."

Here we need to explain that adoption never establishes a physical relationship. It goes without saying that adoption is based on a commitment made toward the adoptee and to the society. Of course, the child will never be the adopting father's physical son. But even though there is no physical connection between the father and son, there is the moral responsibility toward the other, the community, and toward God. We also can explain to our friend that in marriage there is a spiritual dimension as well as a physical one. This idea will be new to a Muslim, but we can refer to many phrases in the Arabic and Muslim culture to reinforce the concept, such as the expressions used in marriage, "their souls became one," or "my soul loves your soul."

Facing Death in War: Verse 16

Muhammad is encouraging his people to fight and not to flee from death and killing. We need to present Jesus' perspective here as the Prince of Peace. We can share the words he said to Peter in the garden: "Put your sword back in its place, . . . for all who draw the sword will die by the sword."[1]

Muhammad's Wives: Verses 30–31

God has special treatment for the wives of the Prophet. If one of them sins, she will be doubly punished, and she will be rewarded twice if she does

---

1. Matt. 26:52–53.

good. We need to share here that God has no favorites. If he is truly just, he will deal with Muhammad's wives the same as with all other women.

Chastity: Verse 35

In this list of characteristics of true believers, we find a phrase in Arabic that says that both men and women will guard their vaginas. It is a slip in the Arabic language. Commentators explain that the vagina is any open place in the man's body where things come out. However, since Muhammad used the same word in many places to refer to the woman's vagina in relation to keeping her chastity, the simple reader will understand it only this way.

Zaid's Wife: Verse 37

Having already set the stage, God now tells Muhammad, "Do not worry about people, worry about me. However, as soon as Zaid (Zainab's husband) has enough sex with her, add her to your wives as a lower wife, so you will be an example to the believers for what you are doing."[2]

Muhammad, the Father to None: Verse 40

The marriage to Zaid's wife is sealed by a very strong statement: "Muhammad never was a father to any one of your men." Here Muhammad puts himself in a very special status, using the titles "Apostle of God" and "Seal of the Prophets." We can compare this with what Jesus did, not only with the disciples, but with all the people around him. He took care of them, far more than a physical father would, and he called them "my children," reflecting God's relationship with mankind.[3] This is in contrast to what Muhammad is doing here in rejecting the idea of taking care of men in a fatherly way.

Muhammad, the Lamp: Verse 46

God calls Muhammad the shining candle. We can build a bridge here, beginning with the psalm that reads, "Your word is a lamp to my feet and a light for my path."[4] From there we can move to what Jesus said of himself: "I am the light of the world. Whoever follows me will never walk in darkness, but will have the light of life."[5] We can then share how Jesus' presence affects

---

2. Gabriel, *Jesus and Muhammad*, 178–79.
3. Cf. Mark 10:24; John 13:33.
4. Ps. 119:105.
5. John 8:12.

us as his followers: "You are the light of the world. A city on a hill cannot be hidden. Neither do people light a lamp and put it under a bowl. Instead they put it on its stand, and it gives light to everyone in the house. In the same way, let your light shine before men, that they may see your good deeds and praise your Father in heaven."[6] This means we are to reflect Christ's image to people, which is quite different from what we find in following Muhammad's example.

Importance of Sex in Marriage: Verse 49

If a man marries a woman and never has sexual intercourse with her, he is not heavily obliged to the woman. He can simply give her a little money and let her go. We need to compare this with the story of Joseph. He was engaged to Mary, and, though he had never touched her, he was burdened as to how he could break their engagement.[7] He did not even have sex with her before the birth of Christ, and yet he took her as his wife and cared for her. Sex is the strongest element in Muslim marriage, however, so we find that if a man does not consummate his marriage sexually, he does not have much responsibility toward his wife.

Muhammad Free to Marry Any Woman: Verse 50

God is assuring Muhammad again that he can take as his wife any woman who offers herself to him. He does not need to worry about the talk of others.

Muhammad's Wives Forbidden to Remarry: Verse 53

We find here God establishing restrictions to insure Muhammad's privacy. Toward the end of the verse, he tells Muslims not to hurt Muhammad or to marry the Prophet's wives after his death. We need to ask our Muslim friend here how Muhammad could be hurt after he dies if someone marries his wives? If he took so many wives from others, why could no one take his? Is he different from the people? Did he not say he is just a slave of God, like others? Why would God treat him so differently, when he is claiming to be like others? We need to share with our friend what the Word of God says about the freedom a woman has to remarry after the death of her husband.[8]

---

6.   Matt. 5:14–16.
7.   Matt. 1:18–19.
8.   1 Cor. 7:9, 39.

God Prays to Muhammad: Verse 56

The Qur'an here says that God and his angels pray to Muhammad.[9] We can ask a very simple question: Who prays to whom? Is it not logical that the lesser prays to the greater? We know that this statement is mentioned many times. Muslims will say it hundreds of times a day. A work of the Holy Spirit has to occur for a Muslim to be able to realize the blasphemy in a statement he has said millions of times since his childhood. We pray to God; God does not pray to man.

God Curses Man: Verse 64

Here we see God cursing people and sending them to hell. It would be a good parallel here to share that Jesus never cursed people, only a barren fig tree.[10] He himself became a curse for us.[11]

---

9. Yusuf Ali translates this incorrectly by saying that God and his angels "send blessings" on the Prophet, but the word used means "pray."
10. Matt. 21:18–19.
11. Gal. 3:13.

Saba

The City of Saba

EARLY MECCAN

Overview

The declaration that only God has the right to be praised begins this sura. He is the owner of all things. We also read in this sura, as we have in many others, that God is comforting, protecting, and defending Muhammad against the ones accusing him of madness and lying. He warns the ones not listening to the Prophet, reminding them of what he did to those who rejected other prophets, like David and Solomon. An important theological point found here is that every soul is responsible for that soul's own deeds. God again speaks against the pride of money and children. Proof is given that Muhammad's words are not just magic and that his message from God is to bring peace to Muslims.

Comments and Possible Bridges

Creation Worships God: Verses 1–10

These verses reveal God's qualities, ultimate knowledge, and control. In verse 9 especially, God warns people about not obeying Muhammad, and God shows his majesty in verse 10, when he says that he gave David a great voice and ordered the mountains to echo his praises to God. Here we can share with our friend from the book of Psalms about Israel's beloved "singer"[1] and can use this as a bridge to ask our friend, "Do you want to know more about his praises that made the mountains rejoice to God?" We can say that the songs are found in the *Zabur* and that we would be glad to share some of them with our friend. We can encourage our friend by saying, "If you repeat these songs with a heart that is truly seeking God, the Creator himself will respond back to you." It is not who David was, but the words God gave him to sing that make the difference. This approach will be very attractive to a Muslim.

Solomon's Bronze: Verses 12–13

In verse 10 the Qur'an also says, "We made the iron soft in your hands" (to reshape). In reading this, no one can deny that Muhammad had a strong background in the Bible, because in the Psalms, David said, "He trains my hands for battle; my arms can bend a bow of bronze."[2] We can connect this with verse 12, which says that God gave brass (bronze) to Solomon. It is true that Solomon brought a huge amount of brass to Jerusalem. He brought so much that the total weight could never be determined.[3] This can be a great bridge to take this verse and explain the meaning of "and we sent to him a spring (fountain) of brass" (*ain al-qatr*). We can tell our friend that God did give Solomon the brass and that he made many things for the temple, but he never supported Solomon with jinn. God gave wisdom to Solomon and to his workers to be able to shape brass and to use wood and stones.[4] Wisdom is from God, but jinn are not. Why would God allow jinn, who the Qur'an says are evil, to support his chosen king?

Solomon's Death: Verse 14

This verse pivots between myth and reality. It says very simply that when God passed the death sentence on Solomon, his corpse was standing, leaning on his cane. Because of the way he died, the jinn were not aware of his death, so they continued serving him in humiliating slavery. Then a worm ate his cane. When his cane broke because of the worm, Solomon fell, and the jinn realized he was dead.

We can ask several questions of our Muslim friends about this account. Jinn are spiritual beings, which are supposed to be more gifted than ordinary

---

1.   2 Sam. 23:1.
2.   Ps. 18:34.
3.   1 Kings 7:47; 1 Chron. 22:14; 2 Chron. 4:18.
4.   1 Kings 4:29–34; 5:13–18; 7:13–14; 2 Chron. 1:11–12.

people. If a human looks at a corpse standing, leaning on a cane, he or she would recognize that the person had died. Why did the jinn not realize it? Does the word *jinn* in Arabic not connote quickness, smartness, or brilliance in an evil sense? Also, what is the purpose of keeping the jinn unaware of Solomon's death? Were they meant to keep serving him even after his death? There is a great saying in Arab literature: "One of the Muslim lady fighters said that it does not hurt the sheep to skin them after they are dead." What benefit would Solomon have in keeping the jinn in humiliating slavery after he died? Can we really believe Solomon would do such a thing? Did Solomon really use and abuse the jinn? Solomon actually died. The verse says that the jinn had not known the "unseen," yet Solomon's death was not "unseen"; it was obvious that he was dead. What, then, does this mean?

Saba: Verses 15–17

The sura moves from the story of Solomon to the warning God gave to the people of Saba, in Yemen, from which the sura gets its name. He gave them two gardens, from which they could eat, but they turned away from God; so he sent a flood and made their land desolate. He threatens those who refuse the message of Muhammad with a similar fate.

Intercessor: Verse 23

This is a very important verse. It says there is no intercessor between man and God, except only one that God allows. We need to share with our Muslim friend that never in the entire Qur'an do we find that this role was given to Muhammad. Though this verse speaks of an intercessor, Islamic theology teaches that there is no intercession between God and man, because every soul is responsible for that soul's own deeds. We need to point out this conflict and show that Jesus actually does qualify for this role as intercessor. He had no human father, is sinless, has divine qualities (raising the dead, opening the blind eyes, etc.), and the *Injil* refers to him as the only intercessor.[5]

Jinn: Verse 41

Those who worship jinn are condemned. We could ask the question: If jinn are so bad or could be a temptation for worship, then why would God support Solomon using them as servants? Worship implies a relationship, and we are not to have a relationship with jinn, which Solomon did according to the Qur'an.

---

5. Rom. 8:31–34; Heb. 7:23–28.

Muhammad, the First Prophet to the Arabs: Verse 44

God is saying that he had never sent a prophet to warn Arabs prior to Muhammad. We need to share with our friend that before Muhammad's time, portions of the Bible were translated into Arabic, and many missionaries went to the Arab world. Otherwise, how could there have been so many Christians in Muhammad's time among the Arabs? There is even the possibility that Muhammad's first wife was Christian, because her cousin was a church leader.[6]

Repentance Too Late: Verses 52–54

God is warning the people about repenting too late to avoid destruction. This is a great opportunity to build a bridge by sharing the story of Esau.[7] When he repented and cried for his birthright, which he had earlier scorned, it was too late. We can then move to the parable Jesus told about the rich man and Lazarus, illustrating how repentance cannot come after death.[8] We can end our discussion with the words of Jesus: "Those whom I love I rebuke and discipline. So be earnest, and repent. Here I am! I stand at the door and knock. If anyone hears my voice and opens the door, I will come in and eat with him, and he with me."[9]

---

6. Gabriel, *Jesus and Muhammad*, 31.
7. Gen. 25–27.
8. Luke 16:19–31.
9. Rev. 3:19–20.

Fatir *or* Al-Malaika

The Originator of Creation or *The Angels*

EARLY MECCAN

Overview

The sura starts with praise to God for his creation and for making his angels messengers to his subjects. The angels are said to have many wings. God knows all the deeds of mankind—believers and nonbelievers. He gives some evidence or signs of his power: making people from dust, knowing what is in a woman's womb, and making fresh and saltwater and the various colors in the mountains. Most of these things have been mentioned previously.

Comments and Possible Bridges

Angels: Verse 1

The first verse recognizes God as the Creator of heaven and earth and praises him for making his angels messengers with two, four, six, and eight wings. We can take our Muslim friend from this point to the only place in the Bible that talks about winged angels, as Isaiah describes the seraphim in God's presence. They have six wings. With two of them they cover their eyes, because no one can see God and live; with two more wings they move in his presence; and with the last two they cover their feet.[1] Then we can

---

1. Isa. 6:1–3.

tell our friend that when Jesus came, all the angels looked upon his face and rejoiced, because it was the first time God revealed himself in such a personal and intimate way to his creation.

God Forcing People to Sin: Verse 8

God tells Muhammad that he can mislead whomever he wants and guide whomever he wants. We need to share with our Muslim friend that God's heart desire is that all people know him.[2] God will never mislead. When people do not follow God, it is their own sin that leads them astray.

The other part of the verse is very dangerous. God tells Muhammad, "Do not lose spirit over them." This means that he should not be sad or destroy himself in grief over them. We need to share here how much Jesus, God incarnate, cried over the lost in Jerusalem. We need to introduce the idea of a suffering God. If God himself suffers over mankind because of his love for them, he certainly expects his prophets to do the same. Paul wrote, "Your attitude should be the same as that of Christ Jesus: Who, being in very nature God, did not consider equality with God something to be grasped, but made himself nothing, taking the very nature of a servant, being made in human likeness. And being found in appearance as a man, he humbled himself and became obedient to death—even death on a cross!"[3]

Jesus knew the cross was before him. He did not waver but walked straight forward to carry his cross. The Bible teaches us not to avoid suffering for others. This is the ultimate love we can have for another.[4]

Sweet and Salt Waters: Verse 12

God shows his greatness by providing saltwater and freshwater, and the most amazing thing is that we can have fish to eat from both kinds. We also can sail a boat on top of either kind of water. Muhammad is here claiming all these things as new proofs of God's might (and thus his role as prophet). We need to share with our Muslim friend that there is nothing new in this revelation. Man had been getting fish out of both kinds of water for thousands of years prior to Muhammad's arrival. What is unique about Muhammad's prophecy? A prophecy brings forth something people do not know in the present or tells people things that will happen in the future. When the prophesied events happen, the prophet will be proved truthful. If they do not happen, he will be a false prophet.

---

2. John 3:16; 2 Peter 3:9.
3. Phil. 2:5–8.
4. John 15:13.

Individual Responsibility: Verse 18

It is clear that the Qur'an is saying that Muhammad cannot be a mediator because every soul must carry one's own sins and cannot carry those of another. See notes on "Individual Responsibility" in suras 6:164; 17:15; 41:46; and 53:38; and notes on "Intercessor" in suras 6:70; 34:23; and 39:43–44.

Dead Cannot Hear: Verse 22

God tells Muhammad not to worry about the dead; he is the prophet of the living. God says, "You cannot make the people in the grave hear you." What a wonderful opportunity to share with our Muslim friend that there was a man who could talk so that even a person who had been dead for four days could hear and come out of the tomb. The one who called was Jesus. Lazarus heard his voice and came out of his tomb to life.[5] We can also set forth the truth that on the end day Christ will call all mankind, living and dead. The people in the grave will hear his voice and come forth.[6] A response can be drawn by asking, "Which prophet do you want to follow?"

Paradise, Garden of Eden: Verse 33

God promises Muslim believers paradise or the Garden of Eden, which is decorated with rings of gold, pearls, and silk. We need to ask our friend: If these things are in paradise, surely they are good. Why, then, would God forbid us from using these good things here on earth? According to the Qur'an, God forbids having these good things here but will provide them in the Garden of Eden. If paradise is better than earth, the blessings of paradise should be far more than silk, gold, pearls, and sexual fulfillment. With these thoughts in mind, we can take our Muslim friend to the paradise that John and Peter wrote about.[7] Briefly we can share that it will not be a physical paradise but a spiritual one, since we will be spiritual beings.[8] We will not have silk, pearls, and gold, but the Bible does mention a different kind of gold. The book of Revelation talks about a kind of transparent gold, which is beyond our imagination.[9] Jesus also said that in his kingdom, there will be no marriage or giving in marriage.[10]

---

5. John 11.
6. 1 Thess. 4:16–17.
7. 2 Peter 3:13; Rev. 4; 5; 21.
8. Phil. 3:21.
9. Rev. 21:18, 21.
10. Matt. 22:30.

Ya-Sin

Abbreviated Letters

MIDDLE OR EARLY MECCAN

Overview

This sura warns blasphemers with the example of the blasphemers of Mecca, whose wickedness was exposed by God. It then gives evidence of God's power by the way he is protecting Muhammad. God tells the believers through Muhammad that the Prophet is not taking his Qur'an from poetry or from his own imagination. The sura concludes with a description of how God created man and is able to raise the decayed bones.

Ya-Sin is usually seen as a title for Muhammad. This sura is considered the heart of the Qur'an and is read at ceremonies after death, since it talks of the hereafter. It is said that God will grant a Muslim rewards equal to the reading of the Qur'an ten times just for reading this sura.[1] This sura and suras 38 and 50 get their titles from the letters found in the first verse.

Comments and Possible Bridges

God Swears by the Qur'an: Verse 2

God swears by the Qur'an that Muhammad is his prophet. We should explain to our Muslim friend that in swearing, the lower swears by the higher,

---

1.   Elass, *Understanding the Koran*, 76.

and the ultimate oath is made in reference to the most ultimate thing. We see in the Bible that when God swears, he swears by himself.[2] There is nothing higher than himself. Yet here he swears by the Qur'an. Good questions can be raised: Is the Qur'an God? The Muslim *tawhid* declares that God is one; then what is the Qur'an? It cannot be God. This means that God is using something inferior to himself to swear by, and that is logically unacceptable.

Straight Path: Verses 3–4

The statement here follows a similar saying found in the Bible, when God said, "I will send my messenger."[3] The dilemma comes in verse 4, which says that Muhammad is on the straight path. Was that while Muhammad was on earth among his followers or was it later on?

This idea of Muhammad being on the straight path leads to the concept of his being the representative or model of the straight path, which goes into the area of perfection or infallibility. Over this issue, Muslim scholars break into two groups. Some say that a prophet is infallible only while he is bringing God's Word; after that he is merely a normal human. The other school says that prophets are always infallible. This misunderstanding comes because, as we have seen, the Qur'an never mentions the downfalls or sins of the prophets when conveying their stories. The Bible is honest in portraying the prophets as fallible men whom God used. Only Jesus was perfectly sinless.

Raising the Dead: Verse 12

God says here that he is the one who raises the dead. We can share that in other parts of the Qur'an he says that Jesus raised the dead.[4] This can help bring our Muslim friend to understand a little more clearly the deity of Jesus.

End Day: Verses 51–54

These verses give an idea of how the end day will come—when the trumpet sounds. On that day, the people will wake from the dead and ask what is happening. They will be told that the trumpet has sounded and it is the end day. Then people will be rewarded exactly for the acts they have committed. We can easily bridge between this verse and what we have in the Bible.[5]

---

2. Gen. 22:16; Jer. 22:5; 44:26; 49:13.
3. Mal. 3:1; Mark 1:2.
4. Sura 3:49.
5. Matt. 24:30–31; 1 Cor. 15:52.

Paradise, Garden of Eden: Verses 55–58

We have in these verses another glimpse of paradise. We can share that when that day comes and the book is opened, only one deed written therein will decide for a person heaven or hell—whether that person accepted Christ or not. We can then share how one can accept Christ.

God Curses Man: Verses 66–67

God declares his power by saying that if he wanted, he could reduce man to an animal or monster. Such an act, however, degrades the image of God in man. God made man in his image, and when he made man, he said, "It is good." There is no intention in God's heart to reduce his image into that of a monster.

God Comforts Muhammad: Verse 76

God is comforting Muhammad again and asking him not to feel sad for the lost state of the nonbelievers. We can relate this to Jesus' tears for the lost of Jerusalem.[6]

Dry Bones: Verse 78

God tells Muhammad that man asks, "Who can bring life from the dry bones?" We can take our friend to the Bible and relate the story of Ezekiel and the dry bones.[7] Then we can point out that Jesus gave life to those who were dead and decaying, as when he raised Lazarus from the dead.

---

6. Matt. 23:37.
7. Ezek. 37.

Al-Saffat

Those Ranged in Ranks

EARLY MIDDLE MECCAN

Overview

This sura begins as the previous one did, with God swearing by something lower than himself. Now he swears by rows of creatures from his creation.[1] God declares his oneness and then talks about life after death. He warns the nonbelievers of the certainty of the coming end day. We also find God again protecting Muhammad from those who say that he is crazy and a madman. A new thing we read in this sura is a strong dispute about the blasphemers' declaration that God has girls and that these girls have sons, and also that God made the angels female. The sura ends by clearing God of all the false accusations.

Comments and Possible Bridges

God Swears by Lesser Things: Verse 1

God swears by some creatures, and as we shared in the previous sura, God cannot swear by a subject inferior to himself.

One God: Verse 4

God is one. This is the center of Islamic *tawhid*.

---

1.   See notes on sura 36:2.

Blasphemers: Verses 15–23

The blasphemers charge that Muhammad's verses proving God's power are just magic. These people are determined to continue to believe in their ancestors. God threatens them through Muhammad, saying they will be destined to hell.

Paradise, Garden of Eden: Verses 43–51

More details are given about paradise. Believers will sit on couches in front of each other and be served drinks from a clear-flowing spring that does not cause drunkenness. There will also be *horiya* there. These are chaste women with big eyes like guarded eggs. We can build bridges here, as in previous verses, by relating to our friend the biblical view of heaven.

Tree of Zaqqum: Verses 51–73

These verses give a description of hell and threaten the blasphemers with it. The Tree of Zaqqum, with its terrifying and bitter fruit, awaits those destined for hell.[2]

Noah: Verses 75–82

God reveals how he punished the people of Noah's day when they did not believe and how he rewarded Noah. We can relate this to the story of Noah from the Bible.

Abraham: Verses 83–113

As we read the story of Abraham here, we find in verse 91 that Abraham went to his family's idols, put food in front of them, and said, "Won't you eat?" When they did not move to eat the food, he broke them. Then Abraham told his family, "See, you worship things you carved." As a result, his relatives got together and tried to burn him.

Verses 97 and 98 are very important verses because they add a new element to the story. The idolaters built a big fire and tried to burn Abraham in it, but God did not let them succeed in their plot. He saved Abraham from the burning fire. Here we need to share that this did not happen to Abraham, but to Shadrach, Meshach, and Abednego. Then we can tell their story.[3]

---

2. See also sura 17:60.
3. Dan. 3.

The story then moves from the fire to the account of Abraham offering his son. As we can see in verse 103, the Qur'an never says that Ishmael was the one who was being sacrificed. It is very clear that the name is not mentioned. However, most commentators will say that God was asking Abraham to give Ishmael, not Isaac, as the Bible says.

Great Sacrifice: Verse 107

Verse 107 is the pivotal verse in the story. God tells Muhammad that he ransomed Abraham's son with a great sacrifice. We know that the ransom should equal the subject ransomed. When a rich man's son is kidnapped, a high ransom will be demanded. When a poor man's son is taken, the ransom will be lower. We can bring our Muslim friend's attention to the fact that there is no ram, even if we search the world over, that would be able to ransom one human soul, because of a person's great value before God. We need our friend to understand that the essence of Christianity can be wrapped up in this verse. The great sacrifice God provided to save not only Abraham's son, but all of mankind, is Jesus, the Son of God. Because he is so special, he could be put on one side of the scale; and even if we put all the lost people of the world on the other side, his sacrifice would be enough, because he is the Great Sacrifice.[4]

Isaac: Verses 112–113

This is an interesting verse. Since the Qur'an never mentions that Ishmael is the one sacrificed, there is a great connection between the story of the sacrifice and the blessing of Isaac. God tells Abraham, "Here is good news. Isaac is a prophet from among the righteous." In the verse that follows, God blesses Isaac's offspring, not Ishmael's. A Muslim, however, will never see this without the power of the Holy Spirit.

Jonah: Verses 139–148

Because Jonah refused to go to the city to preach God's word, he was thrown out of the boat, and the fish swallowed him. However, because he praised God in the belly of the fish, God rescued him. God made a gourd plant to grow over him but does not say why. The story says that the city had more than one hundred thousand people, but it does not mention the name. Though it says the people believed, it does not give details as to how. We can

---

4. Heb. 10:10–14; 1 John 2:2; 4:10.

share the details of the biblical story with our Muslim friends so that they can see the wisdom of God behind the story they know.

Daughters and Sons: Verses 149–153

The pagans were asking if God had only daughters. Muhammad disputes this claim, saying that God does not like girls more than boys, and he denies that God created angels as girls. We can use this verse to build a bridge to talk about the fact that God does not have favorites. In doing so, we can take our friend to the book of Galatians, which says, "There is neither Jew nor Greek, slave nor free, male nor female, for you are all one in Christ Jesus."[5]

---

5.   Gal. 3:28.

Sad

The Letter Sad

EARLY MIDDLE MECCAN

Overview

This sura focuses on showing the resistance of the non-Muslims to Muhammad's call, as well as their envy of him. As usual, God gives many examples of all the previous peoples who took a stand against prophets and encourages Muhammad to stand firm against the attack of the non-Muslims. The sura ends by clarifying Muhammad's mission to the world and God's prayers over him.

This is one of several suras in which the name of the sura is taken from an Arabic letter. Some questions we can ask Muslims in relation to this issue include: What meaning is given to the sura when it is introduced by an Arabic letter? What will happen to the meaning of the letter when we translate this sura? Will it not lose its value? In Psalm 119 in the Bible, we find an interesting use of letters but for quite a different reason. Each section of that psalm features eight lines, all beginning with the same Hebrew letter. The sections proceed successively through the twenty-two letters of the Hebrew alphabet. The purpose of this structure is to help people to remember and memorize the long psalm (song).

Does God speak only in Arabic? It is well known that in the Muslim world Arabic is considered the heavenly language. Early in the Islamic era, translating the Qur'an was forbidden. It loses a lot of its meaning and power when it is put into another language. A lot of the effect of the Qur'an is based on the poetic style of the Arabic language and the music and rhythm in it.

Comments and Possible Bridges

God Swears by the Qur'an: Verse 1

We see God again swearing by the Qur'an. We can ask the same question: Is the Qur'an equal to God? If the answer is yes, the Islamic ideology of Allah as one will be destroyed. See notes on sura 36:2.

Blasphemers: Verses 4–5

The blasphemers again charge that the Qur'an is just magic. They also are amazed by Muhammad's statement that God is one. We can build a bridge of agreement here by taking our friend to the words of Paul, when he said, "So then, about eating food sacrificed to idols: We know that an idol is nothing at all in the world and that there is no God but one."[1]

One God: Verse 7

The blasphemers declare that they had never heard about God being one, but we can share with our Muslim friends that this concept was well known and held by the Christians and Jews of the time. We can remind them of the greatest commandment God gave to mankind in the Old Testament: "Hear, O Israel: The LORD our God, the LORD is one. Love the LORD your God with all your heart and with all your soul and with all your strength."[2]

David and the Disputants: Verses 21–25

This account from the life of David is quite different from the biblical text. Two brothers entered into David's presence, and he fed them. One of the two said that his brother had ninety-nine goats, and he had only one, and yet that brother wanted to take his only goat. David responded quickly and said that this was wrong. He then realized that he himself was wrong. He bowed before God and asked his forgiveness, and God forgave him immediately.

We need to take our Muslim friend to the real story.[3] David was a great king at the time that he took Bathsheba. We can share the details of the story

---

1. 1 Cor. 8:4.
2. Deut. 6:4–5.
3. 2 Sam. 11–12.

of how David had her husband killed and then took her as his wife. We have to tell this story because the Qur'an does not mention details of the prophets' sins, and Muslim commentators will even say that David really did not do anything wrong. The Bible is clear, however, and reveals how the prophet Nathan came to David and confronted the king with his sin. Nathan's story dealt with a poor man, who had one little lamb, and a rich landowner, who came and took the man's beloved lamb. The prophet then looked David straight in the eyes and said, "You are the man!"[4] (i.e., the rich man).

We also need to stress the process of repentance before God. The Bible teaches us that David wept for a long time with a broken heart before God. God forgave him because of his broken heart, but David's sin demanded consequences in the physical realm. Nathan told David that the sword would never leave his family. What he had done in taking a man's wife would be done to his own family. Here will be a great opportunity to share with our friend that while God forgives, in God's justice there are still temporal consequences for our sin.

Solomon's Horses: Verses 30–33

Solomon loved horses, and this is one reason horses are so loved by Arabs as well. We can build a bridge here by sharing how God warned kings of Israel not to accumulate great numbers of horses or go back to Egypt to get them.[5] Yet, we see that this is exactly what Solomon did, as he acquired more than twelve thousand horses during his reign, importing them from Egypt.[6] We can talk about how even things such as horses can become idols in a person's life when that person begins to depend on them more than on God.[7]

Solomon: Verses 34–40

The verb in verse 34 that is translated "tested" ("We did test Solomon") is the same word used when talking about sexual temptation and is better translated "seduced." Of course, we need to share that the Bible tells us that Solomon had many women, with wives and concubines together numbering one thousand. We share this to show, as the Bible says, that at the end of his days, these women turned his heart from God.[8]

---

4. 2 Sam. 12:7.
5. Deut. 17:16.
6. 1 Kings 4:26; 10:26–28; 2 Chron. 1:14–16; 9:25.
7. Isa. 31:1.
8. 1 Kings 11:4.

Verse 34 is a unique verse and a good example of instances in the Qur'an when the meaning of a story or verse is completely unknown and commentators go in many different directions to explain what it means. Here, God is testing Solomon by throwing a body on his seat (throne). Many stories are relayed by commentators as to the identity of the body. In general, it is taken to be a satanic figure, which could be called *Saqr* (stone). Some of the stories say that Solomon wanted to build the temple without making a sound and that *Saqr* could do it. We can find a lot of biblical material mixed in with this story. For example, God gave the commands to Moses that the altar was to be built with undressed stones and without tools.[9] Another story told in relation to this body is that Satan sat on Solomon's throne for forty days, during which he disrupted his kingdom, causing Solomon to suffer.

The following verses say that when Solomon repented, God subjected the wind to his power, and all who gave Solomon a hard time were put in chains. Verse 37 says that God gave evil spirits to serve Solomon. In general, Islam is a spiritual vacuum. The Qur'an does not give many directions in relation to the spiritual world. Even the Holy Spirit is considered an angel. Because the Qur'an records that God subjected Satan and his jinn to serve Solomon, we find that a lot of Muslims, through folk Islam, are open to such use of demonic powers. As Christians, we need to be aware of this and remember the Bible's warnings against Satan and his demons.[10]

Job: Verses 41–44

This is a very short account of the life of Job. Yet, we can use it to share in detail about the conversation between Job and his friends and between Job and God. In verse 42, we read that God healed Job by enabling him to hit the ground and bring forth water to wash and drink, but we can share that it was much more than that. Of course, the washing here can be read as a kind of repentance and spiritual cleansing, because God's restoration of Job follows in verse 43. We need to share here with our Muslim friend that water was not the issue for Job. It was only when Job realized how mighty God is and how, even with all his goodness, he could never measure up to God that God restored him. This is when Job began to have a real, personal relationship with God and said, "My ears had heard of you but now my eyes have seen you."[11] In verse 43, we need to go into more details to say that God restored

---

9. Exod. 20:24–26; Deut. 27:5.
10. Cf. Eph. 6:10–18; 2 Cor. 11:14.
11. Job 42:5.

all Job's possessions twice over, but he gave Job only the number of children that he had lost. Perhaps we can surmise that this was because the children who had died were alive in heaven.

Hell: Verse 62

This verse reveals that some people in hell were wondering why it was that some others, whom they thought would be in hell, did not end up there. We can agree that many will surely be surprised on the end day and even share the words of Jesus, who said, "Indeed there are those who are last who will be first, and first who will be last."[12] This also reminds us that Jesus said, "Not everyone who says to me, 'Lord, Lord,' will enter the kingdom of heaven, but only he who does the will of my Father who is in heaven. Many will say to me on that day, 'Lord, Lord, did we not prophesy in your name, and in your name drive out demons and perform many miracles?' Then I will tell them plainly, 'I never knew you. Away from me, you evildoers!'"[13]

Creation of Man: Verses 71–85

This is similar to the accounts of the creation of man in earlier suras, again revealing that God told the angels to bow in obedience to him. They all did except *Iblis*. See notes to suras 2:30–37 and 7:11 for more on this topic.

---

12.   Luke 13:30.
13.   Matt. 7:21–23.

Al-Zumar

The Crowds

LATER MECCAN

Overview

This sura begins by praising the Qur'an and disputing the heretics who claim that God has a son. It speaks of God's power and then makes a comparison between the righteous and wicked. In the end, however, everyone will die. God, therefore, is calling people to come to him before it is too late. The sura ends with a description of how the end day will come.

Comments and Possible Bridges

God Speaks to Muhammad: Verse 2

God tells Muhammad, "We revealed to you the Qur'an." See earlier notes to suras 3:7 and 6:19.

God Has No Son: Verse 4

This verse gives a very weak argument, saying that if God wanted to have a son (physical), he could choose whomever he pleased, because he is the Mighty One. Using this same argument, we could ask the logical question, Then, why not Jesus? This argument opens up the very possibility the Qur'an tries to deny.

God Does Not Need: Verse 7

If you reject God, it does not really hurt him, nor does he care. Again, we need to share with our Muslim friend that even though God does not need man, as a loving God, he yearns for a relationship with the man he made to love him.

There is no one who can carry someone else's sin. We can have total agreement with our friend on this part of the verse. Every person is responsible before God for his or her own acts (priesthood of the believer). At the same time, however, we need to explain that we have to forgive one another. Also, we should bring our friend's attention to Jesus, the very unique man. He is the second, perfect Adam, the sinless one, the only one who can bear a person's sin, if that person willingly accepts his saving work. Jesus is not just a man, since a man cannot bear another's sins—he is also deity, God in the flesh.[1]

Muhammad, the First Muslim: Verse 12

Muhammad says that he was ordained to be the first Muslim. Commentators say, "or the first one to be led by God's directions."[2] We need to remind our Muslim friend that the Qur'an also says that Abraham was a Muslim,[3] and then ask, "Is Muhammad higher than Abraham? Is he before Abraham?" We need to understand here, in talking with our friend, that the Qur'an recognizes Muhammad as the slave of God and as just a man. Any Muslim will voice this position, yet the reality is that the worldwide Muslim body raises Muhammad sometimes to a higher position than even God himself.

Qur'an Consistent with Itself: Verse 23

This verse says the Qur'an is consistent with itself, but we have found it is not consistent as we have examined its logic, history, and ideology. The verse reads that when the people hear the Qur'an, their skin will be crumbled. The imagination asks, Is it crumbling out of fear or from shivering because of excitement about God's Word? In either case, we can share with our friend that when we read or hear the Word of God, as found in the Holy Bible, we have eternal peace in our hearts.[4]

---

1. John 1:1–14.
2. Committee of the Qur'an and Sunna, *Al-Muntakhab*, 818.
3. Cf. suras 2:131; 3:65–67.
4. Pss. 33; 56; 119:9–17, 105; Isa. 26:3.

Arabic Language: Verse 28

Here the Qur'an calls itself Arabic, and as we noted earlier, many Muslims believe it should not be translated. This verse says the Qur'an is without any crookedness. This could mean without any non-Arabic words, though there are many non-Arabic words included. However, it also could mean without any contradictions or mistakes. It is not within the scope of this book to discuss in detail the historical and linguistic mistakes in the Qur'an. There are many other references that can provide this information.[5] We simply share this verse to make you aware of the claims of the Qur'an in order to raise the issue with Muslim friends, if needed.

Parable of the Owners: Verse 29

God gives a parable about a man who was owned by many partners and another man who was owned by only one. The question he raises is: "Are they equal?" We need to find a kind way to talk about the quality of this parable in comparison to those given by Jesus in the New Testament. Not only were the parables of Jesus more understandable, but many times he also told more than one in order to make sure the hearers understood the spiritual truth he wanted to convey.[6]

Assurance of Salvation: Verse 37

This verse says that if God saves someone, no one can lead him astray after that. We can ask our Muslim friend, "Are you sure of your salvation?" Not a single Muslim will be able to say yes. Then what is the meaning of this statement? After some discussion, we can share that no one can have real assurance until he or she comes to Jesus, and his atoning work takes place in that person's life.[7]

Muhammad Has No Responsibility over Muslims: Verse 41

God releases Muhammad from any responsibility over Muslims; he is not to judge over them. Since he has no responsibility, he has no authority. Jesus, however, took all the responsibility for mankind, to the point of death, and that is why he has all the authority.[8]

---

5. Esack, *The Qur'an*; Safa, *Inside Islam*.
6. Matt. 13; Luke 15.
7. John 10:27–30.
8. Matt. 9:6; 28:18; John 17:2–5.

End Day: Verse 42

Even though this verse is hard to understand, we can go to Paul, who, in explaining the end day, says, "Listen, I tell you a mystery: We will not all sleep, but we will all be changed—in a flash, in the twinkling of an eye, at the last trumpet. For the trumpet will sound, the dead will be raised imperishable, and we will be changed. For the perishable must clothe itself with the imperishable, and the mortal with immortality."[9]

The tombs will give up their dead, and we who are alive will be changed from the body of death into a glorified body, like that of Jesus. So the parallel here is that God will deal with the spirit of man, whether dead or alive. We can also talk about the time when Jesus called Lazarus *asleep*, meaning "dead."[10] When we die, our bodies "sleep" until the end day comes and they are raised to join our spirits in our eternal destiny.

Intercessor: Verses 43–44

Muhammad accuses people of taking intercessors. He rejects the idea of intercessors. Perhaps the Prophet was affected by Orthodoxy or Catholicism, which promote the idea of the intercession of saints. While we reject the idea of multiple intercessors, we cannot agree with our Muslim friend that there is no intercessor between man and God. As verse 44 says, God alone has the power of granting intercession between man and himself. When we say that Jesus is our Intercessor, we mean also that Jesus is God himself and is interceding on our behalf—between sinful man and God the Father. He is the only one who has that right, because he paid the price on the cross. He alone can bring us to his Father.[11]

Christians Are Ignorant Ones: Verse 64

Muhammad calls Christians ignorant because they join others to God in their worship. This label of "ignorant ones" is also used in general for any who do not believe in the God of Muhammad and in Muhammad as his prophet. We can very simply ask, "Did the mighty men of the Old Testament ever acknowledge Muhammad as the seal of the prophets? Can we really call Moses, Solomon, and David ignorant?" Such labels do not encourage understanding.

---

9. 1 Cor. 15:51–53.
10. John 11:11.
11. 1 Tim. 2:5.

End Day: Verse 68

When the trumpet sounds, everyone in heaven and earth will die, except those whom God wills to keep alive. Then the trumpet will sound again, and everyone will be alive. How much time is there between the first and second trumpet? Are there two comings? We can build a bridge with this verse by going to the New Testament, which says that when the trumpet sounds, everyone will stand before God to give an account.[12] We need to ask our Muslim friend, "Are you ready to be in the presence of God at this very second?" Since the Qur'an does not provide assurance of salvation, our friend will be afraid to face God. We can state clearly that only in Christ can we see God and live.

Length of Heaven and Hell: Verses 72–73

Hell is eternal, and so is heaven. This is why we need to make sure before we die which way we are going.

---

12. Rom. 14:12; 1 Cor. 15:51–52; 1 Thess. 4:16–17; 1 Peter 4:5.

Al-Mu-min *or* Gafir

The Believer or *He Who Forgives*

LATER MECCAN

Overview

The sura starts with a description of the qualities of the Qur'an and a call to worship the only God. It tells about the carrying of God's throne and how the angels worship him. God's abilities and miracles are revealed, and a reminder is given to the believers about the end day. The sura then gives a further account of Moses and Pharaoh. At the end of the sura, people are encouraged to see how God dealt with and punished the nations before them.

Comments and Possible Bridges

Forgiveness: Verse 3

This verse says that God is the forgiver of sins. He accepts repentance and is severe in punishment. Perhaps the name of the sura has been taken from this verse. We can agree with our friend that God is the forgiver of sins and share verses from the Bible that relate this truth.[1]

Do Not Dispute with the Prophet: Verse 4

Those who argue with the Prophet are considered blasphemers. We can use this point to take our Muslim friend to the verse that says, "'Come now,

---

1. Mic. 7:18; Matt. 6:9–15; Mark 11:25; Luke 7:49.

let us reason together,' says the LORD. 'Though your sins are like scarlet, they shall be as white as snow; though they are red as crimson, they shall be like wool. If you are willing and obedient, you will eat the best from the land; but if you resist and rebel, you will be devoured by the sword.' For the mouth of the LORD has spoken."[2]

If God himself is asking man to reason with him and have a dialogue, how can we call a person a blasphemer just because he questions us? God made man with a free will to choose. The ability to question or argue is the main essence of the free will, which makes man different and above all the animals. For man to follow without questioning is to reduce him to a mere animal.

God's Throne: Verse 7

This is a unique verse and raises many questions.[3] Is God's throne carried by angels? Does God have a throne? Can we imagine how God looks? For a Muslim, to even think about what God might look like is considered blasphemy, but we can ask our Muslim friend if the throne looks that magnificent, how much more magnificent will be the one who sits on the throne. We can help him begin to realize that if a person can imagine a throne, as in the qur'anic text, why is it that he cannot think of the one who sits on the throne? Another question comes to mind: Are angels intercessors for man before God? How could this be when the Qur'an said earlier that there are no intercessors between man and God? We need to help our Muslim friend see that angels cannot be intercessors, and neither can saints. The only one who can intercede is Christ.

Haman: Verse 24

God says that he sent Moses to Pharaoh and Haman. By relating the story of Haman in the Bible, we can show our friend that Haman was a completely different personality and did not live during Pharaoh's time, but during that of Queen Esther. Also, Qarun is not mentioned in the Bible.[4]

Pharaoh: Verse 26

This verse adds something new to the story of Pharaoh and Moses. Here, Pharaoh declares his desire to kill Moses. According to the Old Testament,

---

2. Isa. 1:18–20.
3. Yusuf Ali translates the first phrase as "Those who sustain the throne," while the word in Arabic is "carry," which leads us to the questions raised.
4. Elass, *Understanding the Koran*, 115.

the pharaoh of the exodus never intended to kill Moses. All of these verses are opportunities to reveal the biblical story to our friend.

Pharaoh Builds a Tower: Verses 36–37

We see Pharaoh asking Haman to build him a tower to reach up to the God of Moses to see if he is truly God. We can share with our Muslim friend that the only time man tried to do something of that nature was with the Tower of Babel. Then we can reveal the confusion between the two stories.[5] Also, if we look at the person of Haman, we know from the Bible that he did build a tower, but it was for a completely different purpose.[6] If we think logically about the qur'anic account here, it does not make sense, since Pharaoh saw the mighty work of God through Moses. He had no need to build a tower to reach God; God was making himself known to Pharaoh. The Bible also reveals to us that though Pharaoh was stubborn and refused Moses' request, he recognized the power of God and feared him.[7]

Life Is Temporary: Verse 39

A great bridge can be built here as we agree with the truth found in this verse that life on earth is temporary but the hereafter is for eternity. We can share the hope we have through Christ, which helps us to not worry about this earthly home, but to look forward to the home to come.

The Bible, a God-given Book: Verses 53–54

The Qur'an testifies that God gave Moses and the Israelites the Book and that it is a guide and a reminder of all the stories for the one who has wisdom to hear. These are two powerful statements, and we can use them to build a bridge by sharing with our friend the wisdom and history we find in the Bible. When we find differences between the stories of the Qur'an and the Bible, we can use these verses to show that if a person is wise, he or she will look at the Bible and seek guidance from the stories found there.

Creation of Man: Verses 67–68

These verses describe how God created man and allows him to grow strong till the time appointed for his death. We can relate this to the biblical account.

---

5.   Gen. 11.
6.   Esther 6:4.
7.   Exod. 8:8, 19; 9:27–28.

Ha-Mim Sajda *or* Fussilat

Abbreviated Letters or *Patterned*

LATER MECCAN

Overview

This sura has two names, *Fussilat*, meaning "patterned" or "explained," and *Sajda*, meaning "prostrate." The sura mainly speaks about the preciousness of the Qur'an and how it rewards and threatens. It reminds the nonbelievers about the mighty power of God and scares them by what happened to 'Ad and Thamud and with the coming end day. God is mighty in power and able to bring life and death. There is a harsh threat for anyone who takes a stand against the Qur'an and Muhammad's message. The sura ends with a declaration of the perfection of the Qur'an and revelation of the final destination of the blasphemers.

Comments and Possible Bridges

Arabic Language: Verses 2–3

These verses give assurance to the people that the Qur'an is from God and in Arabic. See previous notes on suras 12:2 and 39:28 about the Arabic language.

Muhammad Is a Just a Man: Verse 6

As mentioned before, Muhammad says of himself that he is just a man like others. Here we need to bring our Muslim friend's attention to the fact that if Muhammad is just a human like other people, he is therefore not infallible. We can then ask, "Should we follow just a man like us or Jesus, who by his words and actions proved to us that he was not a mere man like us?" He is like God, yet he chose to appear like us in order for us to have a relationship with God.

Creation: Verses 9–12

These verses reveal that God created the earth in two days. We need to bring the attention of our friend to other places in the Qur'an, where it says he created the earth in six days.[1] How do we have such a contradiction in God's Word? With the creation of the mountains, sky, and firmament, it is eight days total. How can this be?

'Ad People: Verses 13–17

God threatens the people by what he did to 'Ad and Thamud. See notes on suras 11:50–60, 61–68; 14:7–9; 51:41–42, 43–45; and 54:9–48.

Enemies of God: Verse 28

This verse speaks of "the enemies of God." This statement refers to the unbelievers. We can build a bridge by sharing that, in fact, we are all God's enemies because of sin, and we all deserve hell. But while we were still sinners, Christ died for us.[2]

Consequences for Rejecting the Qur'an: Verses 40–42

Muhammad here is threatening those who refuse the Qur'an as the authentic Word of God with hellfire and all punishments possible for mankind. This confirms the belief at the heart of Islam that only Muslims are destined to heaven. For this reason, in mainstream Islam, holy war cannot be avoided. Whether it is a literal holy war, killing all infidels in the name of God, or an intellectual holy war, through writings, media, money, and other resources, Muslims have to make Islam the only religion in a land.

Qur'an Heals Those Who Believe: Verse 44

The Prophet Muhammad never healed anyone from sickness or disease, so how can his Qur'an heal people? We can build a bridge here by sharing how Christ healed many of diseases and illness, and how, even today, he can bring healing.

---

1.   Sura 7:54.
2.   Rom. 5:8–11; Col. 1:21–22.

Individual Responsibility: Verse 46

Again we see the Qur'an refer to the fact that each person is responsible for his own acts. See notes on suras 6:164; 17:15; 35:18; and 53:38.

God's Signs Revealed in Man's Soul: Verse 53

The ultimate way for God to prove himself is through his signs (miracles) in the life of a person or within a person's soul. We can connect this with Jesus' encounter with the Pharisees. "Once, having been asked by the Pharisees when the kingdom of God would come, Jesus replied, 'The kingdom of God does not come with your careful observation, nor will people say, "Here it is," or "There it is," because the kingdom of God is within you.'"[3]

---

3.   Luke 17:20–21.

Al-Shura

Consultation

LATER MECCAN

Overview

This sura is called *Shura*, or "Consultation," because it shows Muslims how to do their business in a society based on consultation. There are a lot of issues raised about religion and beliefs from the political point of view in this sura. As usual, however, it begins by showing the importance of the Qur'an. God then takes a stand against the blasphemers in an effort to comfort Muhammad. God's authority over all things is emphasized. Nonbelievers are threatened and challenged to bring something to compare with even the shortest sura from the Qur'an. The wisdom of God is revealed by allowing people to be rich and poor, and by giving sons to some, daughters to others, and a combination to others. The sura continues by referring to all the tragedies that have occurred because of people's sin.

Comments and Possible Bridges

Inspiration as with Other Prophets: Verse 3

The sura begins by revealing that God gave Muhammad a revelation or inspiration as he did other prophets before him. This illustrates a change from previous suras, which usually lift the Qur'an higher than anything else. Here, however, he is comparing the revelation with the previous ones.

Muhammad Has No Responsibility over Muslims: Verse 6

The point is again stressed that Muhammad is not responsible for his people. See previous note to sura 39:41 on the same subject.

Mother of Cities: Verse 7

God reveals that he sent Muhammad an Arabic Qur'an in order to warn Mecca, the Mother of the Cities, and the people around her of the end day. We can agree with the concept of the need to warn people before death, because on the Day of Judgment there will be no more warning, no second chances, only judgment.[1] Jesus came the first time as a Savior to save, and when he left, the Holy Spirit stayed with us to work in the world. But when Jesus comes back, he will come back as Judge. A sword will come out of his mouth (not literally), meaning that he will not say another word but will go to the task of separating the sinners from the righteous.[2] He will take the righteous to his eternal kingdom, and the sinners will go to eternal hell.

Cause of Difficulties: Verse 30

This verse says that when catastrophe or misfortune comes upon a person, it is because of that person's sin. We can agree in part with this verse, for many times we do bring upon ourselves problems because of our sin, but this is not the only explanation for suffering. We can share with our friend several passages from 1 Peter that speak to this subject.[3] We can also explain that God sometimes allows troubles to come into our lives because he knows very well that they can help us to grow. But he is also faithful not to bring us more than we can handle.[4] The account of Job, who was a righteous man yet suffered terribly, is a good example of how God allows suffering to come even to the righteous, but not without a purpose.

How God Speaks His Revelation: Verse 51

God is explaining here how Muhammad received his revelation. When God talks to a person, it is not face-to-face. The person might hear the words but will not see the face of the speaker. God also may send an angel to speak

---

1. Matt. 24:36–51; 25:1–46; Mark 13:32–37.
2. Matt. 25:31–32; Rev. 19:11–21.
3. 1 Peter 2:20–25; 3:13–22; 4:12–19.
4. 1 Cor. 10:13.

his message. We can use this opportunity to share with our friend how God revealed the Bible over a period of 1,500 years, to some forty different writers, and yet the message is consistent and in harmony throughout.[5]

---

5.   Luke 24:13–32; John 1:44–45; Acts 11–26; 2 Tim. 3:15–17.

Al-Zukhruf

Gold Adornments, or Decorations

LATER MECCAN

Overview

The sura starts with a reminder of the importance of the Qur'an to God. Then God talks about those who express sarcasm toward Muhammad's message. Evidences are given in order for man to believe in God. A partial account of Abraham's story is shared. God gives a rebuttal to the blasphemers of Mecca over their accusations that Muhammad is not a good prophet, because he is from neither Mecca nor Taif. In relation to this, God reveals the story of Moses and God's punishment of Pharaoh because of his pride. The sura threatens nonbelievers with suffering on the end day and gives believers a promise of heaven.

Comments and Possible Bridges

Qur'an, Easy for Arabic Speakers: Verse 3

God says that he made his Qur'an in Arabic so that the people will understand. We can raise several questions with our friend over this statement: Is the Qur'an for the Arabs only? Are non-Arabs able to understand the Qur'an? Is God's Word limited to certain languages? Who created the different languages in the world? With questions like this, we can encourage our friend to think freely. We need to state that God's Word should communicate to people regardless of their language, culture, age, or status, and this is the reason we do not have problems with seeing the Bible translated into different languages.

Airplane Verses: Verses 12–14

These important verses are read today in every Muslim airline before the flight takes off. Even though the verses speak about riding an animal, they are the closest thing Muslims can use from the Qur'an for flying in an airplane. The problem occurs when they add verse 14 to it. It reveals a very fatalistic view. When people are flying in an airplane, they do not want to be reminded of their death but encouraged to know that God will keep them safe. The next time we are on an airplane and this verse comes on the little TV screen above, it is a great opportunity to start a discussion. The discussion can begin with many different questions: Are you afraid to die? Where do you think you will go after you die? Would you like to know how to change your eternal destiny just in case the airplane crashes?

Daughters and Sons: Verse 16

Muhammad is mocking the blasphemers by asking, "Do you think that God has the girls and you have the boys?" In the Arabic culture, boys are much more important than girls. Muhammad really wants to mock what they are doing. He is telling them, "Do you think you are so much higher than God that you have the boys and he the girls?" We need to go to Galatians, where we can share that in Christ, and only in Christ, there is no difference between male and female.[1]

Condemnation for Unbelief: Verses 22–25

Muhammad ridicules the nonbelievers for saying they will not change from the beliefs of their fathers and grandfathers. He tells them that they have to be Muslims and threatens them with the same punishment God inflicted on peoples before them. We can ask, "Why does the Prophet Muhammad ask people to change their own religion to become Muslim and even go so far as to threaten them with the sword, while the Muslim himself has no freedom to change his own religion?" If a Muslim changes his religion, he has to be put to death by the Muslim *umma*. Is this not a double standard?

---

1. Gal. 3:28.

We do not have any record in the *Injil* that Jesus threatened those who did not follow him.[2]

Slavery: Verse 32

This verse reveals that the Qur'an justifies slavery. The phrase, "some may command work from others," means in Arabic, "some may enslave others." It is true that in God's almighty creation we find both rich and poor, but this is not only because God has ordained it, but also due to sin and laziness. We need to tell our Muslim friend that we must never enslave one another. We can share honestly that in Christian history as well, we did not until recently understand the need for liberation from slavery. When we study the Bible, we can understand true redemption is in Christ and can be found on many levels. We cannot go back to enslaving one another.

Demons Given to Unbelievers: Verse 36–38

These are very dangerous verses. Here God says that to the one who gives a blind eye to the Qur'an, he will put on him a demon as a twin (intimate companion). We need to share with our Muslim friend that the Bible teaches that though Satan is the prince of this world for now, the Holy Spirit, who indwells every follower of Christ, is more powerful. All who have yet to give their lives to the lordship of Christ are under the power of Satan, which means that they are in a state worse than that of having a demon as a twin. The only thing that can free us from demonic powers is the establishment of a personal relationship with Christ, which leads to the filling of the Holy Spirit as proof of eternal life in paradise. God does not give us a demon as a twin. Therefore, we should be careful to understand from where this verse is coming.

We can also explain that a person does not have to hopelessly endure demonic oppression. Once we accept Christ, the Lord separates all our sins from us, as far as the east is from the west.[3]

Pharaoh: Verse 51

We can build a bridge by relating a phrase from the Bible similar to that which we find here in relation to Pharaoh's pride: "I have dug wells in foreign lands and drunk the water there. With the soles of my feet I have dried up all

---

2. Mark 10:17–23; John 6:66.
3. Ps. 103:12. Most translations of sura 43:38 use "east and west." However, in Arabic it says "two easts."

the streams of Egypt."[4] We can share the importance of remaining humble and not boasting except in the Lord.[5]

Jesus' Humanity: Verse 64

Here the Qur'an is dealing with Jesus and, as always, with the purpose of reducing him to just a man. Jesus is attributed with saying, "God is my Lord and your Lord, so worship him; this is the right path." We can point to a similar expression in the Bible but also reveal its meaning: "Jesus said, 'Do not hold on to me, for I have not yet returned to the Father. Go instead to my brothers and tell them, "I am returning to my Father and your Father, to my God and your God."'"[6]

Paradise, Garden of Eden: Verses 70–71

The picture given of the qur'anic paradise is that of people sitting on couches, being served on golden plates. It has everything that the flesh desires and whatever the eye covets. It is very physical and appeals to the natural man. We need to take our friend here to explain what paradise is as Jesus told us, as he is the only one who has the right to do so. Paradise is far more than physical pleasures. We will have different kinds of joy and pleasures we cannot even fathom now. We will not have wives and husbands, and we will not need to eat or have a couch to sit on because we are tired.[7]

Son of God: Verse 81

This is a very open-minded verse, as Muhammad claims that if he were convinced that God had a son, he would be the first to worship him. Again, we find that he is using the physical word for son (walid). We can share with our Muslim friend that we understand why Muhammad had a problem with God having a physical son. However, if Jesus is considered the spiritual son of God (ibn), then he is the one who can tell us everything about the Father. If Muhammad had really understood this difference, then he surely would have been one to worship Jesus. We can then ask, "Would you like to be open-minded like Muhammad and consider this reality?"

Intercessor: Verse 86

See notes on suras 6:70; 19:81–90; 34:23; and 39:43–44.

---

4. Isa. 37:25.
5. 2 Cor. 10:17.
6. John 20:17.
7. Matt. 22:29–32; Luke 20:34–36.

Al-Dukhan

Smoke, or Mist

LATER MECCAN

Overview

The sura begins with the news that God brought the Qur'an on a blessed night. Then it discusses the accusations of those who denied the Qur'an. A comparison is made between the blasphemers of Mecca (non-Muslims) and the people of Pharaoh, on whom God took revenge. It stresses the point that the end day is a day of judgment and tells about the rewards and punishments.

The name of the sura is taken from one word in verse 10. The commentary that makes the most sense in discussing this verse relates the smoke to the end day, when heaven will come with smoke.

Comments and Possible Bridges

Blessed Night: Verse 3

All Muslims consider the night when Gabriel gave the Qur'an to Muhammad a blessed night. This night occurs during the month of Ramadan, and Muslims regard it very highly. Some Muslims call it the Night of Power and recommend reading the Qur'an throughout the entire night in order to earn multiple merits. We need to remember that Paul said we do not need to consider one day better than any other.[1] If we as humans consider all the days the same, why would God select a certain night to make it so special? Does God listen to us more on one night than on others? Is he busy with other things during the other days?

God, Giver of Life and Death: Verse 8

There are no other gods, but only the one who gives life and death. Here we can share with our Muslim friend that the only person on earth able to give life to the dead was Jesus, and he also passed the sentence of death on a fig tree. Therefore, Jesus has God's characteristics. This is why he is the only one who has the right to redeem lost man for salvation.

Smoke: Verse 10

We can take this verse about the smoke on the end day and relate it to Peter's description of that day. "But the day of the Lord will come like a thief. The heavens will disappear with a roar; the elements will be destroyed by fire, and the earth and everything in it will be laid bare."[2]

If there is smoke as a result of the fire, it will not be for long, because immediately we will be transformed into the spiritual realm.

Revenge: Verse 16

We see a picture of a hateful, mean, and vicious God as he takes vengeance on the nonbelievers. We need to share that when the time for punishment comes, God will not be relishing revenge; he will be sad about those who chose to go to hell. It will not be a mean, evil act on God's behalf toward the lost. He is merciful, gentle, and just; he is never mean. When the judgment does come for the sinners on the end day, their punishment will be severe, not because God is taking revenge, but because they will experience eternity without his presence, and that is the real hell.

God Tempts: Verse 17

God tells Muhammad that he tempted the people of Pharaoh. The people should consider this, or he will do the same thing to them. It is important to share that God does not tempt man with evil. "When tempted, no one should say, 'God is tempting me.' For God cannot be tempted by evil, nor does he tempt anyone; but each one is tempted when, by his own evil desire,

---

1. Rom. 14:5–8; Col. 2:16.
2. 2 Peter 3:10.

he is dragged away and enticed. Then, after desire has conceived, it gives birth to sin; and sin, when it is full-grown, gives birth to death."[3]

God's Indifference: Verse 29

This verse says that the heavens and earth did not feel sad when people went astray. We need to think here about the phrase "heaven's cry." Of course this does not mean rain but rather that heaven or persons in heaven could feel sad over the human losses. Here the emphasis is that God did not shed a tear over the loss of all those people when they were punished. We can ask the question: If God does not concern himself with those who disobey, then why was he so sad when Adam and Eve broke his law and ate from the tree so that he had to expel them from the Garden of Eden? This presents a wonderful opportunity to take our Muslim friends to some of the many places in the Old Testament that say that God was sad because of the sins of the people.[4] God does not rejoice at man's suffering; he suffers when man suffers, because he loves man.

Children of Israel Chosen: Verse 32

God says that he chose the children of Israel above all other nations. What a wonderful bridge we can make here by telling our Muslim friend that since God chose these people and gave them such a high standing, we should look at their Book.

God the Creator: Verse 38

God says that he did not create the heavens and earth just to play with them or for sport. This gives an impression that God cannot have any fun. We can share that it is hard for us to imagine that God does not have a sense of humor. Can he really look down on mankind and not laugh sometimes when man messes up? When he created the heavens and earth, was he so serious about his creation that he did not enjoy creating so many amazing creatures? God is not an old, grumpy landowner. When we try to imagine him enjoying the process of creation, we can also think that perhaps on the seventh day, when he rested, he looked around at all he had created and smiled and perhaps even played.

---

3. James 1:13–15.
4. Gen. 6:6–7; 1 Sam. 15:11, 35; 2 Sam. 24:16; 1 Chron. 21:15; Isa. 63:10; Jer. 42:10; Ezek. 6:9.

Tree of Zaqqum: Verses 43–48

These verses provide a very full picture of hell and the Tree of Zaqqum. We can share with our Muslim friend that Jesus also spoke of hell more than he spoke of heaven, but he told us that hell will not be merely a physical place as related in the Qur'an. We need to explain here the spiritual dimension of hell, that the spirit of a person is tormented forever and ever. From this, we need to look our friend in the eyes and ask that crucial question: "Are you sure you are not going there? I am asking, because I care for you and I want to make sure that you will not go there. That place is not for us. God's intention for that place was for the Evil One and his cohorts."

Paradise, Garden of Eden: Verses 52–57

Just as there will be punishment for the wicked, there will be a reward for the believers. Again the description is one of physical pleasure. Since Muslims are allowed only four wives on earth, in heaven they will have many more than four, and the quality of the women will be amazing. They will be unbelievably beautiful, with big, wide eyes. It is important to share with our friend that there will be no sex after death, nor will we have a desire to fill physical needs, for we will be in the presence of God.

Al-Jathiya

Bowing the Knee

LATER MECCAN

Overview

The sura reveals celestial evidence to prove faith and then curses the nonbelievers. Mention is given of the many blessings God gave to the Israelites as well as the disputes among them that God will solve on the end day. On the end day, he will open the book of each soul. Believers will be rewarded and others punished. The sura ends by giving glory to the Creator of heaven and earth.

Comments and Possible Bridges

Nature Gives Witness to God: Verses 3–5

We can bridge this verse with those in the Bible that say, "The heavens declare the glory of God; the skies proclaim the work of his hands. Day after day they pour forth speech; night after night they display knowledge."[1] The signs of nature become more specific, such as in verse 5, which tells of the turning of the day and night, the water God brings to the earth from heaven, and the effect of wind on nature. We can explain to our Muslim friend the difference between general and specific revelation. It takes a fool not to

---

1. Ps. 19:1–2.

realize there is a creator behind the creation. The general revelation of God is for all mankind, but we need to lead our friend to the specific revelation of God in Jesus, that salvation comes only through him.

Forgiveness: Verse 14

This is a unique verse. Most commentators say that this verse was revealed in the beginning days of Islam, when Muslims were to forgive those outside the faith. Later on, this verse was changed or abrogated, so that Muslims were told to carry out jihad against any who might hurt them. We need to share with our friend that Jesus said, "For if you forgive men when they sin against you, your heavenly Father will also forgive you. But if you do not forgive men their sins, your Father will not forgive your sins."[2] The apostle Paul told the church, "Forgive as the Lord forgave you."[3] These are not only New Testament directions; we can see this rule throughout the entire Bible. God asks all people to forgive and love their brothers and sisters. These are not temporary directions for a chosen few but the main intention God has for mankind.

Children of Israel Chosen: Verse 16

God raised the Jews higher than the other nations. See notes to sura 44:32.

Disputes of the Children of Israel: Verse 17

We see something here that we really have to stop and look at. The disputes among the Jews will never be solved until the end day. It is interesting to note that Muhammad does not offer any solutions to the Jews' problems and does not even say that if they come to Islam, their disputes will cease. The question we must ask, then, is: If Islam does not solve problems among people, then what good is it as a religion?

---

2. Matt. 6:14–15.
3. Col. 3:13.

Al-Ahqaf

Winding Sand-tracts

LATER MECCAN

Overview

This sura starts by emphasizing that the Qur'an is from God. It also threatens those who do not believe in it with the punishment that fell on those who did not believe in the previous prophets. Then it speaks about a group of jinn who began listening to the Qur'an and found it to be almost like the previous books. Then the jinn believed in the Qur'an, and they called their people to believe as well. The sura ends by encouraging Muhammad to have patience amid the rejection from his own people.

The name of the sura is taken from a geographical place where a tribe of people lived. Historians are not sure if the place is between Yemen, Oman, and Hydramaut (in the southeastern Arabian Peninsula) or east of Aqaba.

Comments and Possible Bridges

Opposition to Muhammad: Verses 7–8

Those who opposed Muhammad said that the Qur'an was just magic. Some said that Muhammad fabricated it and then claimed that it was the Word of God, thus making himself a false prophet. His best argument against this was saying, "If I really am a false prophet, God will smite me immediately with his punishment." However, we can counter this attempt by reminding our friend that we have seen a lot of prophets who did not speak the truth and yet lived a long time. God did not smite them immediately. In speaking of false prophets, we can build a bridge to what the Bible says about true and false prophets.[1]

Muhammad, a Warner: Verse 9

God tells Muhammad to tell the opposition some interesting facts about himself. This is a good verse to refer to when we are asked by a Muslim what we think about the Prophet. Here the Qur'an reveals clearly that Muhammad had no new doctrine to offer. He did not know the future destiny of himself or his followers; he was a mere warner. We can compare this to what Jesus said about himself and to the certainty he had about his future as well as that of his followers.[2]

Arabic Language: Verse 12

Muhammad tries to show the people that his Arabic Qur'an is a confirmation of the earlier books given to Jews and Christians. He is emphasizing the Arabic language for the Arabic people. However, there was never a problem in translating the Hebrew Old Testament and Greek New Testament into other languages. The Qur'an, however, emphasizes the language as an important part of the prophecy of God for Islam.

Hud: Verse 21

God warns the people not to be like the people of Ahqaf, who did not listen to their prophet, Hud. Hud warned the people about the winding sand-tracts, from which the sura takes its name. The people group mentioned in this verse is not well known, but the fact that the whole sura carries its name in relation to it adds mysticism to the Qur'an.

It is very important to understand as we deal with Muslims, that there are many areas—such as relationships, places, and names—in which the Qur'an is not clear. A Muslim will say that this is the Word of God and it is very hard to understand, since God is so ultimate in knowledge and we are so limited. The best response we can give to such a view is that God wants to communicate with us and to make things easy for us to understand.

---

1. Deut. 13:1–5; 18:17–22.
2. John 6:47; 14:1–6; 16:27–28.

A good communicator takes things that are very complicated and makes them easy for the ordinary person to understand. We do believe that God is ultimate in wisdom, and as such he is the Great Communicator. When he communicates with those who have totally surrendered themselves to him, he will make ultimate truth easy for them to understand and grasp.

Jinn: Verses 29–32

These are very hard verses to deal with. God says that he gave some jinn to listen to the Qur'an. The jinn then tell their own people (other jinn) that the Qur'an is equal to the word given to Moses. We find that the jinn begin to evangelize each other and call each other to believe in God. No matter what Muslim traditions say about jinn, we need to establish that there is mankind and there are angels; all other spirits are evil ones. Jinn are evil spirits. We need to share with our Muslim friend that all the evil spirits, including Satan, are doomed to hell, and hell was made for them. They cannot be redeemed. Another point is that jinn cannot bear the Word of God. Many places in the Bible, when they saw the Word of God (Jesus) they screamed in torment: "'What do you want with us, Son of God?' they shouted. 'Have you come here to torture us before the appointed time?'"[3] When confronted by the Word of God, they screamed and left the bodies they were possessing. Demons shudder before the Word of God. There is no companionship between light and darkness.[4]

God Comforts Muhammad: Verse 35

God encourages Muhammad to have patience like that of the apostles before him. Again we see that an effort is made to build credits for the Prophet by comparing him to earlier prophets or apostles. Jesus said,

> You have sent to John and he has testified to the truth. Not that I accept human testimony; but I mention it that you may be saved. John was a lamp that burned and gave light, and you chose for a time to enjoy his light. I have testimony weightier than that of John. For the very work that the Father has given me to finish, and which I am doing, testifies that the Father has sent me. And the Father

---

3.   Matt. 8:29.
4.   John 3:19–21; Rom. 13:12; 2 Cor. 6:14; 1 John 1:5.

who sent me has himself testified concerning me. You have never heard his voice nor seen his form, nor does his word dwell in you, for you do not believe the one he sent. You diligently study the Scriptures because you think that by them you possess eternal life. These are the Scriptures that testify about me, yet you refuse to come to me to have life.[5]

---

5. John 5:33–40.

Muhammad

The Prophet

FIRST YEAR OF THE *HIJRA*

Overview

The sura starts with God's disapproval of the works of the nonbelievers. He forgives the believers, and shows the importance of defending the truth, encouraging the believers to fight in the name of God. There must be no hypocrites among the believers, lest they harm their morale. Believers are forbidden to weaken on the issue of killing nonbelievers. (This means they have to be strong and determined to kill them.) The sura ends with a call for spending all they can to provide for the war machine that kills in the name of God (holy war). If we make one statement to sum up this sura, it would be that Muhammad is encouraging people to support the holy war either physically or financially and to have no mercy toward the non-Muslims.

The name of the sura was taken from the prophet of Islam, Muhammad, who is mentioned by name only four times throughout the entire Qur'an. Amazingly, we find that Jesus (*'Isa*) is mentioned twenty-five times. Much research has been done on the name *'Isa* and its origin. It could be the reverse of *Yesua*, or the "Red one." Some even say it could come from *Esau*. Others say it is just the Arabic name of Jesus (*Yesua*). The title "the Christ" is mentioned eleven times in the Qur'an; so a total of thirty-six times "Jesus the Christ" is mentioned, compared to four times for Muhammad. The word "God" is mentioned in the Qur'an about 2,700 times.[1]

Comments and Possible Bridges

Clear Conscience: Verse 2

This verse is very clear that if the Muslims believe in Muhammad's words, God will forgive them their sins and cleanse their conscience. An obvious question we could ask our Muslim friend is: "Are you sure of your salvation?" If our friend is not sure of his salvation, we can then respond by saying that this means his conscience could not be cleansed. If we are cleansed from all our sins, then our consciences will automatically be cleansed, we will be sure of our salvation, and we will know that we will be in the presence of God.

Mutilation of Enemies in War: Verses 4–6

Here is a very bloody verse. We hear God say to the Muslims in verse 4 to chop the necks of the unbelievers and to tie down whoever is left after that. We need to share with our Muslim friend that a loving God could not encourage such treatment, even of an enemy. The ultimate Revelation of God came to us to say, "You have heard that it was said, 'Love your neighbor and hate your enemy.' But I tell you: Love your enemies and pray for those who persecute you."[2]

When we look around today, we find that this verse of the Qur'an is being applied in many countries. We need to realize that while moderate Muslims try to wash their hands of this blood, this is the heart of Islam and is found in the heart of Muhammad's sura. Also, in the same verse, Muhammad says that whoever dies killing others in God's name will make it to heaven. We could ask here: Can God not defend himself? Would he really make killing in his name a way to get to heaven? Do we have to kill to show our love for God?

Way (Cause) of God: Verse 7

The verse says that if you help God to have victory, God will make you victorious. Of course, he was talking here about a physical fight. Can we help God physically to kill someone? Is not God ultimate in power? Is it our war or his? On the other hand, we need to share with our friend the verse that

---

1. Shafaey, *Al-Daleel al-Mufahres*, 128–64, 585, 792.
2. Matt. 5:43–44.

says, "Do not take revenge, my friends, but leave room for God's wrath, for it is written: 'It is mine to avenge; I will repay,' says the Lord."[3] God is in control of each person's destiny. We are not called to kill in the name of God but to give life in his name.

Paradise, Garden of Eden: Verse 15

We can see here again the picture of a physical paradise. It includes rivers of fresh water, fresh milk, delicious wine, honey, and all the fruits one can eat. See previous notes about the Islamic view of paradise on suras 13:23; 16:31; 18:31; 35:33; 37:43–51; 43:70–71; and 44:52–57.

Obey God and Muhammad: Verse 33

We see here that the Qur'an is putting Muhammad in the same position with God. Muslims are called to be obedient to both God and Muhammad. Anyone who does not believe in Muhammad is a blasphemer. In denying Muhammad, one denies God. So, when the verse reads, "Obey God and Muhammad," it is making Muhammad equal to God. We can see the strength in such a position, when we are sharing with our friend, and talk about some of the contradictions in Muhammad's position, lifestyle, and so on. Our friend will immediately make a simple claim that we must obey God and Muhammad.

Way (Cause) of God: Verse 38

Muslims are encouraged to spend from the best of their goods in the way of God (for the holy wars), and they are reminded that whatever they have, they are very poor in comparison to God's richness.

---

3. Rom. 12:19.

Al-Fat-h

Victory

AH 6 (FEB. 628) MEDINAN

Overview

This sura talks about the great victory God gave to Muhammad, the great effect of spreading Islam, and how God kept the believers' hearts steadfast. It then tells about Muhammad's appointment and how the allies of those who refused to go out with Muhammad in his wars lied.

Comments and Possible Bridges

Muhammad's Sins Forgiven: Verses 1–2

God tells Muhammad that he gave him the victory, and then as proof, he tells him that he has forgiven all his sins, those in the past and in the future. In many places in the Qur'an and *Hadith*, Muhammad very clearly states that he did not know his final destiny on the Day of Judgment. We can share with our Muslim friend that there are some contradictions here. If all the Prophet's sins, past and future, are forgiven as the verse states, then the assurance of salvation has to be granted. We can then share here that the real source of forgiveness and assurance can be found by reviewing what the Qur'an says about Jesus and accepting him not only as prophet and miracle worker, as the Qur'an shows him, but also as Savior, as the Bible reveals him to be.

Human Characteristics of God: Verse 10

Those who pledge their allegiance to Muhammad pledge it also to God. The hand of God is over their hands. We see here again that Muhammad puts himself at the same level as God. An important part of the verse speaks of "God's hand." In Islamic thought, there is no one like God. If you ask how God looks, a Muslim will be quick to say there is no one like him, meaning that a Muslim cannot imagine what he looks like or compare him to anyone. Yet here the Qur'an compares God to a man by speaking of God having a hand and putting it on other people's hands. We can take our friend to the Bible, where we find the expression "God's hand" used many times.[1] We can find agreement from our friend in the fact that God's hand was used to anoint his prophets and messengers. We have a tradition in the Christian church of laying hands on a person to consecrate that one for ministry. This is symbolic of God putting his hand over the believer's hands.[2]

Condemnation for Unbelief: Verse 13

If anyone does not believe in God and Muhammad, he is destined to hell. The Qur'an here is calling all non-Muslims blasphemers, destined to hell.

Spoils of War: Verses 18–19

When the believers pledged their allegiance to Muhammad as their warrior leader, God rewarded them with the booty from the battle. We need to share with our Muslim friend that what we take from war after killing the owner is not a gain. What good is it if a person wins the whole world and loses himself?[3]

God's Word Does Not Change: Verse 23

Though this verse is meant to apply to a specific situation (holy war), we can use it in a general sense to understand from it that God's Word is unchangeable. Moving from this point, we can then ask our Muslim friend how this works, since it directly contradicts the idea of abrogation, which is also found in the Qur'an. Examples of such changes in the Qur'an are the direction for prayers, which changed from Jerusalem to Mecca; and Christians being accepted as believers in the beginning but later on rejected, with the revelation that only Muslims can go to heaven.

---

1. 1 Sam. 5:11; 2 Chron. 30:12; Job 19:21; Eccl. 2:24; 9:1. The phrase "hand of the Lord" is used even more.
2. Acts 6:6; 13:3.
3. Mark 8:34–38.

Religion of Truth: Verse 28

This verse says that God sent Muhammad with the true religion and put this religion above all religions. God was satisfied with Muhammad as a final witness. We can ask our Muslim friend which religion has the higher moral authority, Christianity or Islam? After we listen to the response, we can take our friend to the Sermon on the Mount, which contains the highest human ethics voiced since the beginning of time. This is the ultimate ethical code, to which no other religion has ever come close. We need to share with our friend that Jesus was the final revelation of God, and as he hung on the cross, he said, "It is finished."[4] God said all he wanted to say through Jesus' coming. So actually the final testimony was Jesus.[5]

Treatment of Non-Muslims: Verse 29

This verse reveals a double standard in relating to people. Among themselves, Muslims should be merciful, but with the unbelievers they should be cruel and harsh. We can share that the Bible teaches us to treat the strangers among us like our own people, to love our enemy, and to bless those who curse us.[6]

Zabbeeba: Verse 29

The Qur'an says here that the faithfulness of their prostration (bowing down in prayer) will show on their faces. Though this should be a symbol of righteousness, we see evidence today of attempts by some Muslims to exaggerate the mark on their foreheads to proclaim their greater holiness. The next time we come in contact with a Muslim with a big scar on his forehead, we can take opportunity to ask such questions as: How long have you had that scar (*zabbeeba* or raisin)? How long did it take to develop? How hard do you hit the ground with your forehead? Why do people have it in different places? Do they not bow in the same manner all the time? Is it more important to have this mark of righteousness on the forehead for everyone to see, or have our heart marked by the seal of his Holy Spirit as we worship God in the spirit?

---

4. John 19:30.
5. Rev. 1:8; 21:6; 22:13, 18–19.
6. Deut. 24:17–18; Matt. 5:43–48; Luke 6:27–31; Rom. 12:20–21; Heb. 13:2.

Al-Hujurat

The Inner Apartments, or Rooms

AH 9 MEDINAN

Overview

The sura in general starts by giving instructions to Muslims on how to respect their prophet, Muhammad, and how to control some of their relationships. The name of the sura is taken from verse 4, which speaks of those who call to Muhammad to leave his rooms (of his house) and come outside.

Comments and Possible Bridges

Muhammad's Elevation as Prophet: Verse 1

The Qur'an gives the highest supremacy to Muhammad by saying that Muslims cannot make a religious or worldly decision better than Muhammad and God. One more time, we see the highest authority is given to Muhammad, since the people cannot hear God. We could ask how we can be sure that this is God's Word and not just Muhammad's, since we have already discussed some of the contradictions in the Qur'an?

Behavior in the Prophet's Presence: Verses 2–4

God tells the Muslims to never raise their voices above Muhammad's. They also are forbidden to speak strong words against him, meaning to refute him or argue against what he is saying. In general, Muslims should show total submission to the Prophet. As background to this verse, commentators say there was an argument between Abu Bakr and Omar, and their voices started getting loud; therefore, this verse came from Muhammad.[1] Again, we see God reacting to Muhammad's needs, not acting from his own essence.

Another command from God to the believers is that the Prophet should be highly respected. They are not to challenge his words or call him to come out to them; they have to go to him, as a way to show respect. We stand before all this self-exaltation with the words of Jesus about himself: "Whoever wants to become great among you must be your servant, and whoever wants to be first must be slave of all. For even the Son of Man did not come to be served, but to serve, and to give his life as a ransom for many."[2]

Sinful Nature of Man: Verse 7

This verse makes it appear that man will always seek the good and hate wickedness. We need to explain to our Muslim friend that human nature is a fallen nature. While God did make Adam and Eve in a perfect condition, once they sinned, the flesh became dominant in their lives. We inherit this sinful human nature from them. Therefore, the reality is that mankind likes to sin.[3] The fallen nature pushes us to sin, not to believe in God.

Quarrels Between Believers: Verse 9

Instructions are given on how to deal with Muslims who begin to quarrel with each other. If one party goes too far, then they are to be fought until they come to submission. We can point out to our friend that Jesus said, "If a kingdom is divided against itself, that kingdom cannot stand."[4] We also should share the principle of the body. Members of the church have to be different (as different parts of the same body), and they have to like each other and work together, regardless of their differences. As Christians, we see differences as a positive thing, not a negative one.[5] However, we must admit that disputes do happen, and the Bible gives us clear directions on how to handle them.[6]

---

1. Ibn Kathir, *Tafseer al-Qur'an al-Azeem*, 4:185.
2. Mark 10:43–45.
3. John 3:19.
4. Mark 3:24.
5. 1 Cor. 12.
6. E.g., Matt. 18:15–17; 1 Cor. 6:1–6.

Moral Directives: Verses 11–12

These verses give commands for believers to live by. They should not mock each other, be arrogant, have doubts, or gossip. We can build a bridge by saying that the *Injil* also encourages followers of Christ to abstain from such behavior. However, it is important to share with our friend that without being changed on the inside through a relationship with Christ, we can never achieve such high moral standards.

Purpose for Mankind: Verse 13

Muhammad gives the reason that mankind is on earth. He explains that all mankind came from Adam and Eve so that we may know each other. We can agree that it is true that we are all brothers in humanity through Adam and Eve. However, we need to share that we can also become brothers and sisters in the spiritual dimension through Christ.

The Qur'an here expands the purpose of mankind so that in knowing each other, we will also know that the one who submits to God the most is the one God prefers the most. We need to explain that the main reason God created people and made them different is not to choose the best from among them but to have a relationship with them.

Obey God and Muhammad: Verse 14

This is another dangerous verse. When the Arabs told Muhammad that they believed, he was not satisfied. He told them that it was not enough that they said they believed, they had to submit to God and his apostle. They had to be Muslims. Once more, the Qur'an makes the exclusive place in paradise for Muslims only and no one else.

Qaf

The Letter Qaf

EARLY MECCAN

Overview

This is another sura named for a letter. See sura *Sad* for discussion on the letters as titles. The beginning of this particular sura offers proof that Muhammad is the Apostle. The non-Muslims refused the idea of a prophet coming from non-Hebraic tribes. Muhammad then offers a lot of evidence for the power of God. On the end day, some of the ones destined to hell will start blaming the demons for leading them astray. Their attempts to deflect blame will not be helpful, and God will throw them all into hell and then send the believers to heaven.

Comments and Possible Bridges

God Swears by the Qur'an: Verse 1

As with other suras, this one begins with God swearing by the Qur'an. See notes on suras 36:2 and 38:1.

Nature, a Proof of the Qur'an: Verses 2–11

These verses describe nature and claim that it is a miracle on behalf of the Qur'an.

God's Relationship with Man: Verse 16

When talking about how close God is to a Muslim, most Muslims will quote part of this verse, saying that God is as close to man as his jugular vein. When we hear this, we need to understand that they do not mean that there is a personal relationship between God and man, but only that God knows man very well. We can, however, lead them to the next level of understanding by saying that it is true that God knows man, even with all his faults, and yet he wants to have a personal relationship with him. Then we can explain how one can have this relationship.

Evil Spirits as Companions: Verses 23–27

The Qur'an says that on the end day, each person's evil spirit companion, which has been accompanying him during his life on earth, will come before God and give an account of the bad deeds committed. We can ask, "Do you want to have companionship with a demon?" Then we can share that when a person accepts the lordship of Christ, that person will never again be subject to demons but will be freed from the authority of sin and evil. The only way to get rid of that personal demon is through Christ. As we look at the Muslim world, we see many demon-possessed Muslims going to Christians for healing.

God Does Not Get Tired: Verse 38

This verse stresses the point that God did not get tired after creating the world. The Bible tells us that God rested on the seventh day.[1] What a wonderful bridge we can make here when we explain that God was not tired, yet he rested and took joy in the work of his hands.

End Day: Verse 44

The name for the end day used here should not be translated "the day of gathering." The word suggests that a person is trying to put more things into a space than the place is designed for. This gives the impression that the people will be gathered, pressed, and pushed into hell. Christianity has never used this expression for the end day.

---

1.   Gen. 2:2.

Al-Zariyat

The Winds That Scatter

EARLY MECCAN

Overview

The sura begins with an emphasis on Muhammad's message and a defense of the Prophet and the Qur'an, along with a threat to the blasphemers. It then gives an account of the angels' visit to Abraham. Wonders of the creation are also described in this sura. Unlike the previous sura, the main reason given for the creation of man and jinn is for them to worship God. The sura finishes with a threat to those who did not believe in Muhammad.

Comments and Possible Bridges

God Swears by Lesser Things: Verses 1–8

The sura gets its name from its first verse, as God swears by the winds that move the clouds. The verses that follow offer more items by which he swears. See notes on suras 36:2 and 37:1.

Abraham: Verses 24–31

This is a new account of Abraham's meeting with the angels, as he offered a fatted calf to feed them. In verse 29, we read that Sarah stabbed her face when she heard she might have a son in her old age. As the account here is very limited, we can offer to take our Muslim friend to the Bible and share details about how Abraham hosted the three angels, why there were three angels, and what he told them.[1]

Sodom and Gomorrah: Verse 33

God smites Sodom and Gomorrah with stones made out of mud. We can explain that the Qur'an is not clear here what kind of stones they were. We can offer more details from the biblical account.[2] See notes on suras 7:4 and 15:61–74.

Pharaoh: Verses 38–40

Pharaoh was a sign of those who disbelieve. See notes on suras 10:90–92; 20:57–71; and 26:18–21.

'Ad People: Verses 41–42

The 'Ad people also were disobedient, and God destroyed them with a wind.

Thamud: Verses 43–45

When the people of Thamud ignored God, he sent an earthquake to destroy them. Their judgment is a warning to the nonbelievers.

Purpose for Mankind: Verses 56–57

God says that he created man and jinn to worship him. God does not require from them any food, because he is the one who provides for all. We can share with our friend (as mentioned in notes on suras 6:100 and 15:26–27) that God did not create jinn. God created a perfect angel, named the Morning Star.[3] Jesus did not accept testimony from evil spirits.[4] Paul did not accept testimony from evil spirits.[5] God would never allow worship from an evil spirit. They cannot even stand in his presence but shudder at the thought of him.[6]

---

1. Gen. 18.
2. Gen. 18–19.
3. Isa. 14:12.
4. Luke 4:35.
5. Acts 16:17–18.
6. James 2:19.

Al-Tur

The Mount

EARLY MECCAN

Overview

The sura begins with God swearing by six of the greatest things. Then it talks about God coming to these five things. A description of paradise is given. Muhammad challenges the nonbelievers to bring only one verse like the Qur'an. The sura ends with praise of God day and night.

Comments and Possible Bridges

God Swears by Lesser Things: Verses 1–6

The sura starts with mention of Tur, which is the mountain in the Sinai where God spoke to Moses. He then swears by the written word and by a scroll unfolded. We could draw the attention of our friend here to the fact that when God brought his words to Moses, it was on stone tablets, not on a leather scroll. Altogether, God swears by Mount Sinai, the written word given to Moses, the filled house of prayers (Ka'ba), the people bowing down before God, the heavens spread above, and the sea. See notes on suras 37:1; 51:1–8; 56:75–77; 68:1; 79:1–3; and 81:15–19.

Paradise, Garden of Eden: Verses 19–24

These verses offer further descriptions of paradise and add a new element not previously seen in the Qur'an. Verse 24 states that in paradise the Muslim believers will be served by young boys who are as cute as pearls. Commentators discuss a variety of origins for these boys. Some say they are the offspring of the nonbelievers or that they could be completely different beings, such as the *horiya*. Even though Muslim countries take a harsh stand against homosexuality, there is an indirect understanding that these boys could be for the sensual pleasure of the believers in paradise.

Opposition to Muhammad: Verses 29–30

These verses indicate the opposition Muhammad had from the non-Muslims. Muhammad's denials here reveal that his opponents were calling him a priest, poet, and even a crazy man.

Assurance of Salvation: Verse 31

Muhammad tells the nonbelievers, "Wait," meaning wait till the end of all things. Not only does he tell the nonbelievers to wait, but he also says that he will be waiting too. We should ask our friend if this means that the Prophet was not sure of his salvation. Maybe he was assured that he was a believer in the God of Islam and that he was a believer in all the words he said in the Qur'an, but he was never a believer in the saving power of Christ. This verse provides further proof that he was never sure of his eternal destiny.

Nothing Like the Qur'an: Verse 34

The Prophet continues talking to the nonbelievers and dares them to produce one verse like that found in the Qur'an. See note to sura 17:88 on the same subject.

Al-Najm

The Star

EARLY MECCAN

Overview

God reveals this sura with the claim that even if the stars fall, his words are correct. Then an account is given of Muhammad's journey to heaven. Muhammad talks about how dumb the blasphemers are for worshiping idols, calling the angels female, and bragging that God has girls and they have boys. God then comforts Muhammad by telling him to leave them alone, for he will take care of them and punish them as he did the people who rejected the previous prophets.

Comments and Possible Bridges

Stars: Verses 1–2

God swears that even if a star falls down, Muhammad is telling the truth and has never misled. Commentators vary on the understanding of this verse. Some say that it refers to when the star goes down in the west as the dawn rises. Other commentators find the meaning of the falling star to be one thrown at Satan. Some others say that even if the Qur'an falls down, Muhammad will not. The problem with this interpretation is that it makes Muhammad higher than the Qur'an.

Satanic Verses: Verses 1–20

Though we would not want to refer to these verses in this way, it is important to know the source of what are known as the "satanic verses," based on the writings of Salman Rushdie. At the beginning of the passage, Muhammad encourages these three gods to serve as mediators between the people and God. When he was rebuked by his followers that this was against the main theme of his preaching (God is one), he gives in a later verse a reversal of this statement by removing these three gods and saying that God is one and can have no mediator.[1] The main question to ask is why God would reveal something to Muhammad that was known to be false?[2]

Muhammad's Visit to Paradise: Verses 7–18

These verses describe the Prophet's vision or visit to paradise. The words literally read that he and Gabriel were closer than two ends of two bows or even closer. It should have read that they were as close as two ends of *one* bow or closer. When tension is put on the bow, the two ends come very near to each other. This is meant as an allegorical expression, but it is important to make a point when the Qur'an is clearly not correct in order to help our friend focus on what the words of the Qur'an really mean instead of merely on what a commentator says about them. This may begin to raise questions in our friend's mind.

Lat, 'Uzza, and Manat: Verses 19–20

These verses tell about three idols that were worshiped during Muhammad's time. At the beginning of his ministry, he encouraged Muslims to use them as mediators to God (see above notes to verses 1–20). Later on, he came out so strongly against idols that he developed the ideology that God is one. In these verses, he is mocking these three gods.

Sins Vary in Size: Verse 32

This verse indicates that Muslims should avoid big sins but assures them that God is gracious to forgive the smaller ones. It is important to share with our friend about the biblical concept of sin.[3] In God's eyes all sins are offensive and worthy of judgment.

---

1. Ibn Kathir, *Tafseer al-Qur'an al-Azeem,* 4:228.
2. Elass, *Understanding the Koran,* 33–34.
3. Matt. 5.

Individual Responsibility: Verse 38

The Qur'an stresses strongly that no soul can bear the sins of another. We can agree with our Muslim friend in this; no one can redeem another's sin. There is only one person who can redeem all of mankind's sin—Jesus. We also can share with our friend that even though we cannot be responsible for someone else's sin, we can be a reason for someone else to sin.[4]

Works: Verses 39–41

We will be rewarded for our works. Here we need to share with our Muslim friend that the Bible tells us that all our works are like filthy rags before God.[5] When asked what works God requires, Jesus replied, "The work of God is this: to believe in the one he has sent."[6] Our works cannot gain us God's acceptance or salvation. The apostle Paul said God accepts us by grace, not on the basis of our works. If he accepted us by our works, we would have reason to boast, which would lead to sin.[7]

4.   Luke 17:1–3; 1 Cor. 8:9–13.
5.   Isa. 64:6.
6.   John 6:29.
7.   Rom. 11:6.

Al-Qamar

The Moon

EARLY MECCAN

Overview

Some verses reveal the position of the blasphemers toward Muhammad's miracles and their insistence in not believing him. The sura then gives an account of some earlier nations that rejected their prophets and received God's punishment. It ends by threatening the blasphemers of Mecca and saying they are no better than the nonbelievers who came before them. It describes how God will drag the blasphemers on their faces to hell in order to give them a glimpse of what is to come. Believers, of course, will be granted paradise.

Comments and Possible Bridges

Split Moon: Verses 1–2

This sura begins with the statement that the time is near and the moon is split. Some commentators say that this verse means the end day is near, at which time the moon will be caused to split. The more common view, which has been proved by many *hadith*, relates to claims by Muslims that the moon split twice during Muhammad's time (in Mecca). When the people of Mecca asked Muhammad to show them a miracle, he showed them the moon split into two pieces, and they saw Mount Harat between them. Other *hadith* say that the moon was split into two pieces, and that each piece was on a separate mountain. Some others say they saw the mountain between the two halves of the moon.

Verse 2 reveals that the nonbelievers did not believe this sign and said that it was continuous magic. There is a good question to ask here: Why would God split the moon? We can share with our Muslim friend that in the Old Testament, we also read about God performing miracles of the same nature. He stopped the sun twice. He stopped it once to give more time for Joshua to win a battle[1] and another time to show a king that he would add fifteen years to the king's life.[2] Such miracles obviously require great power, but it is also important to note that God has a purpose in all he does. He may stop the motion of the whole universe to show his love toward one little creature. It makes sense for him to stop the sun's motion to control time, but splitting the moon had no real purpose. For how long was the moon split? How did he put it back together? Yes, we know that he can do all things, yet he is bound by his nature and does not do miracles in nature for no reason.

Condemnation for Unbelief: Verses 9–48

As we have seen in previous suras, accounts are given of many nations that refused to believe the prophets of God. They include the people of Noah's time, the people of Sodom and Gomorrah, 'Ad, and Thamud, and Pharaoh's people. God threatens those who do not believe Muhammad and his miracles with the same punishments given to the people in these examples. It is very important to understand the fear factor involved here. We need to share with our Muslim friend that God does not want to threaten us all the time. In working with Muslims, we need to give a message of hope more than a message of threats.

---

1. Josh. 10.
2. 2 Kings 20.

Al-Rahman

Most Gracious

EARLY MECCAN

Overview

The title of this sura speaks of God's grace, and the chapter begins by pointing out that God is the merciful one. Then it reveals God's great power and majesty over man and jinn, heaven and earth. The sura then talks about the punishment of criminals and the reward of believers. A special poetic phrase appears thirty-one times in the sura and reads, "Then which of the favors of your Lord will you deny?"[1]

Comments and Possible Bridges

Creation Worships God: Verses 5–6

We can ask how the stars and trees can bow down to God. It is good to help our friend to see this allegorically and then to take this Muslim person into more depth with verses from the Psalms. What is given in the Qur'an about creation is not as detailed as what we find in the Psalms.

Multiple Paradises: Verses 46, 54, 62

Verse 46 refers to two gardens or paradises. Perhaps they became two here to make the poetic rhyming work in Arabic, but if we really take it

---

1.   The phrase begins at verse 13.

literally, we need to ask what the two paradises mean. If paradise is the ultimate joy and pleasure for mankind, how can there be two ultimates? Even if God were trying to rhyme here, would that make him change the truth? We can go on to explain to our friend the meaning of paradise to the Christian mind. (See also verse 54, which also refers to two gardens.) Verse 62 speaks of not just two but four gardens!

Paradise, Garden of Eden: Verses 56, 72–74

These verses reveal that in paradise believers will be given women who have never been touched by man or jinn. They will be waiting in tents for the believers to come and enjoy them. Again we need to explain to our Muslim friend that the idea of providing perfect, sexually desirable women for men is not in God's mind. There are many problems with these verses. Does this mean that in other places outside of paradise, women have been touched (in the sexual sense) by jinn? Here we need to refer to the restrictions God put to keep the satanic world away from the human world.

Al-Waqi'a

The Inevitable Event, or the End Day

EARLY MECCAN

Overview

This sura starts by explaining what will happen on the end day. It then lists the three different kinds of people and what has been prepared for each kind. A description is given of God's power over creation and how important it is to worship God. The importance of the Qur'an is again emphasized, and the sura ends with elevating God as the Most High.

Comments and Possible Bridges

End Day: Verses 1–6

These verses provide an explanation about how the end day will occur. The earth will be shaken, and the mountains will become like dust.

Mankind Sorted: Verses 7–10

On the end day, all mankind will be divided into three groups:

1. The people of the right, who are blessed and wonderful
2. The people of the left, (who are destined to hell)
3. The foremost, which are the ones who are closest to God

Nations Included in Paradise: Verses 13–14

The majority of those found in paradise are from nations before Muhammad's time. Only a minority will be Muslims. A good question we can ask our friend is, "What do you think about the fact that even the Qur'an says that Muslims will be the minority of those closest to God?"

Paradise, Garden of Eden: Verses 15–37

Again we see that believers in paradise will be served by young boys (see notes to sura 52:19–24). There also will be wonderful women with beautiful, big eyes. Several verses are given to provide a prolific explanation of the women who will be given to the Muslim men in paradise. God designed these women in a special way. They are always virgins. They are always young. We can ask our male Muslim friend if he would really want his wife to be a virgin every night in bed. In the Arab world, the virginity of the girl is very important. This is the way a man makes sure that no one else ever touched his wife. The culture tries to glorify the first night of marriage, when a man breaks his wife's hymen, making it possibly the most important ritual in the whole wedding celebration. It depends upon the country and restrictiveness of the culture, but if we really ask that hard question of a man about this first night, we will learn that he was even more afraid than his wife was. If anyone says that he enjoyed it, he will not be normal. Is this a picture of paradise—having a woman be a virgin all the time?

Because of what Muhammad explained about these women in paradise, one of the women asked Muhammad, "Who is better, Prophet Muhammad, the women of earth or the women of paradise?" He said that the women of earth were better. She asked: "Why?" He replied, "By her prayers and fasting and worship. Once in paradise, God will make their faces shine with light and cover their bodies with silk. They will be white in color and wear green garments, yellow ornaments, and golden combs. They will be immortal and never die. They will refer to themselves as the soft ones; they will never be wrinkled. They are the ones who have existed forever. They are always agreeable. They never mock. Blessed are the ones who will have them." Then Um Selma asked, "If the woman is married to more than one man, then dies and goes to paradise, who will be her husband there?" Muhammad replied, "Um Selma, she will be given a choice to choose. Then she will choose the best man who was kind and nice to her on earth, and he will be given to her."[1] We can compare the Prophet's answer to what Jesus said: "At the resurrection people will neither marry nor be given in marriage; they will be like the angels in heaven."[2] As man draws near the end of life, his desire for sexual pleasure will end.[3]

From this discourse, we still see the view that the Prophet was preparing the woman to be even better than the *horiya*, but the ultimate goal is still for her to be a source of pleasure for her husband in paradise. We need to proclaim that the ultimate purpose for women in paradise will not be for them to please their husbands but to worship God. Therefore, the ultimate purpose for men and women in God's kingdom will go far beyond their sexual being. We will not be trying to please one another sexually, intellectually, or in other ways; but in heaven, in God's presence, our eternal goal will be to enjoy his presence, which brings eternal joy. The main focus eternally will be God, not man.

Hell: Verse 41

This verse describes the punishment for the "companions of the left hand." In hell they will be in the midst of fire and boiling water, and they will drink like a diseased camel, raging with thirst.

God Swears by Lesser Things: Verses 75–77

God swears by the positions of the stars and says that it is a great oath, and this great oath is to prove that the Qur'an is mighty. Our question again should be: Which is greater, God, the position of the stars, or the Qur'an?

Only the Clean Can Touch the Qur'an: Verses 78–79

These verses say that no one who is unclean can touch the Qur'an. Can the unclean make God's Word defiled? We can help our Muslim friend by sharing that God's Word is really needed only for the unclean, because the clean ones do not need God's Word. The unclean cannot defile God's Word, because a true word from God will cleanse the defiled person. Jesus was the Word of God. He touched many unclean people. They were cleansed immediately. They received immediate physical healing and also spiritual

---

1. Ibn Kathir, *Tafseer al-Qur'an al-Azeem*, 4:262.
2. Matt. 22:30.
3. Eccl. 12:5.

healing from their sins. When we come into contact with God's Word, we do not pollute it; rather, God's Word purifies us.[4]

We also can address this issue in relation to another matter concerning the Qur'an. If in the beginning the Qur'an was written on pieces of bone and clay and on people's chests, then how can it not be touched by the unclean?

---

4.   John 15:3; Eph. 5:26.

Al-Hadid

Iron

AH 8 IN MEDINA

Overview

This is the first in a series of ten suras, all given during the years in Medina, with each focusing on a special aspect of life. The sura begins with praise of God and the reasons he is due praise. He owns heaven and earth, and this encourages man to give in the name of God. The sura then shows the believers that on the end day their lives go before them, and the hypocrites will be waiting to have light from the believers. Man should humble himself before God. The chapter reveals the destiny of believers and nonbelievers and speaks about the earthly life and the great reward of the end day. Whatever comes our way is written in the book, and believers are encouraged to surrender to God's destiny. The sura draws to a close as it tells about the messengers or apostles sent to mankind, encouraging the believers to continue their faith.

Comments and Possible Bridges

God, the First and Last: Verses 3–4

God is the First and the Last. We can share that one of Jesus' titles is the Alpha and Omega,[1] and in Jesus all things are created, the seen and the

---

1. Rev. 1:8; 21:6; 22:12–13.

unseen. Verse 4 reveals that God created the heaven and the earth. We can tie these two verses of the Qur'an together to show Muslims the deity of Christ.[2]

God Knows Man's Heart: Verse 6

God knows the secrets of man's heart or the depths of his heart. We can share with our Muslim friend that Jesus read people's thoughts. We can tell about Jesus being in a house when several men opened the roof to let down into the room their paralyzed friend, trusting Jesus to heal him. Before Jesus healed the man, he said,

> "Son, your sins are forgiven." Now some teachers of the law were sitting there, thinking to themselves, "Why does this fellow talk like that? He's blaspheming! Who can forgive sins but God alone?" Immediately Jesus knew in his spirit that this was what they were thinking in their hearts, and he said to them, "Why are you thinking these things? Which is easier: to say to the paralytic, 'Your sins are forgiven,' or to say, 'Get up, take your mat and walk'? But that you may know that the Son of Man has authority on earth to forgive sins. . . ." He said to the paralytic, "I tell you, get up, take your mat and go home." He got up, took his mat and walked out in full view of them all. This amazed everyone and they praised God, saying, "We have never seen anything like this!"[3]

Jesus knows man's heart. He did not need anyone to tell him.

God Does Not Need: Verse 11

The richness of God is a common thread in Islam.[4] God does not need man. God almighty is transcendent. He is over all and yet not connected. In this verse, as the Prophet is encouraging people to give money (for war purposes or spreading the Qur'an), he says, "He who gives lends to God, and God will pay him back well." But if God is so rich, why is Muhammad asking here for people to lend God money? Does he not have all the money in the world? Is this money for God or for human purposes?[5]

---

2. John 1.
3. Mark 2:5–12.
4. See also the same idea in verse 24.
5. See also verse 18.

Source of the Light of the Believers: Verse 12

A picture is drawn here of the believers in paradise. They walk with light between their hands. We can deal with this verse in one of two ways. We could refer to the statement, "Your word is a lamp to my feet and a light for my path."[6] Then we can share with our friend that this is not our light but God's light, when he leads us in our daily life through his Word.

However, if we want to deal with it another way, we can show that believers will shine like stars in eternity, not because of their works, as commentators state, but because on a certain day they accepted Christ as Savior. This is what gives us a place in paradise. Then, as we start walking like Jesus and reach out to those who do not know him, he shines through us. Thus, the main reason for believers to shine in eternity is not because of their works, but due to the presence of Christ in their lives.[7]

Hypocrites Borrow the Light of the Believers: Verses 13–15

Verse 13 is very complicated. We can approach it in various ways. In looking at the first part of the verse, when the hypocrites ask to borrow light from the believers, we can share the parable of the ten virgins.[8] Certainly Muhammad had heard this story, but we need to present it in a way our friend will understand. First of all, we can state that it will not be the hypocrites who will ask for the light from the believers. Instead, it will be the ones who did not meet with the Bridegroom, who is Jesus. Therefore, if we have Jesus, we have the light. If we do not have Jesus, it will be too late to go back and ask for the light when the end day comes.

The rest of verse 13 puts a fence or divider between the two different kinds of people, as it reveals the difference between heaven and hell. In verse 14, the Qur'an is very clear that when the end time comes, there will be no more reconciliation between the good and bad. The decision is final for those who are destined for either heaven or hell. We can share with our Muslim friend how important it is for us to know our eternal destiny right now. We cannot wait till the end day when our works will be put on the scale and hope we do not discover that we are one atom short on the right side and thus destined to hell. We cannot gamble with our eternal destiny by just hoping and expecting that we will make it when we get to the scale. We need to explain that in

---

6. Ps. 119:105.
7. Matt. 5:16; 13:43; 2 Cor. 4:5–6; Phil. 2:15–16.
8. Matt. 25.

Christ our salvation is secure. Our eternity will be guaranteed. We need to ask our Muslim friend to make a decision right now.

Life Is Temporary: Verse 20

This verse emphasizes the reality that life is temporary and we should not crave for the good things in this life or the way of the wicked. We can relate this to the Scripture that says, "The senseless man does not know, fools do not understand, that though the wicked spring up like grass and all evildoers flourish, they will be forever destroyed. But you, O LORD, are exalted forever."[9]

Another good passage to speak on this subject is, "As for man, his days are like grass, he flourishes like a flower of the field; the wind blows over it and it is gone, and its place remembers it no more. But from everlasting to everlasting the LORD's love is with those who fear him, and his righteousness with their children's children."[10] As we share these passages, we should remind our friend that because life is temporary, we need to be prepared for the eternal and sure of our destination.

Predestination: Verse 22

The Qur'an teaches that everything is written and thus predestined. We need to share with our Muslim friend that God is not static but dynamic. He did not create the world, write down everything that would happen, and then step out of the universe. God designed the world and is the one who continues to make it run. He is engaged in his creation. Because both the Qur'an and the Bible say that our works are important, we must take responsibility for our actions. We also can ask why God judges us according to our works, if they are already predestined? We cannot blame God for everything that happens in our life, and especially not for our eternal destiny. That is in our own hands, and we must make the choice through our decision to follow Christ or not.

Iron: Verse 25

Here we find the one word (*iron*) from which the title of the sura is taken. The commentators say that with iron we can make weapons for killing and, in peace, we can make tools that make life easier. Iron is being put at the

---

9. Ps. 92:6–8.
10. Ps. 103:15–17.

same level as the Qur'an and the law, as it is used to test people's faithfulness to Islam. We could sincerely ask our friend, "Why would the entire sura take its name from this one word? Is this such a great revelation that the sura should be named for it?" If we look at the world today, even though iron is an important metal, it is not the main one used in either weaponry or tools. There are many other useful metals that were not known in Muhammad's time. And the reality is that iron by itself is not as good as many other metals unless it is mixed with other metals to get the right alloy for the best use. All this will help our friend question why the Qur'an would use one word to sum up an entire sura, which says so much more and even greater things than that held in this one word. We can also ask, "How can iron test one's faith? What do you understand from this verse?"

Monasticism: Verse 27

We can agree with our friend that the New Testament does not teach about monasticism, and we can explain to him why it did not call for monks. Jesus said of his followers: "I have given them your word and the world has hated them, for they are not of the world any more than I am of the world. My prayer is not that you take them out of the world but that you protect them from the evil one. They are not of the world, even as I am not of it. Sanctify them by the truth; your word is truth. As you sent me into the world, I have sent them into the world."[11] God does not want to take us from the world (to put us aside in monasteries) but to leave us in the world so we can shine as his lights and share Jesus with others.

On the other hand, even though we do not find anything specific about monks in the New Testament, we can relate it to Paul's own example and words. He devoted himself exclusively to preaching the gospel and giving his life for its sake.[12] We also know that he said that those who are unmarried are free to focus on what pleases the Lord.[13] There are many different kinds of monks—those who live in monasteries and those who live among us. Mother Teresa lived among the people. All the popes lived among us, yet they were previously monks. Christianity did not invent monasticism, but monasticism came as a result of some who were striving to live a good Christian life and

---

11.   John 17:14–18.
12.   Acts 18:5.
13.   1 Cor. 7:32.

escape the temptations of the world.[14] We can share with our Muslim friend that in monasteries people devoted their lives to worshiping God. They never killed each other, but loved each other greatly, serving one another. It is not a bad invention, as the Qur'an calls it here, because sometimes monasteries were the only way for a Christian group to withdraw from the world and to keep their faith going. Most of the ancient biblical writings were copied and kept in monasteries.

If we continue in the verse, we read that some Christians believed and God rewarded them. We must ask: In whom did they believe? Was it in Muhammad or Jesus? The answer is Jesus, because this was prior to Muhammad's time; and also, if they believed in Muhammad, they would no longer be called Christians. Contradiction comes in the same verse, which says, "But a lot of them (referring to Christians as nonbelievers) are so wicked." The ultimate purpose of this verse is to put Christians down and reduce their value to zero.

God's Preference: Verse 29

All of the above was mentioned to make Christians realize that they have no power and can do nothing without God's preference. When Muhammad says "God" here, he means the God of Islam. Thus he is inferring that the Christians can do nothing without Islam. It would be good here to share with our Muslim friend that we agree that neither Christians nor anyone else can do anything without God. Only through Christ can we do all things. If we have no relationship with Christ, God is far from us. He will never listen to us, and he will have no relationship whatsoever with fallen man. He gives his preference only to those who accept his Son.[15]

---

14. *World Book Encyclopedia*, 13:701.
15. John 1:16–17; Rom. 5:15; Eph. 1:5–10; 2:4–10.

Al-Mujadila

The Woman Who Pleads, or Debate, Argument

AH 5–7, MEDINA SURA #2

Overview

This sura talks about old marriage practices in pre-Islamic times. When Aus, son of Samit, tried to apply the old principles, a verse was given to Muhammad. The sura tells how Muslims are to deal with each other and with Muhammad. It ends by encouraging Muslims to agree with Muhammad and God first, even if it goes against their own fathers, mothers, and tribes. Then they will be called the *umma*.

Comments and Possible Bridges

Divorce: Verses 1–4

This is a classic example of the impossibility of understanding the Qur'an without the use of other sources. In pre-Islamic times, if a man told a woman, "You are for me like my mother's back" (i.e., your body is like my mother's body), this statement was equal to divorce. The story goes that the wife of Aus went to Muhammad and pleaded with him against her husband, who had used this statement to divorce her. While she was speaking to Muhammad, God gave him a verse to declare that this old practice of *zihar* does not make her divorced. His argument as we read here in verse 2 is that this word will not make her his mother, meaning that she will still be his wife.

In other places, the Prophet says that a man can divorce his wife by saying, "You are divorced," three times. By emphasizing that she does not become his mother, he means that she can be lawful to the man later on, because in Islam, a man can remarry his wife again. In *Gahalia* (pre-Islamic times)[1] when a man says to a woman, "You are my mother," he really means, "I will never touch you again." A serious question needs to be raised here. Is it true, from what we understand Islam to teach, that when a man divorces his wife three times and wants to marry her for a fourth time, he cannot do so until he lets her marry someone else first? Which practice really has a higher moral value, the old or new?

The verses that follow (3 and 4) are an effort to subdue the *Gahalia* divorce practice. If the *zihar* divorce is not from God, however, then why should one need to do something to recant the decision, as the Qur'an instructs here? It appears that the people did not easily accept this teaching from Muhammad. As the title of the sura suggests, they became argumentative when he tried to get them to accept these new directions from him.

God's Presence Among Men: Verse 7

The verse emphasizes God's omniscience and omnipresence. We can agree that God truly is characterized by both of these qualities, but we also must share with our friend that God cannot be in the midst of any people who are gathered to do evil. He is holy; he cannot look upon sin or walk among the wicked. We need to share with them Jesus' words: "For where two or three come together in my name, there am I with them."[2] This means that as believers in Christ gathered together to do good as he did, he will be with them.

Rules for Conduct with the Prophet: Verses 12–13

These verses require Muslims to pay alms or perform a good deed before being allowed to speak to Muhammad. We can ask why this was required. Was the Prophet different from any other man? Are there places in the Qur'an that require the same acts before talking with God? Does the Qur'an raise Muhammad to the level of deity? Did the Qur'an give Muhammad

---

1.   The word *gahalia* means "time of ignorance." However, we might question how ignorant the people were if their practices were higher than those the Prophet proposed.

2.   Matt. 18:20.

some privileges never given to other men (i.e., like the sexual power of forty men, and that his wives should never be touched by other men)? Why does the Qur'an make such distinctions while at the same time emphasizing the equality and brotherhood among men in Islam?

Obey God and Muhammad: Verse 22

The Qur'an reveals a very important law here, adding to what we have read previously. It requires Muslims to obey Muhammad and God, even against their fathers, sons, brothers, or their own tribe; otherwise, they will not make it to heaven. We need to share with our Muslim friend that with God, no one else can be in the center of our relationship and worship to him. The one we must adore more than our wife, children, parents, brothers, or sisters is God in the person of Jesus.[3]

---

3. Matt. 10:37.

Al-Hashr

The Gathering, or Banishment

AH 4, MEDINA SURA #3

Overview

The entire sura is basically about how God punished a group of Jews who made a deal with Muhammad and then broke it. It shows how Muhammad punished them severely. This refers to an incident with a Jewish tribe of Banu Nadhir, who were opposing the Muslims during the battle of Uhud. After a standoff, they left, some going to Syria or Khaibar.

There is not much in this sura to bridge. The main point we can use here is the *umma* versus the spiritual kingdom.

Comments and Possible Bridges

Jews Forced Out of Homes: Verses 2–4

After he praises God, the Prophet says that God drove out the Jews from their homeland. In reality, Muhammad and his people made the Jews leave their homeland. As they left, they were allowed by Muhammad to carry whatever they could on the back of the camels. They took as much as they could, but whatever they left was destroyed behind them.

Muhammad says that they became the enemy of God and him, which justifies the fact that he expelled them from their homes. We should share with our Muslim friend that the kingdom of God does not consist of buildings, camels, or articles; it is a spiritual kingdom that starts from within and in the present. We can do a study or have a discussion about the differences in how Muhammad dealt with issues on a political and cultural level and how Jesus dealt with them on a spiritual level.[1]

Spoils of War: Verse 7

God gives the best share of the bounty to Muhammad for him to use for what he needs and to give the rest to the poor. We can contrast this to the fact that Jesus' followers never fought a war for him, and he never received any spoils or bounty.[2]

---

1. Matt. 5–7; 22:18–22.
2. Matt. 8:20.

Al-Mumtahana

The Woman to Be Examined

AH 8, MEDINA SURA #4

Overview

This sura begins by forbidding the believers from having relationships
with non-Muslims, because the nonbelievers will take advantage of them. It
then reveals with whom the Muslims are allowed to relate, being basically
the ones who do not kill them. They are forbidden to deal with any who take
a stand against Muslims and kill them. The sura continues by talking about
women who left their blasphemer husbands in order to convert to Islam and
about the Muslim women who went to the nonbelievers. It ends with a verse
about the women who came to pledge themselves to Muhammad, so that
Muhammad could ask God's forgiveness for them.

Comments and Possible Bridges

Enemies of God: Verse 1

For Muslims, there is to be no relationship with the enemy. We can share
the words of Jesus here:

> You have heard that it was said, "Love your neighbor and
> hate your enemy." But I tell you: Love your enemies and
> pray for those who persecute you, that you may be sons

of your Father in heaven. He causes his sun to rise on the evil and the good, and sends rain on the righteous and the unrighteous. If you love those who love you, what reward will you get? Are not even the tax collectors doing that? And if you greet only your brothers, what are you doing more than others? Do not even pagans do that? Be perfect, therefore, as your heavenly Father is perfect.[1]

God Loves the Just: Verse 8

A Muslim can have a relationship with a non-Muslim as long as the non-Muslim did not fight him or kick him out of his own home. This verse is a good bridge to our Muslim friend, as we share that Christianity is the religion of peace. It is fundamental to Christianity that we are to love our enemy and to protect our enemy's possessions.[2] This demands a Muslim to have a relationship with us and becomes a bridge for the gospel.

Women Who Come to Islam: Verse 10

We should ask how we can test a woman's, or anyone's, faith. After a woman proclaims her faith in Islam, it becomes lawful for a Muslim to marry her. It will not be a sin for a man to have sexual relationships with her, as long as he pays her wage. We can ask what the wage is for having a sexual relationship with a woman. If a man pays a woman wages and marries her, knowing that he has the right to divorce her at any time, and she then goes to another Muslim who pays her wages and marries her, is this considered marriage? Jesus brought the issue all the way to the origin of God's design for man and woman, when he said there should be one man for one woman for a lifetime. Adam never had another wife, and Eve never had another man.

Asking Forgiveness for Others: Verse 12

When a woman comes to Muhammad and she pledges loyalty to God, Muhammad then will ask God's forgiveness for her. This is a very dangerous verse. It makes Muhammad a mediator between these women and God, which is refuted by the majority of Muslims. The only person who can mediate between God and man is Jesus, not Muhammad. See notes to suras 6:70; 14:41; and 19:81–90.

---

1. Matt. 5:43–48.
2. Rom. 12:20.

Al-Saff

Battle Array

AH 3, MEDINA SURA #5

Overview

This sura speaks about how God loves people to fight for him in one line (i.e., battle formation). It then credits Moses and Jesus with calling the Israelites stubborn, blasphemers, and people who want to dim God's light. It ends by encouraging Muslims to fight in the name of God by giving of their money and souls. Believers also are encouraged to be with God as the disciples were with Jesus.

The name of the sura means "to get together to be one line fighting the enemy," and this reflects the heart of the sura. We also find in it the most devastating weapon the Qur'an uses to destroy Christianity. (See comment on verse 6.)

Comments and Possible Bridges

Kill in the Name of God: Verse 4

God loves the people who kill in his name to be as one line. In looking at this verse, we need to realize first of all that God does not need anyone to kill in his name. Why would God want the people who kill in his name to be together in unity? Muhammad asked the people to be in such a formation because in unity there is power. We can ask our friend, Does God need human power on his side? Once we receive a response, we can share what God says in Scripture: "The battle is the LORD's."[1] So we do not need to go to war, but to bring peace.

Jesus Foretells Muhammad's Coming: Verse 6

This is one of the most dangerous verses in the Qur'an. It puts words into Jesus' mouth that he never said. It reveals Jesus saying that there is a prophet who will follow him, and his name is Ahmed. Most of the commentators will say that Ahmed is Muhammad. However, if we look at the root of the two words, they are different; and thus Ahmed is a completely different word. Ahmed is not the Prophet Muhammad.

We need to share with our Muslim friend what Jesus told his disciples: "If you love me, you will obey what I command. And I will ask the Father, and he will give you another Counselor to be with you forever—the Spirit of truth. The world cannot accept him, because it neither sees him nor knows him. But you know him, for he lives with you and will be in you."[2]

This coming one is neither Ahmed nor Muhammad. He is one the world cannot see—the Holy Spirit, who teaches us about Jesus and glorifies him. The Holy Spirit is the proclaimer of Jesus. The Qur'an, however, says that Jesus is the proclaimer of another prophet to come, Ahmed. Jesus proclaimed, as he hung on the cross, "It is finished."[3] What Jesus accomplished for mankind was all that was needed. Jesus himself is the good news. Jesus was not proclaiming good news about another person, because he himself was the good news. Through him, we can have the perfect relationship with God the Father, the Son, and the Holy Spirit.

The same verse says that when Ahmed came (at a later time after Christ) with miracles, they said of him that he was doing his signs with great magic. Of course, the Qur'an never says that these miracles came literally by Muhammad's hand. Commentators refer to his greatest miracle as being the Qur'an, and it was this that Christians called great magic.

This is one of the verses in the Qur'an that puts a great wedge between Christians and Muslims and makes very clear that these two religious groups cannot live together. Either a person believes in Islam and denies the fundamental, basic beliefs of Christianity or vice versa.

---

1. 1 Sam. 17:47. See also 1 Chron. 5:22; 2 Chron. 20:15–17; Ps. 24:7–10; Hos. 1:7; Zech. 10:5.
2. John 14:15–17.
3. John 19:30.

Light of God: Verse 8

This verse says that Christians want to quench God's light by defaming the Prophet and Qur'an. We need to share with our Muslim friend that Christians believe in Jesus as the Light of God. When Christians share about Jesus, they are not dimming the light but shining the light. "When Jesus spoke again to the people, he said, 'I am the light of the world. Whoever follows me will never walk in darkness, but will have the light of life.'"[4]

Helpers of God: Verse 14

We find a great contradiction in the ideology of Islam. As we saw in verse 6, Muhammad was trying to destroy Christianity. However, in this verse he is using it as an example. He is encouraging Muslims to be in one accord with God and attributes to Jesus these words to his disciples (which are not found in Scripture): "Who will be my helpers to God?"

We can use this as a great bridge by sharing that it is true that Jesus' disciples were on God's side. We should tell our friend that this verse shows us that the Prophet Muhammad himself declared that Christians are the helpers of God. Then we can move on to ask if our friend would like us to help him or her understand God more (i.e., help our friend to know God's way).

---

4.   John 8:12.

Al-Jumu'a

The Assembly, or Friday Prayer

AH 2–5, MEDINA SURA #6

Overview

The beginning of the sura praises God and thanks him for sending a prophet for the Arab nation. God then condemns the Jews for leaving the *Tawrat* and for saying they are special friends of God.

Comments and Possible Bridges

Muhammad, the Unlettered Prophet: Verse 2

The use of the Arabic word for "unlettered" is interesting, because the word is very similar to the word for "heathen," which is used to speak of Gentiles, or heathen, in contrast to the Jews. Most of the commentators indicate the word means "illiterate," in order to emphasize the miracle of the Qur'an in an even greater way. In other words, if Muhammad were illiterate, then the Qur'an is even more of a miracle.

However, there is some evidence that Muhammad was able to read and write.[1] Also, if we take this word to mean God brought out a prophet from among a group of illiterate people, it will make the Qur'an say things that are not there. We know that Arabs during Muhammad's time had a

---

1. Esack, *The Qur'an*, 102.

very well-developed Arabic language, which was written and read. Before Muhammad's time there were great poets, and the greatest of their poems were called *hangings*, as they were hung in public places for all to read.

Children of Israel: Verse 5

Muhammad's attitude toward the Jews obviously has changed. On the one hand, he knew that they had the *Tawrat*, and he referred to them as people of the Book. On the other hand, he still called them donkeys.

We can see a parallel to this verse in Scripture. The Bible tells us not to cover the mouth of an ox while it is treading the grain.[2] Even a beast of burden is worthy of honor. We can share with our Muslim friend that because God is great in mercy, he will bless the Jews, because it was through them that he sent his Scriptures.

We can also use the verse in another way. If we know the entire Book and yet do not believe in it by accepting Jesus Christ as Savior, we will be as foolish as a donkey. How tragic it is to see the amazing way God brought salvation to man and yet not stretch out our hands to receive it when it is within our reach.

Friday Prayer: Verse 9

This verse encourages Muslims to pray on Fridays and thus established Friday as the Muslim day for prayer. Here we can ask with our friend, "If prayers are a reflection of a love relationship between man and God, should we pray only on Friday?" We also can share in relation to this verse the words of Jesus: "Yet a time is coming and has now come when the true worshipers will worship the Father in spirit and truth, for they are the kind of worshipers the Father seeks. God is spirit, and his worshipers must worship in spirit and in truth."[3] Though we can explain to Muslims why most Christians choose Sunday to join together in worship, we also should remind them that because God is a spirit, we can worship him in the spirit any day.

---

2. 1 Cor. 9:9.
3. John 4:23–24.

Al-Munafiqun

The Hypocrites

AH 4–5, MEDINA SURA #7

Overview

This sura gives some characteristics of the hypocrite and then ends by encouraging Muslims to give to the holy war. It seems that Muhammad struggled, because he could not know the people's hearts. When people came to him and said that they were Muslim but he later discovered that they were not with him, he blasphemed them.

Comments and Possible Bridges

Hypocrites: Verses 4–10

Several verses provide us with a description of those Muhammad saw as hypocrites. They looked very good from the outside and even spoke good words; but when they were told to come to him to seek God's forgiveness, they refused, believing they were without sin. Their money was the main thing they refused Muhammad. The Prophet tried to encourage them to give money for his cause by telling them that at death their money would be worthless. The hypocrites are seen as primarily any who did not want to help Muhammad.

We need to share with our Muslim friend that Jesus never asked people for money. He asked for their hearts first. When Jesus said we put our treasures where our hearts are,[1] he was telling us that our first allegiance is to be to God alone, to seek his kingdom. He never asked money for himself but did ask some to give to the poor and not to worry about earthly treasures, encouraging them to focus on the treasure to come, which is heaven.

---

1. Matt. 6:21; Luke 12:34.

Al-Tagabun

Mutual Loss and Gain, or Quarreling

AH 1, MEDINA SURA #8

Overview

The sura begins by glorifying God and threatening the people with what happened to those before them who did not listen to the prophets. It condemns the blasphemers because they do not believe in the resurrection. The people are encouraged to believe in God and in Muhammad as his prophet and light. People are asked to obey God and Muhammad. God tells the believers that their money and children are a temptation, so they should not get so busy taking care of them that they are drawn away from God.

Comments and Possible Bridges

Nature Gives Witness to God: Verse 1

Compare this verse with the psalms on God's creation. Also see notes on suras 33:190 and 45:3–5.

Creation of Man: Verse 3

We can compare this with the verse in the Bible that says after God created man he saw that all his creation was "very good."[1]

---

1.   Gen. 1:26–31.

Muhammad, the Lamp: Verse 8

The Qur'an calls Muhammad the light of God. While Muslim commentators say the Qur'an is the light, we know that the Qur'an *is* Muhammad. He is the one who proclaimed it to mankind. We need to tell our friend that Jesus said, "I am the light of the world."[2] Using "the" here means he is the "only" light of the world. We cannot have any other light but Jesus. We can share with our friend from the Old Testament about the time when some of the priests brought foreign or unauthorized fire to the altar and they were killed instantly.[3] There is only one holy fire; there is only one holy light. Anyone besides Jesus who claims that he is the light is blaspheming against the Bible.

Condemnation for Unbelief: Verse 10

The Qur'an exclusively condemns all non-Muslims to hell.

Family as Enemies Among Us: Verse 14

The Qur'an says that we can find enemies in our own household. We can agree with our Muslim friend in this to a point, because Jesus also said that members of our household can prove to be enemies,[4] but we cannot stop there. We must continue by saying that loving anyone more than God can hinder us from loving God, and because of human weakness, intimate family relationships will be the most prone to hinder a person from loving God.[5] The more we love God, however, the more we are able to love our family, and not only our family but our enemies as well. This is the wonder of the gospel—Jesus tells us to love our enemies and do good to those who mistreat us. Even if our families work against the will of God in our lives, we are to love them because Christ loved us first.[6] In this way, we may win them to Christ.[7]

God Does Not Need: Verse 17

Muslims are encouraged to give of their money to God with the promise that he will double it back to them and grant them forgiveness. However, we can again talk about the fact that we cannot lend to God if he is all richness, as the Qur'an says in other places. See notes on suras 14:7–9 and 57:11.

---

2. John 8:12.
3. Lev. 10:1–2.
4. Matt. 10:34–36.
5. Matt. 10:37.
6. Matt. 6:43–44; Luke 6:27–36.
7. 1 Cor. 7:16.

Al-Talaq

Divorce

AH 6, MEDINA SURA #9

Overview

The main focus of this sura is divorce. It provides rules on how to deal with a divorced woman and to take care of her financial needs. The end of the sura reminds Muslims of God's grace in bringing them the Qur'an, which brings them from the darkness into the light.

We need to look at the whole issue of divorce in Islam, remembering what Jesus said when asked if it was lawful for a man to divorce his wife. He brought the issue all the way back to the first couple on earth. We need to share with our Muslim friend that God's wisdom from the very beginning is for marriage to be between one man and one woman for a lifetime. Also, we need to share the difference between Muslim marriage, which is considered a contract, with both parties agreeing on certain issues, versus Christian marriage, which is considered a covenant, not to be broken except by death. A very important element in the covenant is that God is involved in this relationship. It has a spiritual dimension that is not found in the contract marriage.

Comments and Possible Bridges

Divorce: Verses 1–6

God tells Muhammad that it is lawful for a man to divorce his wife. We need to notice that he never gives any reason why a man may divorce his wife. Thus, in Islam, a man does not need a reason to justify a divorce. These verses focus only on how to financially provide for the woman after the divorce. A divorced woman needs to stay in her own home, as long as she did not commit adultery. When a man wants to divorce his wife, he has to wait until after her period has finished, without touching her. She is not allowed to remarry before three months have passed in order to make sure she is not carrying any children from her previous husband. If a man wants to bring his divorced wife back after he has divorced her three times previously, in the interim she first has to sleep with another man, called a *mediator*. See notes on suras 2:227–235 and 58:1–4.

Some commentators say that this sura came after Muhammad divorced Hefza and her people asked Muhammad to take her back because she was a good woman. God then revealed to Muhammad these directions about the right to divorce. We can use this topic to discuss both marriage and divorce in the Muslim and Christian contexts and what God intended.

Seven Heavens: Verse 12

While this verse, as in sura 17:44, talks about the seven heavens, it also says there are seven earths. This raises some questions we should ask: Are their seven earths? Do we have any scientific evidence of this? Is the Qur'an talking about layers of the earth? Does it have seven layers? What does this mean to Muslims?

Al-Tahrim

Holding to Be Forbidden, or Forbidden Things

AH 7, MEDINA SURA #10

Overview

Muhammad became angry with some of his wives, so he stopped having sexual relationships with them. When some of them told him this was not lawful for him to do, God gave him this sura to agree with them by saying that he should not abstain from sexual relationships with his wives. He also talks about the fight against the blasphemers and the need to be harsh with them. The sura ends with the statement that everyone is responsible for oneself; neither the husband nor the wife is responsible for the other.

Comments and Possible Bridges

Muhammad's Wives: Verse 1

God tells Muhammad that he does not have the right to withhold sex from any one of his concubines but that he should return to them. We can ask our Muslim friend, "Do you think the sexual life of his prophet Muhammad was so important that God put aside all other things in the universe to address such an issue? What is the wisdom behind it? How does this help others get closer to God?"

Sincere Repentance: Verse 8

The first part of this verse contains an important note to discuss with our friend. We cannot have sincere repentance without Jesus, who is able to pay for all our sins. Sincere repentance alone does not bring forgiveness from God. This verse says that when a person sincerely repents, God will pay for his sins. In Christ, we will know instantly that our sins are forgiven, not just hope that they will be paid for in the future. The Qur'an uses the word *kafara*, which means to cover or pay the wages of sin in order for forgiveness to come. We need to share with our friend that in the Garden of Eden, God covered Adam and Eve with leather clothing.[1] (An animal had to die in order to do so.) For the son of Abraham, a ram was killed instead of his son. Sin needs a blood sacrifice, which means a soul for a soul. Without the blood of Christ, the cleansing of sins is impossible.

Noah's Wife: Verse 10

We see the Qur'an putting Noah's wife and Lot's wife both in hell. We know that Noah's wife is the mother of the believers; she is exactly like Eve, because out of this woman, God refilled the earth with mankind. She was a good woman. Lot's wife changed into a pillar of salt, so it is obvious that she did not trust in God.

The Qur'an uses these historic people as a parable. But in the Bible, when Jesus tells a parable, it is a simple story that is easy to understand in order to explain a spiritual truth that is hard to comprehend. Such stories drew people's hearts toward God; they helped the people come closer to him. If their hearts were against God, the parable would cause them to drift even farther away.

Pharaoh's Wife: Verse 11

Here God is using a supposedly historic event as a parable. This verse gives an account of Pharaoh's wife asking God to build a house in paradise and to save her from Pharaoh. The Qur'an puts Pharaoh's wife at a very high stature—becoming one of the five best women of the Qur'an.

God gives an example of two different kinds of women in verses 10 and 11, the good and the bad, in order to explain the point that the husband is not responsible for his wife. We agree with the concept that everyone is responsible for one's own sins, and we can explain that to our Muslim friend; but we do not agree with the details of the stories.

---

1.   Gen. 3:21.

Jesus' Birth: Verse 12

This is a pivotal verse in the Qur'an, as it equates Jesus with the Spirit of God (see suras 4:171; 19:17–20; and 21:91). We can work from here to build a bridge in discussing the Trinity.

Al-Mulk

Dominion

MIDDLE MECCAN

Overview

This sura speaks about the mighty power of God and reveals the final destiny of the blasphemers, when they will be thrown into hell. The angels will mock them because they did not obey Muhammad.

Comments and Possible Bridges

God Created Death: Verse 2

This verse reads that God created death. We need to share with our Muslim friend that the good God cannot create anything bad. Even Satan, when God created him, was a perfect angel, but he fell when he turned his face away from God. God did not create death, but it was the natural result of sinning against God. Eternal separation from God is eternal death and hell. That is why our friend needs to make a decision now to choose God.

Stars: Verse 5

God decorated the skies with stars and used these stars like darts to shoot Satan. We can share with our friend that the Bible says God created the stars to give guidance at night and to show his glory.[1] We can ask how God

---

1. Gen. 1:16–17.

could use a star to shoot the Devil. As we ask what this verse means, we can find the opportunity to share that perhaps the idea comes from a verse that records Jesus saying, "I saw Satan fall like lightning from heaven."[2]

God Knows Man's Heart: Verse 13

This verse provides a great bridge to reach our friend. The psalmist recognized that God knows everything in him. He wrote, "Where can I go from your Spirit? Where can I flee from your presence? . . . For you created my inmost being; you knit me together in my mother's womb. I praise you because I am fearfully and wonderfully made; your works are wonderful, I know that full well. My frame was not hidden from you when I was made in the secret place. When I was woven together in the depths of the earth, your eyes saw my unformed body. All the days ordained for me were written in your book before one of them came to be."[3]

God sees us even as we are being formed in our mother's body. We cannot escape from God, because he knows every beat of our hearts. We know that we are sinners; who are we mocking—God or ourselves? We need to be serious in making a decision now to get fully cleansed from our own sin and have assurance of salvation.

God the Creator: Verse 23

God made us. He made our ears, eyes, and hearts. We can challenge our Muslim friend by asking, "Since God made our ears; can he not hear us? If he made our eyes, can he not see us? Would he make our hearts and yet be heartless? He made our mouths; can he not speak to us?" Because God created us in such a specific and unique way, he is seeking a personal and specific relationship with us.

---

2. Luke 10:18.
3. Ps. 139:7, 13–16.

Al-Qalam *or* Nun

The Pen or *The Letter* Nun

EARLY MECCAN

Overview

In this sura God defends Muhammad and encourages him to stand fast and not give up. It gives an account of what happened to the people of Mecca as an example and encourages believers by a description of the great heavens waiting for them. The sura ends by encouraging Muhammad to remain patient and have endurance.

Comments or Possible Bridges

God Swears by Lesser Things: Verse 1

God swears by the pen. See notes on suras 37:1; 51:1–8; 52:1–6; and 56:75–77.

God Comforts Muhammad: Verse 2

God reassures the Prophet that he is not crazy. We can relate this to Jesus, when the Jews accused him of being possessed. Jesus was sure of his state of mind and responded, "'I am not possessed by a demon,' said Jesus, 'but I honor my Father and you dishonor me. I am not seeking glory for myself; but there is one who seeks it, and he is the judge.'"[1]

---

1.   John 8:49–50.

Muhammad, a Model Man: Verse 4

This verse continues God's attempts to comfort the Prophet by telling him that he is a man of high character or morals. All Muslims consider Muhammad to be the perfect Muslim whom they should follow, because his manners were the greatest. Very gently we can ask whether having him as our example and model would allow us to marry thirteen wives, as he did, or to marry ten-year-old girls, as he did. Our friend may answer that the commentators say he was a very special person and that God gave him very special powers (the sexual power of forty men). Then our question could be: Is God setting for us a standard that can never be followed? In contrast, Jesus said, "I tell you the truth, anyone who has faith in me will do what I have been doing. He will do even greater things than these, because I am going to the Father."[2] We can follow Jesus and his life example without any hesitation.

Patience: Verse 48

God encourages Muhammad to be patient and not like Jonah, who cried out in agony and asked God to smite the nonbelievers. We need to share the true story of Jonah. Jonah's primary problem was not impatience but that he did not want God to bless the non-Jews. Even after he shared with the people of Nineveh, he left the city to wait for God's punishment to rain down on them. When God did not punish them but instead forgave them, Jonah became angry. He did not want them to be blessed. We can share here that when man turns from his bad deeds and submits to God through Christ, God will stop the impending punishment and will restore the relationship.

God Comforts Muhammad: Verse 51

It seems that many people were calling Muhammad crazy and did not believe his message, because this point is brought up several times in the Qur'an. We can approach this in two ways. First, it is good to take a stand for our own beliefs, no matter what people call us. However, we need to honestly consider what other people say about us, for there may be some truth in it. Second, why did the people call him a lunatic? We can ask our friend if he knows of anything in the *Hadith* that would have led people to reach such a conclusion about the Prophet. Such a question will begin to plant a seed of doubt in our friend's mind as to why the issue was raised so often with Muhammad. Perhaps there was some evidence to encourage the people to call him crazy.

---

2.   John 14:12.

Al-Haqqa

The Sure Reality, or the Resurrection

EARLY MIDDLE MECCAN

Overview

This sura explains the resurrection (not of Jesus, but of people on the end day). It speaks about the people who went astray before and how they went to destruction. A description is given of how the trumpet will blow and of what will happen to the heavens and earth. The people on the right are promised paradise; those on the left, hell.

Comments and Possible Bridges

End Day: Verses 13–32

The beginning of the resurrection starts with one blow of the trumpet, and then the earth and the mountains will instantly become like dust. The heavens will split open, and we will see the throne of God. All books will be opened. The person who gives his book with his right hand is destined to paradise. The one who gives his book with his left hand will be destined to hell.

We need to share with our Muslim friend that the picture is very close to what we have of the second coming in the book of Revelation. The difference is that we see heaven and hell not merely as physical places, but as spiritual ones. Also, we do not believe that each person will give his or own book but that God holds the book in which the deeds of man are recorded. The Bible tells us, "All the nations will be gathered before him, and he will separate the people one from another as a shepherd separates the sheep from the goats. He will put the sheep on his right and the goats on his left. Then the King will say to those on his right, 'Come, you who are blessed by my Father; take your inheritance, the kingdom prepared for you since the creation of the world.' . . . Then he will say to those on his left, 'Depart from me, you who are cursed, into the eternal fire prepared for the devil and his angels.'"[1]

The decision will be made by God, not by the person who gives his own book. The decision is not based on our works, which are written in the book offered by our right or left hand, but on whether or not the person during his lifetime accepted the only solution for salvation.

Qur'an Not from a Poet or Priest: Verses 41–42

These verses are a defense of the Qur'an against the accusations of it being the words of either a poet or priest. We can ask several questions. Verse 42 says the Qur'an is not the words of a priest, but didn't Muhammad know a Christian priest? Did he not surely talk about Christianity with a priest or monk? Wasn't Buhayira a monk whom Muhammad knew well? Did Muhammad come across Christians in his caravans while he was working for Khadija, before his marriage to her? Any of these questions will lead our friend to realize that it was easy for Jews and Christians to assume that the Qur'an came from a priest, since so many of its words are similar to what we find in the Bible.

---

1. Matt. 25:32–34, 41.

Al-Ma'arij

The Ways of Ascent

LATE EARLY OR EARLY MIDDLE MECCAN

Overview

The main focus of this sura is the threatening of nonbelievers with the awful things that will happen on the resurrection day. No one can redeem another—not a friend, son, or brother. Even if it tried, the entire population of the earth could not redeem a single individual. The sura also reveals that human beings do not have any power over good or evil. It ends with Muhammad suggesting that the lost be left to their own folly till the end day.

Comments or Possible Bridges

End Day: Verses 4–15

The eschatology of Islam has to be put together from a collection of scattered verses throughout the Qur'an. Here it says that the end day will be as long as fifty thousand years. We need to share what Jesus said: "Therefore keep watch, because you do not know on what day your Lord will come. But understand this: If the owner of the house had known at what time of night the thief was coming, he would have kept watch and would not have let his house be broken into. So you also must be ready, because the Son of Man will come at an hour when you do not expect him."[1] The day of resurrection will come swiftly and without warning. We also can share another verse from the Bible, which says, "'For my thoughts are not your thoughts, neither are your ways my ways,' declares the LORD."[2] God's thoughts are not like ours, nor is his timing like ours.[3] A thousand years being as one day with the Lord is not speaking about the end day in particular, but it reminds us that God is in total control of time.

Verse 10 also reveals that on the end day, each person will be so concerned with his own destiny that no one will bother to ask after his friend's fate. We can agree with this in the sense that on that day, each person will have to give an account for himself.[4] We can then ask our Muslim friend, "What account will you give for yourself?"

On the end day the lost one wishes he could use his own children, wife, or brother, or even his entire tribe to ransom himself in order to be saved from the coming hell. But we know that no one ransoms another on the end day, for it is a day when every person will stand before God to give account for himself alone. Of course, we have to continue to share that our salvation is not by works but only through acceptance of the atoning work of Christ.

Also as we talk about these verses (11–15), we should help our friend to see how the Qur'an indicates a person will be willing to sacrifice even those closest to him in order to save his own skin. This is a very selfish idea, and we can ask how a person could be so quick to turn against his loved ones. We can lead our friend to realize that if people are assured of their eternal destiny, they will not have to be afraid of turning on their own family in the end day.

We need to share the view the Bible shares with us about the end day. When a nonbeliever faces God in all his holiness, the main thing he will realize is how much of a sinner he is. He will be wishing to be hidden from God's face, not wishing to be ransomed by others, because he already knows that it is too late.

Characteristics of a Good Believer: Verses 22–35

A list is given of the good deeds and works of the believers. None of them require a personal relationship with God. It says these are the kinds of works

1. Matt. 24:42–44.
2. Isa. 55:8.
3. Ps. 90:4.
4. Matt. 12:36; Rom. 14:12.

that will take them to heaven. We need to share with our friend that before good works, faith is needed, and only one kind of faith saves—faith that is in Christ crucified and in his atoning blood for the lost.

Nuh

Noah

EARLY MECCAN

Overview

This sura speaks about Noah. However, most of the information here is given in other accounts in earlier suras. Indeed, far more detail is given about Noah in the previous suras than in his own sura.

We cannot find enough information in the Qur'an to make the account of Noah's story complete. For this reason, a lot of folk stories have been added to the Islamic view of Noah. One such story is that on the day the flood came, people stood over their own children in order to catch the last breath as the water was rising. If we can take our friend with us to the very first book of the Bible (Genesis), we can share the wonderful, intact, and logically understood story of Noah.

Comments and Possible Bridges

Noah: Verses 21–28

Noah tells God that the people are not listening to him and have gone too far in their deceptions. We read in verse 26 that it is Noah who asks God to destroy mankind with a flood. As he stresses the need for the punishment of others, Noah asks blessings for himself and his family.

We need to share with our Muslim friend that Noah was a righteous man; he did not ask for God's punishment to come on mankind. God was the one who determined that. He saw that all mankind had gone astray, and he was grieved and decided to destroy all living things on the earth.[1]

1. Gen. 6:5–7.

Al-Jinn

The Spirits

LATE MECCAN

Overview

In this sura God tells Muhammad to inform the people that even the jinn heard the Qur'an, while they were eavesdropping, and some of them obeyed it. Muhammad also is to tell them about the good jinn and the bad jinn. The sura goes on to tell that when God called Muhammad to be his disciple, the jinn surrounded him. It also lists Muhammad's limitations.

Comments and Possible Bridges

Jinn Hear and Believe the Qur'an: Verses 1–2

Muhammad is told that some of the jinn listened to the Qur'an, called it amazing, and believed. There are great problems in this first verse. When it says the jinn called the Qur'an amazing, this means they liked it, agreed with it, and thought it contained the most wonderful words in the world. We need to remind our Muslim friend that Adam was cast out of the Garden of Eden because he did not obey God's command. Satan and his cohorts (i.e., all the jinn, demons, and fallen angels) do not like God and do not like to hear his words. In reality, they are his first enemies. Why would they call his words amazing?

Jinn Give Testimony About God: Verse 3

We find the jinn saying that God is great and that he did not have a wife or son. Jinn cannot give a testimony about God because they are liars, and thus everything they say about God will be lies in order to deceive man.

Jinn: Verses 4–14

The "believing" jinn seem to be saying here that before they heard the Qur'an, they thought that there were some among the jinn and mankind who might tell lies about God (i.e., that he has a son); but once they heard the Qur'an, they realized that truly God has no son. If we take this explanation for the verse, which is debated by commentators themselves, we run into a problem. Not only is this taking the word of the jinn, who are known liars, but it is also accepting that the jinn were saved after hearing the Qur'an. We need to share with our Muslim friend that all evil spirits, including jinn, are destined to hell, and nothing can change that.

Verse 6 tells us that people put a burden on the jinn, and thus the jinn became tired. We can ask a good question here: Can the jinn carry a man's burden? If a man cannot carry a man's burden, how can the jinn?

These verses reveal that the jinn spoke in the Qur'an and told us that some of them are good, because they believed when they heard the Qur'an, while others are bad. Verse 14 is interesting in that it reveals clearly that some of the jinn are considered Muslims. We can ask our friend, "Has anyone actually seen these jinn? Are they still around today and among the Muslims?"

Al-Muzzammil

Folded in Garments

EARLY SURA, ABOUT 10–11 YEARS BEFORE THE *HIJRA*

Overview

In this sura, God tells Muhammad to put aside considerable time during the night to pray and recite the Qur'an; however, by the end of the sura, he reduces the time. God again advises the Prophet to be patient with those who are taking a stand against him, and he threatens the nonbelievers with the punishment given to Pharaoh and others who did not listen to the prophets sent to them.

The sura does not offer much we can use as a bridge since it basically encourages Muslims not to be relaxed and comfortable but to wake up in the middle of the night when it is not convenient in order to pray to God. We can use this to share with our Muslim friend that while it is important to direct our thoughts and prayers to God always, we also must realize that God made night for rest so that we can wake up after that good night's rest to face the day with a clear mind. It is only then that we can really have a thoughtful relationship with God.

We need to warn our friend about looking at prayers as good works. There are even some Christians who pray for hours, fast, and even lash their own bodies in an attempt to get closer to God. However, we can share what Martin Luther learned, since he too used these means to try to get close to

God. He found that through all these religious works he never really had a true relationship with God. That came only when he discovered that the righteous will live by faith (in Christ), and only then did he find peace.

Comments and Possible Bridges

Prayer: Verse 20

God praises Muhammad and his friends who were praying two-thirds, one-half, or one-third of the night. However, after that, he tells Muhammad that he does not have to do that but can do much less. We can share with our Muslim friend that it is not the amount of worship God wants but the quality and the heart behind the worship.[1]

---

1. Ps. 51:6, 16–17; Hos. 6:6; John 4:21–24.

Al-Muddaththir

One Wrapped Up

EARLY SURA (LIKE 73)

Overview

This sura encourages Muhammad to warn his people and speak about the end day and about what will happen to the people of the right and the people of the left.

The most important thing we catch in this sura is the music. It consists of very short sentences and is very strong in rhythm.

The sura was given at a time when the Quraish came against Muhammad and accused him of being a priest, lunatic, or magician. The defenders of the Prophet rejected this accusation. Muhammad then took his cloak around himself, and Gabriel came and told him, "Hey, you in the cloak; you who are covered. Go and tell the people (the message of the Qur'an)."

Comments and Possible Bridges

End Day: Verses 7–11

Muhammad is explaining the end day and warning the nonbelievers about hell.

Condemnation for Unbelief: Verses 38–47

Once again, Islam is revealed as the only way to make it to heaven. All other souls are in agony on the end day. Only Muslims, the people of the right, will make it to heaven. We need to remind our friend here that Jesus referred to the people on his right hand as those who had accepted him as Savior. These would be the ones who go to heaven.

Several reasons are given for why people go to hell: not praying as Muslims, not feeding the poor, doing bad deeds, and not believing in the end day. These are not the real reasons people go to hell. People go to hell because they do not accept the only solution God has for them—the blood of Jesus.

Al-Qiyamat

The Resurrection

EARLY MECCAN

Overview

This sura speaks about the resurrection and the terrible things that will happen in that day. Muhammad, however, was comforted because the whole Qur'an was collected in his bosom. The sura also shows how the faces of the believers and nonbelievers will look on the end day and speaks about the condition of the dying person.

Comments and Possible Bridges

End Day: Verses 7–9

Signs are given for the end day. The most important, in verse 9, is that the sun and moon are joined together. We need to share with our friend that on the end day, there will be no sun or moon, as all the elements of the universe will be destroyed by fire, but there will be a new heaven and new earth.[1]

End Day: Verses 21–36

These verses provide more details about the condition of people on the end day. While this sura is about the end day, a full account is not given. In

---

1.   2 Peter 3:10–13; Rev. 21:1.

reality, if we collect all the information on the end day given in other suras, we will find more than what we have in this sura. Yet with all we find in the Qur'an, we do not have enough to put together a clear and complete picture of the end day and resurrection.

Overall, the resurrection here means the resurrection of people, good or bad. But we can use this to build a bridge for our friend with the first resurrection that ever occurred—when Christ rose from the dead as the first resurrected man. We need to share with our friend that as Jesus rose from death and took a glorious body, believers in Christ at the final resurrection also will receive glorified bodies to live eternally with him. All others will be resurrected to spend eternity in hell. It is a must here to take our friend to the book of Revelation for a wonderfully complete picture of these end-time events.

Al-Dahr *or* Al-Insan

Time or *Man*

EARLY MECCAN

Overview

This sura talks about the creation of man and his ability to accept or refuse God. It then speaks about the punishment of the nonbelievers and the rewards of the believers. God talks with Muhammad and orders him to be patient. The sura ends by telling of God's mercy.

There are several questions in relation to this sura. Even though this whole sura is supposed to be about the creation of man, we find that we do not have much about how or why man was created, how he lived in the Garden of Eden, or his fall. Nor do we know how he came to know Eve and have his first children from her. The Qur'an does not answer such questions. This is why we need to take our Muslim friend to the Bible, which can answer all these questions.

Comments and Possible Bridges

Value of Man: Verse 1

The first verse is a question, asking about the time when man was worth nothing. We need to share with our friend that after God created the heavens and earth, he then created man. He looked upon all he had made and saw that it was "very good." Man was created in God's image. That is why man will always have value, even when he feels he is nothing.[1]

Creation of Man: Verse 2

Logically this verse should refer to Adam's creation, since the entire sura talks about the creation of man. Should it not, then, talk about man's creation from the dust of the earth, as it does in other suras, rather than from seminal fluid?

Paradise, Garden of Eden: Verses 12–21

These verses describe the paradise to which believers will go after death. The most important thing, found in verse 19, is that in paradise there will be young, fresh boys who are as pretty as pearls to serve the believers. But is it not better if the angels were serving people in paradise, since they are already there? What is the purpose of having young boys?

Muhammad Not to Obey the Blasphemers: Verse 24

God tells Muhammad not to obey the blasphemers. If God was forbidding this, does this mean the Prophet was planning to obey them? Was the Prophet tempted by the nonbelievers?

Prayer Times: Verses 25–26

God is telling Muhammad to pray much and to always mention God's name. We need to share that in sura 73, God cut down the time one needs to spend in prayer. Why do we come here and find him telling the Prophet to pray always, without any limitations or clear direction about how many times?

---

1. Jer. 31:3; John 3:16; Heb. 2:5–9.

Al-Mursalat

Those Sent Forth

EARLY MECCAN

Overview

The most important thing this sura presents is evidence for the coming of the day of resurrection. Nonbelievers are threatened many times with what they can expect if they do not believe, and good news is given to those going to heaven.

The title of the sura comes from its first word, *sent*. According to the commentators, this refers to the verses of the Qur'an that are sent forth. Without a commentary, however, it would be impossible for a Muslim or Christian to understand what this means. While we understand that God sent some verses of the Qur'an to warn man about the day of resurrection, we do not find in this sura any details about how the resurrection will happen. However, we can use this lack of information to take our friend to the Bible, which does give details.

Comments and Possible Bridges

End Day: Verses 1–10

God swears by the words of the Qur'an that the end day is surely coming. The end day will come when the stars are wiped away, the sky is split open, and the mountains explode into dust. We need to take our friend to the book of Revelation to give a complete picture of the end day and how it will happen.

Woe to the Rejecters of Truth: Verses 15, 19, 24, 28, 37, 40, 45, 47

God threatens the nonbelievers using the same sentence: "Woe to the Rejecters of Truth." The repetition of this phrase serves only to contribute to the rhythm of the sura, making it musical and poetic. We can talk about the beauty of poetry in God's Word and read to our friend from the book of poetry in the Bible, Psalms, or from poetry found in the books of the prophets. As we compare the poetry of the Bible and the Qur'an, we can see which touches the heart of our friend more.

Al-Nabaa

The News

MIDDLE MECCAN

Overview

This sura also talks about the resurrection. Threats are made to those who do not believe in it. Some evidence of the resurrection also is given, along with some signs as to how it will happen. The sura ends with a warning about the coming end day.

Comments and Possible Bridges

Great News: Verses 1–3

The sura opens with a question about what the people are marveling over. The answer comes—it is the great news. The verses continue by saying that the people cannot agree about this great news.

The common understanding is that this great news refers to the end day. However, we need to share that *the* great news, the ultimate news, is not the end day but what can happen today when a person accepts the greatest news of all, that Jesus Christ came to be the Savior of the world.[1] There is little to dispute about the timing of the end day. Jesus said no one knows when that

---

1.   Acts 5:42; 10:36; 13:32–39.

day will come.[2] Many people have predicted the date of its arrival but have been proven liars time after time.

End Day: Verses 4–20

These verses give some geographical facts and phenomena that are presented as evidence of the end day. For example, verse 6 says that the land is flat (which is not true), and verse 7 says that the mountains are as pegs that give stability to the earth (also not true, as seen in previous explanations). Other evidence of the end day is that God created us in couples, made the night to stay calm and the day for work to be done, made a great lantern (sun), and brought the rain. We need to ask our Muslim friend what these facts have to do with the end day. How do they prove it? When we look around us at God's creation, how does that make us think of the end day?

When the verse reads that God created us in pairs, we can ask our friend how many pairs of humans God created. In reality, he created only one pair—Adam and Eve. Every other human was born of them or their descendants, not created in pairs. When a man is born, he grows to a certain age and makes a choice to find a wife and to marry. So God does not create every pair of humans on the earth.

The explanation of the end day does not add much more to what is found in previous suras. We can refer to previous notes (e.g., to suras 1:4; 3:9; 21:47; 25:23–30) to build bridges on this topic.

---

2. Matt. 24:3–44.

Al-Nazi'at

Those Who Tear Out

EARLY MECCAN

Overview

The sura starts with God swearing by those who "tear out." The word *nazi'at* means "tear out," but Muslim commentators give many explanations for the identity of the ones who tore out. Various answers include angels, spirits of nonbelievers, death, stars, or the bows of the battle. With this amount of discussion over just the name of the sura, we need to understand that the explanation of the material could take any direction based on what the particular scholar considers the subject of this one verb.

After talking about Moses and Pharaoh, God comforts Muhammad by revealing what is waiting for those who are not faithful. When the blasphemers ask about the time of the resurrection, verses are given to show that Muhammad's job is only to warn people of the end day, but he does not know when it will be.

Comments and Possible Bridges

God Swears by Lesser Things: Verses 1–3

As in many other suras, the beginning verses record God swearing, this time by those who extract (pull out) some from sinking, thus in some way giving proof of the coming end day.

End Day: Verses 6–14

These verses give an explanation of what will happen on the end day. It will include earthquakes, and the hearts of those who face that day will tremor. They will lower their eyes in humility and see themselves as corroded bones. Here we need to stop and share with our friend that on the end day, even if we are corroded bones, the Bible says that when the trumpet sounds, the grave will give up all the dead.[1] There will be no corroded bones. The sea will give up all those who drowned, the living ones will be changed, and the mortal will be dressed with immortality and ready to live forever and ever. All are destined to live forever, either with Christ in his kingdom with the Father or with Satan and his cohorts. We need to make the choice now.

Timing of the End Day: Verse 44

This is a very important verse, for it clearly states that no one but God knows the time of the end day. We can use this verse to build a bridge, taking our friend to the Bible, where Jesus himself did not claim to know the hour, but he did something very important in the meantime. He encouraged us to watch and to have the wisdom to know the seasons, and he gave many signs for the end day.[2] We cannot find anything of this nature in the entire Qur'an. All the statements stop with "only God knows the hour," which fits with the main frame of the Islamic thinking pattern.

Though Jesus did not claim to know the hour, he did tell us that the coming of the end day will be sudden and that it might come at any minute.[3] We need to be ready, because he might come at any time; and with this we can cross the bridge to share the urgency of accepting Jesus now.

---

1. 1 Cor. 15:52; 1 Thess. 4:16.
2. Matt. 24 is an excellent chapter to read with our friend.
3. Matt. 24:44; 1 Cor. 15:52.

'Abasa

He Frowned

EARLY MECCAN

Overview

This sura, commentators say, starts with God gently correcting Muhammad for avoiding Ibn Ummi-Maktum, a blind man who came to ask guidance of the Prophet. Muhammad was busy with the leaders of Quraish, hoping that through them, he could lead many to Islam. The sura ends with a description of the end day and the two kinds of people: believers and nonbelievers.

A question needs to be asked of our friend in relation to this sura: Would God only gently rebuke this obvious hypocrisy of Muhammad in disregarding the poor, blind man, in open preference for the rich and powerful? Where is God's justice? We can share with our friend many places where the Bible says that God defends the needy, the hungry, the widows, and the children.

Comments and Possible Bridges

Muhammad and the Blind Man: Verses 1–10

The sura gets its name from the frown that came upon Muhammad's face when he saw the blind man. God says Muhammad did not give him the attention he deserved, but ignored him. We need to share with our Muslim friend what Jesus did.[1]

There are many accounts of Jesus dealing with the blind in the Gospels. This is a great opportunity to read several of them with our friend.[2] One blind man in the Bible was a beggar, and when he cried to Jesus, Jesus healed him only because he asked him to do so. In another account, Jesus took a blind man by the hand and led him outside the village in order to deal with him without distractions.

The reason God tells Muhammad not to frown on the poor and needy is so that they might listen to his words and come to know God. When Jesus met the blind and needy, instant change took place. There was no "perhaps" about their coming to know God, but an assurance that when they met with Jesus, healing would take place and sins would be forgiven.

End Day: Verses 33–41

More explanation is given about the end day. On that day, a person will flee from his brother, mother, father, friends, and children. We need to share that the order of these relationships is incorrect. The brother should not be the closest one to the person; the closest one should be his wife. The Bible says that a man will leave his father and mother and cling to his wife, and they will become one flesh.[3]

However, if the Qur'an wants to show that the end day will be such a stressful day that a person will flee, let go, or drop, even those closest to him, we would expect the list to start with children, especially young ones. When a father and mother love their children, they will protect the little ones even with their own lives.

---

1. As noted earlier (see comment on sura 25:2–3), it is better to compare the Qur'an to Jesus than to compare Muhammad to Jesus. In this case, the comparison is between how Jesus dealt with a poor, blind man and how the Qur'an dealt with the same kind of man.
2. Matt. 9:27–30; 12:22–23; 20:30–34; Mark 8:22–26; 10:46–52; John 9.
3. Gen. 2:24.

Al-Takwir

The Folding Up

EARLY MECCAN

Overview

In this sura, a revelation is given of what will happen on the end day, showing the power and might of the Qur'an. God tells Muhammad that the Prophet is not crazy and then threatens the lost. The sura also tells about how good the Qur'an is.

The name of the sura is taken from the first verse, and again the commentators give many explanations for one Arabic word.[1] The word actually refers to collecting things together into a ball. However, commentators say that it is an explanation for what will happen to the sun on the end day. Some take the word to mean that the sun will get dark. Other meanings are that the sun will be gone, vanished, the light will be gone, and the sun will be made like a ball and thrown away, put down, or put into hell. Again, these explanations give various indications of how the sura will read in relation to the end day. Therefore, we need to bring our Muslim friend to read of the end day in the Bible, which reveals a great harmony. The Bible says that in the new world prepared for God's followers there will be no more sun. It says that the new city will have no sun, because the Lamb will be the light for the New Jerusalem, forever and ever.[2]

---

1. Ibn Kathir, *Tafseer al-Qur'an al-Azeem,* 4:430.
2. Rev. 21:23; 22:3–5.

One other point about the explanations about the sun can be made. We know that the sun is already a big, rotating ball of gases fueled by nuclear reactions within this star. So to use the phrase "to gather and make a ball out of it" is redundant. Why should a ball be made out of an already existing ball? Our hope with this approach is to get our Muslim friend to think for himself.

Comments and Possible Bridges

End Day: Verses 1–3

The end day will come when the stars have no light and the mountains move from their place. We can compare this with another place in the Qur'an, which says the mountains will be dust, and then ask which is going to happen to the mountains. However, instead of pushing this discrepancy too far, we can tell our friend that on the end day, there will be no mountains, because "the elements will be destroyed by fire, and the earth and everything in it will be laid bare."[3]

God Swears by Lesser Things: Verses 15–19

God swears by the stars, the morning, and the night in order to confirm that the words of the Prophet are correct. As we have shared before, the greater cannot swear by the lesser.

God Comforts Muhammad: Verse 22

God declares to the people that Muhammad is not crazy. We can ask why God tries to prove this point so many times in the Qur'an. We can encourage our friend to try to see Muhammad through the eyes of the people who lived during his time in an effort to give our friend a greater understanding of his prophet.

---

3. 2 Peter 3:10.

Al-Infitar

The Cleaving Asunder, or Splitting Apart

EARLY MECCAN

Overview

This sura gives an account of the horror that will happen on the end day, when the soul knows its destiny. It then rebukes the arrogant persons who forgot their Creator and shows there are angels in charge of man. The reward for believers is revealed, as well as details of the horrible fate of those going to hell.

Comments and Possible Bridges

End Day: Verses 1–4

These verses give an account of the celestial phenomena in the end day, which have been mentioned previously.

Scroll of Deeds: Verses 10–12

Commentators say that God appointed angels to keep up with man and to write down the good and bad deeds. We can agree that man's deeds will be written down, but the Bible teaches us that it is written before his own creation.[1] God does not need two angels to write down the deeds of a person,

---

1. Ps. 139:16; Rev. 17:8; 20:11–15; 21:27.

because he knows all things even before they happen. God will bring into judgment whatever a person does; but we need to share with our Muslim friend that once we accept Christ, even though God knows everything we have done, he will forgive us immediately and separate us from our sins as far as the east is from the west.

Al-Tatfif *or* Al-Mutafifeen

Dealing in Fraud or *The One Who Cheats on the Scales*

EARLY MECCAN

Overview

This sura begins by threatening those who cheat on the scales. God guides us in using the right measure in buying and selling. He threatens these people, warning them that it is written in the book. Then he begins addressing the righteous people, comforting them and telling them what a wonderful paradise is waiting for them.

Comments and Possible Bridges

Fraud: Verses 1–4

God rebukes those who make the measure of things they want to buy look like less, while making that which they want to sell look like more. Here we can bring in the verse from the Bible that reads, "Give, and it will be given to you. A good measure, pressed down, shaken together and running over, will be poured into your lap. For with the measure you use, it will be measured to you."[1]

Yes, God is concerned about justice, and he wants us to be just in buying and selling.[2] Because God is ultimate in justice, we know that even if a

---

1. Luke 6:38.
2. Lev. 19:35–36; Prov. 11:1; 16:11.

person steals one penny, he will realize deep in his heart that he is a thief. We can share with our Muslim friend that we are made in God's image, and therefore this ultimate sense of justice is implanted in each one of us. But even if we know this, our conscience can never save us but only reveal to us our sin and shortcomings. We need the Holy Spirit to give us the power to overcome these temptations to commit fraud, because the conscience is corrupted and easily swayed by evil.

Nearest to God: Verse 28

There is a spring in the paradise from which only the nearest to God can drink. These are the elite or selected ones in paradise. We can use this concept to share with our Muslim friend that this elite group will be led to the spring of the living water by Jesus,[3] but in order to obtain this status, they have to know him as Lord and Savior. We can then tell them how to do that.

---

3. Rev. 7:17.

Al-Inshiqaq

The Rending Asunder

EARLY MECCAN

Overview

This sura, like the previous ones, reveals some signs of the end day. Everything man does is written, and every person will give his own book (account) on that day.

Comments and Possible Bridges

End Day: Verses 7–10

These verses give an account of two different sets of people. Those who give their books by the right hands will be destined to paradise. Those who keep their books behind their backs will be sent to hell. We need to remind our Muslim friend that on the end day every knee will bow before Jesus.[1] The ones who have accepted him as Savior during their lifetime will be invited into heaven. "When the Son of Man comes in his glory, and all the angels with him, he will sit on his throne in heavenly glory. All the nations will be gathered before him, and he will separate the people one from another as a shepherd separates the sheep from the goats. He will put the sheep on his right and the goats on his left. Then the King will say to those on his

---

1. Phil. 2:9–11.

right, 'Come, you who are blessed by my Father; take your inheritance, the kingdom prepared for you since the creation of the world.'"[2] It is, therefore, not the believer's right hand that will matter, but Christ's, as he calls those who have trusted in him to sit on his right.

Consequences for Rejecting the Qur'an: Verse 21

The best explanation for this verse, if we consider that it is talking about the end day, is that when people heard the Qur'an and did not bow down, they were sent to hell. We need to remind our friend once again, that it is not the Qur'an that pronounces the final verdict on our eternal destiny, but the word that comes out of Jesus' mouth like a sword. It is Christ who will judge the nations.[3]

2. Matt. 25:31–34.
3. Acts 10:42; 17:31; Rev. 6:10; 19:11–16.

368

Al-Buruj

The Zodiacal Signs

EARLY MECCAN

Overview

The sura starts with God swearing by different things, and then it gives an account of people like Pharaoh and Thamud. God blesses the believers and comforts them with the assurance that throughout history believers have suffered, so they should not be discouraged. The sura ends with the statement that the Qur'an is the main corner of righteousness or right.

Comments and Possible Bridges

Qur'an Tablet Preserved: Verses 21–22

This is a mighty Qur'an and is written on the tablet that is preserved. Here we can ask, "Is the Qur'an eternal?" If the answer is yes, it creates a problem, because we cannot have two eternals—God and the Qur'an. We can lead up to another question by saying that if the Qur'an is written on a tablet, it has to be very old, maybe even older than the Ten Commandments, which were written on tablets by God's finger. This creates a big problem with the issue of abrogation. If God wrote the entire Qur'an on one piece or tablet, why would there be changes between the first suras and those that came later?

Al-Tariq

The Night Visitant, or Star

EARLY MECCAN

Overview

In the beginning God swears by the heavens and stars, which reflect his mighty strength. He assures man that he is in control over all the souls of mankind. He asks man to consider his beginning and then mentions how he created man. He swears again that the Qur'an is the final word, even though the blasphemers denied it.

Comments and Possible Bridges

Creation of Man: Verses 5–7

These verses say that man was created from gushing water. The Qur'an stated many times previously that man was created from the dust of the earth. However, we can understand that the Qur'an here is trying to give an explanation of how conception occurs, because verse 7 gives further details that are sexual in connotation. This infers that God creates man from the man's ejaculation. We need to share with our Muslim friend that man is not "created" when a man and a woman come together, because the creation of man occurred only at the beginning of time with Adam and Eve. However, God allows man to procreate through the sexual act in order to continue his species.

Al-A'la

The Most High

EARLY MECCAN

Overview

The sura starts with adoration of the Highest and how he created everything so perfectly, such as the meadows. Then God says that he will make Muhammad read the Qur'an, and in doing so, he will memorize it, not forgetting any of it. The people demand that Muhammad read the Qur'an. The sura ends with agreement to whatever was given to Moses and Abraham.

Comments and Possible Bridges

Revelation of the Qur'an: Verses 6–7

God tells Muhammad that he will make him read the Qur'an so that he will not forget. We can point out to our friend that when God spoke to people in and through the Old and New Testaments, and these people had a willing relationship with God and loved him, all of them had great assurance of their destiny. Why would God speak so clearly to Muhammad and yet not give him the most important thing—the assurance of being with God eternally? Our friend may not agree with this assessment, but we can remind him or her that there are many statements from Muhammad, especially in speaking to Aisha, that revealed that he was not sure of going to paradise.

God then makes an exception for Muhammad, knowing that he might forget, as God allows, some of the written word of the Qur'an on the tablets. A great dilemma here will face any Muslim thinker—if God allows Muhammad to forget some, that means we will never be able to have the full text of the Qur'an God wrote on the tablet. What is the wisdom in God writing the tablet in full, when we cannot read all of it? Does God want us to know all his thoughts or all he had in mind to share with man or not?

As the discussion develops, we can take our friend to the Bible to tell about the personal relationship God has with each believer. Jesus said, "You are my friends if you do what I command. I no longer call you servants, because a servant does not know his master's business. Instead, I have called you friends, for everything that I learned from my Father I have made known to you."[1] God calls us sons, not slaves, and the Father shares his secrets with his son, not the slave. In such a relationship, God will never hide a part of his will from the one he loves.

---

1. John 15:14–15. See also John 8:34–36.

Al-Gashiya

The Overwhelming Event

LATE EARLY MECCAN

Overview

This sura speaks about the end day and shows that there are two groups of people. Some are going to be sad, knowing they are going to hell; while others will be happy, knowing they are going to heaven. Some evidence of the assurance of the end day is then given.

Comments and Possible Bridges

End Day, Overwhelming Event: Verse 1

Another phrase is used to describe the end day—*the overwhelming event*, from which the sura takes its name.

Faces in Heaven and Hell: Verses 2–12

These verses describe how the people's faces will look when the end day arrives. The people going to hell will have no food; and even if they have bad food, it will not give any satisfaction. We need to share that on the end day people are not going to be eating and drinking; nor will there be any food, either good or bad. People will either go to heaven, where they will find great spiritual satisfaction, or to hell, where they will suffer for eternity.

Verse 12 also mentions the bubbling spring in paradise, from which we can draw a parallel to the living spring in Jesus. See notes on sura 83:28.

Al-Fajr

The Break of Day, or Dawn

ONE OF THE EARLIEST SURAS

Overview

The sura begins with God swearing by the dawn and ten nights. Then he threatens the people with what happened to Thamud and Pharaoh, on whom he poured out his wrath.

Comments and Possible Bridges

Love of Money: Verse 20

God rebukes the ones who love money. We can draw a bridge by sharing that we also find this issue addressed in the New Testament, which says, "For the love of money is a root of all kinds of evil."[1] We can use God's blessings for good, but when we come to love money or things more than God, we sin.

Assurance of Salvation: Verses 27–30

Most Muslims use these verses extensively as a source of hope in making it to heaven after death. We can ask our friend, "How can a soul be content without the assurance of salvation and knowing its final destiny?" Verse 28 says, "Oh my spirit, come back to God content." Solomon says the soul will

---

1. 1 Tim. 6:10.

go back to God, the one who gave it.[2] The soul that goes back to God without having accepted Christ will never be content. We should advise our Muslim friend not to be ruled or deceived by the good, rhythmic words of these few verses. When the matter comes to eternity in either heaven or hell, we cannot trust our feelings or gamble our eternal destiny on them. We need to make sure with our entire mind, soul, and body that we will make it to heaven; only through Christ can we have that assurance.

---

2.   Eccl. 12:7.

Al-Balad

The City

EARLY MECCAN

Overview

Here God swears by Mecca, where Muhammad grew up and which he loved. God also swears by man, whom he says he created to suffer. Then, once again he describes heaven and hell.

Comments and Possible Bridges

Creation of Man: Verse 4

This verse clearly says that God created man for agony. We need to share with our Muslim friend the biblical picture of God's creation, which is quite different. God made Adam and Eve in his own image—perfect, complete, and ultimately satisfied. Then Adam and Eve sinned and brought agony on themselves. The Creator is perfect; he cannot create anything less than that. We can tell our brother or sister Muslim that when we sin, we grieve God's perfect heart. The only way to come back to him is through Jesus. Through him, we can be complete again and meet with God.

Good and Evil Come from God: Verse 10

This is another dangerous verse, for it says that God led man to the way of evil and the way of good. God gives man a free will, and man himself chooses either to go in the way of sin and destruction or in God's way. We need to make it clear to our friend that he or she has to make the same choice, and we can ask, "Which way will you chose?" Instead of God leading the way, we can say that he reveals to man the options of good or evil but clearly tells man that the way of good is that which leads to him.[1]

---

1. Luke 6.

Al-Shams

The Sun

EARLY MECCAN

Overview

We do not find anything new in this sura except the story of the female camel.

Comments and Possible Bridges

God Swears by Lesser Things: Verses 1–6

See notes from suras 37:1; 51:1–8; 52:1–6; 56:75–77; 79:1–3; and 81:15–19 on this issue.

Good and Evil Come from God: Verses 7–8

God created man's soul and gives it *fajur* (debauchery) or righteousness. We should share with our friend that God will never enlighten a soul to evil, because he is a righteous God. See notes on sura 90:10.

Thamud: Verses 11–15

These verses give further details about the sins of the people of Thamud. The story behind God's camel (the female camel) is that God told the people not to kill it but to let it drink freely. However, the people of Thamud did not believe God's word and killed the camel, so God destroyed the whole group. He flattened their village to the ground. We can begin a discussion of this story by asking where this female camel came from. It is not mentioned in other places in the Qur'an. Would God level a city because of a camel?

Al-Lail

The Night

ONE OF THE FIRST SURAS

Overview

God swears by the night, day, and the creation of man. He then gives the difference between good and bad people. He warns the bad people about hell. In general, he encourages people not to be poor with God but to share their money with those in need.

There is not really much to build bridges from.

Al-Dhuha

The Glorious Morning Light

EARLY MECCAN

Overview

This sura tells more about Muhammad's personal life—how he was orphaned, lost, and found by God. He was poor, but God made him rich. Then the Qur'an encourages people to take care of the orphans and to give to the ones who ask for help.

Comments and Possible Bridges

Adoption: Verse 6

God found Muhammad orphaned and took him in. We need to share with our Muslim friend that as God adopted Muhammad, because he had no father, we need to be like God and to adopt orphans. Is it not important that we do good deeds like God? Most Muslims, however, will say there is no adoption in Islam, and we need to be aware of the reason as discussed in a previous sura: Muhammad wanted to marry the wife of his adopted son, so all adoption practices were canceled.[1] We can talk about the allowance for adoption in the Bible, because it sees the need of the child who has lost his parents to be raised

---

1. See sura 33.

in a warm, loving atmosphere. In discussing this issue, we can then move on to talk of how God adopts us as his children through Christ.[2]

Grace of the Lord: Verse 11

We are told to proclaim God's grace. It is appropriate, then, to ask our Muslim friend, "What can you tell us about God's grace?" We can follow this up with, "How can we tell about something we never tasted? How can we taste something we never knew?"

The grace of God is provided because his justice is satisfied by Christ on the cross. "Surely His salvation is near to those who fear Him, that glory may dwell in our land. Mercy and truth have met together; righteousness and peace have kissed. Truth shall spring out of the earth, and righteousness shall look down from heaven."[3] His salvation is through the cross of Christ. If one rejects the cross, he will never be able to taste, understand, or experience grace. It is very hard for a Muslim to tell people about God's grace.

---

2. Eph. 1:4–5; James 1:26–27.
3. Ps. 85:9–11 (NKJV).

Inshirah

The Expansion

EARLY MECCAN

Overview

God here is saying that he lightened Muhammad's chest and made him happy and took away the sins that broke his back. He gave him great wisdom: take the good with the bad, but if hard times come, God will make it easy or provide comfort.

We can refer to a previous sura, which talked about the assurance of salvation for Muhammad.[1] If God took all his sins away, why would he not be sure that he was going to heaven? However, we know that only in Jesus can we have complete peace in the depth of our heart. Only God through Jesus can provide for every seeker what this sura provides for Muhammad.

---

1.   Sura 48:1–2.

Al-Tin

The Fig

EARLY MECCAN

Overview

We see God here swearing by figs, olives, Mount Sinai, and Mecca. In verse 4, he says that he created man perfectly, which contradicts what we read in sura 90:4. The Qur'an says in verse 5 that God made man into the lowest of the low. We need to share with our friend that what breaks man down and puts him under is not God, but sin. Truly God created man perfectly, as verse 4 says, but then Adam and Eve ate from the tree and brought ruin upon themselves.

Iqraa *or* Al-'Alaq

Read or *The Clot of Congealed Blood*

EARLY MECCAN

Overview

This sura begins, "Read in the name of God the Creator." Verses 1–5 are considered the first verses revealed to the Prophet Muhammad. The background of this sura is when Gabriel came to Muhammad and told him to read. Muhammad replied that he would not read. The angel again said, "Read." Muhammad said, "I am not a reader." Then Gabriel said a third time, "Read in the name of the Creator." Then Muhammad trembled and went to Khadija, told her he was so cold, and asked her to cover him. He asked Khadija what she thought had happened to him, because he was so afraid. She told him, "Be glad; it is the glad tidings." Then she took him to her cousin Waraqa, Ibn Nofel. He was a Christian monk who used to write the Bible in Arabic. He translated much of the New Testament into Arabic and was now very old. Khadija asked him to listen to Muhammad. Waraqa asked Muhammad what he saw. When Muhammad talked to him, Ibn Nofel told him, "What you have is like the book of Moses."[1]

---

1. Ibn Kathir, *Tafseer al-Qur'an al-Azeem,* 4:480.

Comments and Possible Bridges

Revelation of the Qur'an: Verse 1

We can talk about the revelation of the Qur'an in order to build bridges and to get our friend to think about Islam's book. We can begin by drawing a parallel between Muhammad's story and God's call of Moses. Moses too had excuses for God and said, "'O Lord, I have never been eloquent, neither in the past nor since you have spoken to your servant. I am slow of speech and tongue.' The LORD said to him, 'Who gave man his mouth? Who makes him deaf or mute? Who gives him sight or makes him blind? Is it not I, the LORD? Now go; I will help you speak and will teach you what to say.'"[2] What is the relationship between the account in the Qur'an and this one from the Bible? There are so many similarities, perhaps because Ibn Nofel already had a great amount of the Bible translated into Arabic.

Another very important approach we can take with this verse is to say that God is telling Muhammad alone to read. We can show our Muslim friend that God wants each one of us to read his Word and know his heart.[3]

Omniscience and Omnipotence of God: Verse 14

God sees all things. Knowing that God watches everything and sees all we do encourages us to live upright before him in everything we do in life.[4]

---

2.   Exod. 4:10–12.
3.   1 Cor. 1:25–27; Eph. 1:7–10.
4.   Ps. 33:13; Matt. 6:2–6.

Al-Qadr

The Night of Power or Honor

MECCAN OR MEDINAN

Overview

God brought down the Qur'an on the night of power. Commentators say that God gave the Qur'an from the tablet in one night. However, it was given to Muhammad in bits and pieces throughout the twenty-three years of his prophethood.

Comments and Possible Bridges

Night of Power: Verses 3–5

This night is so mighty that it is better than one thousand nights. This means that if a person fasts, says his prayers, or does good works on this night, they will be worth more than one thousand months of good works. For this reason, most Muslims spend the whole night reading the Qur'an in the belief that heaven is much more open and God can hear them better. It is also understood that the angels move up and down on this night and that everyone is at peace till the dawn. See also notes to sura 44:3.

As we look at these verses, we need to share that all nights are the same. There is no night better than another in God's eyes. We do not even know the exact date Jesus was born, though this is a special day to us. However, we can call any night a mighty night when we submit in total surrender to God and have a relationship with him. Of course to us as Christians, the most meaningful night or day is the one in which we submitted our lives to Christ.

Al-Baiyina

The Clear Evidence

EARLY MEDINAN OR LATE MECCAN

Overview

In this sura, God promises the nonbelievers help, yet throughout the sura he calls the Christians and Jews blasphemers.

Comments and Possible Bridges

Consequences for Rejecting the Qur'an: Verses 1–6

The people of the Book and the blasphemers were scattered till this sura came to decide who would make it to heaven or not. This means they were not judged until the coming of this sura. All the people of the Book and the pagans who did not believe will go to hell. Of course the Prophet is referring here to belief in Muhammad and the Qur'an, which ultimately means that all Christians are destined to hell. A true Christian cannot agree that Muhammad is a prophet from God. A true Christian will not take the Qur'an as the Word of God. Therefore, all Christians, from Muhammad's point of view in this verse, are destined to the fire of hell.

Al-Zilzal

The Convulsion, or Earthquake

EARLY MEDINAN

Overview

On the end day an earthquake will take place. The dead will come out of their graves to see their destiny.

Comments and Possible Bridges

Scales: Verses 7–8

These two verses summarize the most important aspect of the entire Qur'an—not an atom's weight of a good work will be wasted. This shows us indirectly the accuracy of God's balance, which weighs the good deeds with the bad deeds. We can ask our Muslim friend, "What happens if your scale is missing one atom of good works?" Of course, he will reply that he will not make it to paradise. We can then ask, "What will it take to tip the scale?" We need to know this before the end of the days, because after that there are no corrections allowed.

Al-'Adiyat

Those That Run

EARLY MECCAN

Overview

God here is swearing by fast horses. We need to remember that Muhammad liked horses very much.

Comments and Possible Bridges

Man Is Ungrateful: Verse 6

Man never appreciates what God does for him. He is grateful only to the one he thinks did him good or who gives him something. We can share that if our relationship to God is personal and we receive something from God, then we will be grateful to him. We can challenge our Muslim friend to have this kind of relationship with God. This could be the verse that will change his entire life.

We also could approach this verse from the angle that if God creates man for agony and toil, as the Qur'an tells us,[1] then why should man be grateful for such a life? From here we can begin to share with our friend that God created us to have an abundant life through Christ, and for this we can be more than grateful.

---

1. Sura 90:4.

Al-Qari'a

The Day of Noise and Clamor

MECCAN

Overview

This sura speaks about the end day. On this day people will be like fluttering butterflies and the mountains will be like a flying flock of wool. The one whose scale is heavy with good works will be happy. The one whose scale is light will head to destruction.

Comments and Possible Bridges

End Day: Verses 1–11

Again we need to share with our Muslim friend that salvation is not by works but by grace.

Al-Takathur

Piling Up

EARLY MECCAN

Overview

This sura rebukes those people who become busy in having many children. They have become so preoccupied with their children that they have forgotten about God. They will go to hell.

Comments and Possible Bridges

Wealth and Sons: Verses 1–8

We need to share with our friend that having an abundant life, full of children and wealth, is not the problem. It is in loving those things more than God that the problem occurs. We do need to be aware of where our ultimate love lies as this sura says.

Al-'Asr

Time Through the Ages

EARLY MECCAN

Overview

In this sura, God swears by time. If man does not consider time, he will be the loser.

Comments and Possible Bridges

Life Is Temporary: Verses 1–3

We can share with our Muslim friend that the Bible also talks about time: "Show me, O LORD, my life's end and the number of my days; let me know how fleeting is my life. You have made my days a mere handbreadth; the span of my years is as nothing before you. Each man's life is but a breath. Man is a mere phantom as he goes to and fro: He bustles about, but only in vain; he heaps up wealth, not knowing who will get it. But now, Lord, what do I look for? My hope is in you."[1] We ask God to let us realize our days so that we can serve him more effectively.

---

1.   Ps. 39:4–7.

Al-Humaza

The Scandalmonger

MECCAN

Overview

In this sura, God threatens those who make fun of people by words or signs, as well as those who collect a lot of money and think that their money will make them immortal.

Comments and Possible Bridges

Immortality: Verse 3

This verse gives a picture of a person who thinks his money will make him immortal. We need to share here that a person's soul is immortal, whether he has money or not. The question is where he will spend this immortality. Again, money is not the issue, but loving it is.

Hell: Verse 6

Hell is described here as the burning fire of God. We need to share with our Muslim friend that there are two kinds of fire. First, there is the burning fire of God—holy fire.[1] (We can share the story from the Old Testament of the holy fire and the foreign fire.)[2] The holy fire of God purifies man's soul

---

1. Deut. 4:23–24; Heb. 12:28–29.
2. Num. 3:2–4.

and brings him closer to God. The fire of hell is different; it is not from God. It is the absence of God, and this fire is painful and destructive. We need to ask our Muslim friend which fire he or she would like to choose today.

Al-Fil

The Elephant

EARLY MECCAN

Overview

This sura refers to a historic account when some people from the south brought elephants to try to destroy the house of God (Mecca). It deals with an event in about AD 570, when Mecca was besieged by the Abyssinian (Christian) army, which allegedly was defeated by a flock of birds throwing stones.

Comments and Possible Bridges

Elephants: Verses 1–5

We can begin discussing this sura by asking a series of questions in order to try to see how much our friend understands the sura itself. How did birds bring pebbles from hell to destroy the army? How big of a stone can a bird carry? By asking such questions we can try to help our friend understand the difference between the myth and reality he or she reads in a text.

If this were really a miracle, then why do we not see people turning to God as a result? What was the purpose of the miracle? Does God really receive the glory? Were there really elephants in the desert? Is there a historical record of this account other than the Qur'an?

Quraish

The Quraish, or Custodians of the Ka'ba

MECCAN

Overview

In this sura, God blesses the Quraish and his holy house. He tells the people how he sent the enemies away but let the Quraish live close to him. He gave them the privilege of going in winter to Yemen and in summer to Syria, and no one stopped the caravans or hurt them. This is a great blessing.

Comments and Possible Bridges

Quraish: Verses 1–4

Here we need to ask an important question. If what God did for the Quraish is such a blessing, then why did Muhammad do the opposite of all this by declaring war on the caravans and fighting throughout his life to capture cities and places for Islam?

Al-Ma'un

Neighborly Needs, or Helping Others

EARLY MECCAN

Overview

In this sura, God is talking about the hypocrites. When they pray, their minds are not on what they are saying.

Comments and Possible Bridges

Prayer: Verses 3–7

We need to share with our Muslim friend that if we pray the same prayer every time for many years, it will become so habitual that we cannot help just praying with our mouth while allowing our mind to wander far away. The real hypocrisy is when we do not pray with all our mind and heart. A true believer in Christ is not reciting certain memorized prayers five times a day but is having a dialogue with God. He speaks, and God listens; God talks, and man listens and obeys.

Al-Kauthar

Abundance

EARLY MECCAN

Overview

God in this sura says to Muhammad that he gave him almost everything in life and after. Therefore, he should pray to God and give a sacrifice.

Comments and Possible Bridges

God's Blessings: Verses 1–3

We need to share with our Muslim friend that not only does God bless prophets and leaders, but his blessings also come to us all. Also, God does not ask for a sacrifice only when he gives us blessings. He asks for a different kind of sacrifice, a continual sacrifice of our deeds, actions, and will in total submission to him. He is more pleased with the worship attitude than with physical sacrifices.[1]

---

1. Matt. 9:12–13; Rom. 12:1–2; Heb. 10:5–10.

Al-Kafirun

Those Who Reject Faith, or the Blasphemers

EARLY MECCAN

Overview

This is a very dangerous sura. God tells Muhammad not to compromise. In the first verse he calls all non-Muslims blasphemers, because non-Muslims do not pray to the same God to whom Muhammad prays, nor do they worship the same God. And a Muslim will never accept the god of a non-Muslim. The sura ends with Muhammad saying, "You have your religion and I have mine." Here Muhammad puts the separation between Muslims and all others. In reality he is saying all non-Muslims are blasphemers.

Not all Muslims will take this stand. Some will pull verses from the Qur'an that support their being friendly to non-Muslims, while others will be fundamental and take to heart such verses as those in this sura to justify even murder.

Al-Nasr

Help, or Victory

AH 10 (LAST SURA)

Overview

This sura glorifies the thousands of people coming into the religion of God (Islam).

Comments and Possible Bridges

Conversion: Verses 1–3

During our discussion of this sura, we need to bring out the fact that many people did not hearken to Islam willingly but because they were given only three choices by their Muslim conquerors: convert to Islam, pay the ransom, or be killed by the sword. Because many people did not have the money for the ransom and did not want to be killed, they converted to Islam.

We can ask our Muslim friend a question: If freedom were given to the people of a certain Muslim country to be able to change their religion without punishment (when a Muslim abandons Islam, according to *sharia*, he or she must be put to death), how many people do you think would remain Muslim?

Al-Lahab

Flame, or Father of Flame

EARLY MECCAN

Overview

This sura gives a brief account of Abu Lahab (Father of Flame), the enemy of God and Muhammad. God would send him to hell, along with his wife, who used to carry firewood.

Comments and Possible Bridges

Abu Lahab: Verses 1–5

Abu Lahab, one of Muhammad's uncles, tried to get the Quraish to boycott Muhammad's clan. As a result, Muhammad led the Muslims to live in the desert, and this became known as the year of hunger.[1] He took a strong stand against his uncle.

We can ask this question as we learn from our friend more about this incident: If Abu Lahab was the one who did wrong to Muhammad and God, why did God punish his wife too? Is that fair?

---

1. Gabriel, *Jesus and Muhammad*, 42–43.

Al-Ikhlas

Purity

EARLY MECCAN

Overview

This is a very important sura in Islamic theology, because it refers to the nature of God as one. He is solid and undivided. He did not give birth to anyone. No one is equal to him.

This is said to have been one of Muhammad's favorite suras, and the recitation of sura 112 is considered equal to the recitation of one-third of the Qur'an.[1]

Comments and Possible Bridges

One God: Verses 1–2

We can use this sura as a bridge to reveal to our Muslim friend the true nature of God, who is a person. We are created in his image. We have in our nature three different characteristics: body, soul, and mind. God is the same, yet without our limitations: the Father (mind), Jesus (body), Holy Spirit (soul). Three distinct persons, yet they are one. This is the same way that we are. We have different characteristics but are still one person.[2]

---

1. Elass, *Understanding the Koran*, 76.
2. See also sura 5:73.

God Has No Son: Verses 3–4

God did not give physical birth from himself, but the Son was with God from the very beginning. That Son appeared to us in the person of Jesus when he was born on earth through the Virgin Mary.

Al-Falaq

The Dawn

EARLY MECCAN

Overview

God is telling Muhammad to come to him for protection from the evil, dark nights and from the evil eye. This sura is used often in defensive incantations.[1]

Comments and Possible Bridges

Evil of Created Things: Verse 2

This verse can be very dangerous for it talks about the evil of created things. Our question should be: Did God create evil? How does this fit with the Bible's statement that all God had created was good?[2]

Evil Eye: Verse 5

Can the evil eye affect Muhammad? Was he afraid of the dark of the night? We need to take our friend to where the Bible teaches us that once we are born again and the Holy Spirit is inside of us, the Evil One cannot touch us.[3] Sin has no power over us anymore. Magic does not affect the believer.

---

1. Elass, *Understanding the Koran*, 78.
2. Gen. 1:31.
3. 1 John 4:4.

Al-Nas

Mankind

EARLY MECCAN

Overview

In this sura, God tells Muhammad to ask for God's help and protection from the gossiper of evil, who gossips in the people's chests. Some of these whisperers are men, and some jinn.

Comments and Possible Bridges

Fear: Verses 1–6

We need to share with our Muslim friend that the Bible says, "I can do everything through him who gives me strength."[1] Christ will give us courage and strength, not the spirit of fear at the gossip of men or demons. Evil spirits do exist. Satan uses his cohorts (fallen angels) as well as nonbelievers to attack God's people. However, once we are believers in Christ, we are protected against the accusations of Satan. We have a high priest pleading for us day and night in God's presence. We must tell our friend, "My brother, if you do not have Christ in your life, you will live your life not only afraid of Satan and people but even afraid of yourself. Come to Christ; know him as Savior, and receive the assurance that your name is written in the Book of Life."

---

1. Phil. 4:13.

Brief Outline of Important Dates in Islam

Meccan Period: 611–622
611—First revelation
613—Revelations resumed

Medinan Period: 622–632 (AH 1–11)
623—Fast of Ramadan; Mecca as Qibla
624—Battle of Badr
625—Battle of Uhud
627—Battle of the Trench
632—Death of Muhammad
651—Revision of the Qur'an by Uthman

Taken from Stanton, *The Teaching of the Qur'an*.

Biblical Names Found in the Qur'an

Qur'anic Name	Biblical Name
Adam	Adam
'Aziz (nobleman)	Potiphar
Bilqis	Queen of Sheba
Daoud	David
Elias	Elijah
Gabrille	Gabriel
Galut	Goliath
Habil	Abel
Haman	Haman
Haron	Aaron
Hawa	Eve
Ibrahim	Abraham
'Imran	Amram
'Isa (Al-Messih)	Jesus (the Christ)
Is'haq	Isaac
Isma'il	Ishmael
Khider or Salah	Melchizedek
Lut	Lot
Madyan	Midianites
Maryam	Mary
Musa	Moses

Nuh	Noah
Pharaon	Pharaoh
Qabil	Cain
Qarun	Korah
Shatan, Iblis	Satan, the Devil
Talut	Saul
Yahya	John the Baptist
Yunus (or Zun-nun, his title)	Jonah
Yusuf	Joseph
Zakariya	Zechariah

Biblical References by Topic

Characteristics of a Good Believer, Rom. 10:1–13; Heb. 11:6; 12:1–3
Children of Israel, 1 Cor. 9:9
Circumcision of the Heart, Deut. 30:6; Rom. 2:29
Clothing Instructions, Ps. 101:2–3; Luke 11:34–36; Titus 1:15–16
Condemnation for Unbelief, Mark 10:17–23; John 6:66
Consequences for Rejecting the Qur'an, Acts 10:42; 17:31; Rev. 6:10; 19:11–16
Created in the Image of God, Lev. 18:23; 20:15, 26; Deut. 27:21; Dan. 4
Creation, Gen. 1:27; 11:1–9; Ps. 19:1; 89; 139; 148; Isa. 40:22; 49:15; 66:13;
    Matt. 23:37
Creation for Man's Benefit, Gen. 1:28–30
Creation of Man, Gen. 1:26–31; 2:7; Deut. 32:10–11; Ps. 91:4; 139; 139:13–16;
    Isa. 49:15; 66:13; Matt. 23:37
Creation Worships God, 2 Sam. 23:1; Isa. 6:1–3; John 4:24; Phil. 2:9–11
Cursed Tree, Mark 11:12–14; John 15

Daughters and Sons, Gal. 3:28
David, 1 Sam. 17
David Singing Praise to God, 2 Sam. 23:1
David and the Disputants, 2 Sam. 11–12; 12:7
Day Is like a Thousand Years, A, Ps. 90:4; 2 Peter 3:8–9
Day of Judgment, Isa. 40:15; Matt. 5:22
Dead Cannot Hear, John 11; 1 Thess. 4:16–17
Demons Given to Unbelievers, Ps. 103:12
Difficulties, Cause of, 1 Cor. 10:13; 1 Peter 2:20–25; 3:13–22; 4:12–19
Divorce, Deut. 24:1–4; Matt. 5:31–32
Does God's Word Regress? Matt. 5:44
Do Not Dispute with the Prophet, Isa. 1:18–20
Dog as Example of a Sinner, 2 Peter 2:22
Dress of Righteousness, Gen. 3:21; Isa. 61:10; Luke 15:11–31
Dry Bones, Ezek. 37

End Day, Gen. 2:24; Ps. 90:4; Isa. 55:8; Matt. 12:36; 24:30–31; 24:42–44; 25:31–
    34; 25:32–34, 41; Luke 17:21; John 11:11; Rom. 14:12; 1 Cor. 15:51–52;
    15:51–53; 15:52; Phil. 2:9–11; 1 Thess. 4:16; 4:16–17; 1 Peter 4:5; 2 Peter
    3:10–13; Rev. 21:1
End Day, Timing of, Matt. 24; 24:44; 1 Cor. 15:52
Enemies of God, Matt. 5:43–48; Rom. 5:8–11; Col. 1:21–22
Every Knee Shall Bow, Phil. 2:9–11
Every Soul Will Taste Death, Rom. 6:23
Evil Eye, 1 John 4:4
Evil of Created Things, Gen. 1:31
Eye of the Needle, Matt. 19:23–24; 19:25–26
Eyes Blinded, Hearts Hardened, Ears Deaf, Matt. 13:10–15; Mark 2:1–12;
    John 9

Failure to Keep the Law, Matt. 5:17–20; 15:1–20; 23
Faith, Then Works, Rom. 3:21–26; James 2:14–26
Family as Enemies Among Us, Matt. 6:43–44; 10:34–36, 37; Luke 6:27–36;
    1 Cor. 7:16
Fasting, Isa. 58:1–7; Matt. 6:16–18
Fear, Phil. 4:13
Food Restrictions, Matt. 15:11; Acts 10; 15:20; 2 Cor. 3:6
Forgiveness, Mic. 7:18; Matt. 6:9–15; 6:14–15; Mark 11:25; Luke 7:49; Col. 3:13
Fraud, Lev. 19:35–36; Prov. 11:1; 16:11; Luke 6:38
Furqan, John 13:34–35

God Comforts Muhammad, Matt. 23:37; John 5:33–40; 8:49–50
God Could Send All to Hell, 1 Tim. 2:3–4
God Curses Man, Matt. 21:18–19; Gal. 3:13
God Does Not Get Tired, Gen. 2:2
God Does Not Love the Blasphemers, Prov. 15:9; John 3:16; 1 John 4:7–12
God Does Not Love the Joyful Ones, Num. 16:1–35; Luke 16:13
God Does Not Need, Gen. 6:6–8; 18–19; 2 Sam. 24:16; Ps. 78; 116:15; Prov. 8:31;
    Jer. 42:10; Mark 15:41; John 1:1–14; 4:6–7
God Forcing People to Sin, John 3:16; 15:13; Phil. 2:5–8; 2 Peter 3:9
God Knows Man's Heart, Ps. 139:7, 13–16; Matt. 9:4; 22:18; Mark 2:5–12;
    Luke 9:47; John 6:15
God Loves the Just, Rom. 12:20
God Seals the Heart, 2 Cor. 1:22; Eph. 1:13
God Swears by the Qur'an, Gen. 22:16; Jer. 22:5; 44:26; 49:13
God Tempts, James 1:13–15
God Tests the Believers, Exod. 16:4; 1 Kings 19:4; Prov. 17:3; Jonah 2:1; Matt. 4:3;
    26:36–44; John 4:23; 1 Thess. 2:4; James 1:13; Rev. 12:9
God Willing, Prov. 11:14; 29:18; James 4:13–17
God, Giver of Life and Death, Judg. 14:14; Matt. 21:19–20
God, the Creator, Ps. 14:1; Rom. 1:20–23, 26a
God, the First and Last, John 1; Rev. 1:8; 21:6; 22:12–13
God's Blessings, Matt. 9:12–13; Rom. 12:1–2; Heb. 10:5–10
God's Human Characteristics, 1 Sam. 5:11; 2 Chron. 30:12; Job 19:21; Eccl. 2:24;
    9:1; Acts 6:6; 13:3
God's Indifference, Gen. 6:6–7; 1 Sam. 15:11, 35; 2 Sam. 24:16; 1 Chron. 21:15;
    Isa. 63:10; Jer. 42:10; Ezek. 6:9; 1 Tim. 2:3–4
God's Lack of Responsibility for Man, John 6:38–40
God's Preference, John 1:16–17; Rom. 5:15; Eph. 1:5–10; 2:4–10
God's Presence Among Men, Matt. 18:20
God's Provision in the Wilderness, Exod. 16
God's Signs Revealed in Man's Soul, Luke 17:20–21
God's Timing, Isa. 40:31

Jihad, Matt. 5; Rom. 12:9–21; Col. 1:3–17
Jinn, Matt. 8:29; John 3:19–21; Rom. 13:12; 2 Cor. 6:14; Heb. 1:7; 1 John 1:5
Job, Job 42:5
Joseph's Dreams, Gen. 37:5–7
Joseph's Brothers Before Him in Egypt, Gen. 42:37; 43:8–9
Joseph's Interpretation of Dreams, Gen. 37:8, 10
Joseph, Interpreter of Dreams, Gen. 41:15–16; Acts 16:16–40
Joseph and Potiphar's Wife, Gen. 39:8–10
Joseph Proves His Identity to His Father, Gen. 45:25–28; 49
Joseph, the Concept of Sowing and Reaping, Gen. 27:14–27; 37:31–35
Joseph Thrown into a Well, Gen. 37:19–22
Justice and Mercy of God, Ps. 85:10

Keys of the Unknown, Matt. 16:16–19; Eph. 3; Col. 2
Kill in the Name of God, 1 Sam. 17:47; 1 Chron. 5:22; 2 Chron. 20:15–17; Ps.
    24:7–10; Hos. 1:7; Zech. 10:5; Matt. 5:44; 13:24–30
Kill Your Neighbor, Matt. 28:18–20

Law and Grace, John 1:17; Gal. 5
Life Is Temporary, Ps. 39:4–7; 92:6–8; 103:15–17
Light of God, John 8:12
Light of the Believers, Hypocrites Borrow, Matt. 25
Light of the Believers, Source of, Ps. 119:105; Matt. 5:16; 13:43; 2 Cor. 4:5–6;
    Phil. 2:15–16
Lot, Gen. 13–19; 14; 19:24
Love of Money, 1 Tim. 6:10
Loving Family More Than God or Muhammad, Matt. 10:37
Luqman, Exod. 20:12; Matt. 5:38–42; Eph. 6:1–3; James 1:5; 3:13–18

Made to Be God's, Ps. 139; Eph. 2:4–10
Man, Responsible to Change, Rom. 7:21–25
Marriage Issues, 1 Sam. 11–12; Matt. 19:4–6; 1 Cor. 7:1–5; 2 Cor. 6:14; Eph.
    5:25–33; Col. 3:18–19; 1 Peter 3:7
Marriage, Importance of Sex in, Matt. 1:18–19
Mary, Revelation of Jesus' Birth to, Luke 1:34–35
Men over Women, Eph. 5:22–33
Monasticism, John 17:14–18; Acts 18:5; 1 Cor. 7:32
Moon, Split, Josh. 10; 2 Kings 20
Moses, Exod. 7:8–13; 19–34
Moses Kills the Egyptian, Exod. 2:11–15
Mother of Cities, Matt. 24:36–51; 25:1–46; 25:31–32; Mark 13:32–37; Rev.
    19:11–21
Mountain Miracle, Exod. 13:21; 14:19; 40:36–38; Isa. 4:5

Muhammad and the Blind Man, Matt. 9:27–30; 12:22–23; 20:30–34; Mark
    8:22–26; 10:46–52; John 9
Muhammad, Asks for Forgiveness, Mark 2:1–12
Muhammad, a Warner, John 6:47; 14:1–6; 16:27–28
Muhammad, Ashamed to Proclaim, Jer. 1:7–8; 2:2
Muhammad's Elevation as Prophet, Matt. 3; 17; 20:26–28; John 14:21
Muhammad, the Father to None, Mark 10:24; John 13:33
Muhammad's Justification as a Prophet, Exod. 20:18–21
Muhammad, a Model Man, John 14:12
Muhammad Has No Responsibility over Muslims, Matt. 9:6; 28:18; John 17:2–5
Muhammad, Satan's Effect upon, Matt. 4:1–11; Heb. 4:15
Muhammad, the Lamp, Lev. 10:1–2; Ps. 119:105; Matt. 5:14–16; John 8:12
Muhammad's Wives Forbidden to Remarry, 1 Cor. 7:9, 39

Nature Gives Witness to God, Ps. 19:1–2
Nearest to God, Rev. 7:17
New Earth, 2 Peter 3:11–13; Rev. 21
No Burden More than We Can Bear, 1 Cor. 10:13
Noah, Gen. 6:5–7; 7:9–10; 9:28–29
Noah, Acting in Faith, Gen. 7
Noah, Ridicule, Gen. 6–7

Oath-Taking, Matt. 5:33–37
Obey God and Muhammad, Matt. 10:37; 1 John 1:1–3
Omniscience and Omnipotence of God, Ps. 33:13; 145; Matt. 6:2–6
One God, Deut. 6:4–5
Opposition to Muhammad, Deut. 13:1–5; 18:17–22
Origin of Evil, Matt. 4:10
Origin of Sin, Isa. 14:12–15; Ezek. 28:11–19
Orphans, James 1:27

Parable of the Owners, Matt. 13; Luke 15
Parable of Two Men, Luke 18:9–14
Parables, Matt. 20:1–16; 22:1–14; 25:1–30; Mark 4:26–34
Paradise, Garden of Eden, Eccl. 12:5; Matt. 22:23–32; 22:29–32; 22:30; Luke
    20:34–36; Phil. 3:21; 2 Peter 3:13; Rev. 4; 5; 21; 21:18, 21
Peace on Him, Matt. 3:13–17; 11:11
People of the Cave, Gen. 2:20–25
Pharaoh, Exod. 5:2; Isa. 37:25; 2 Cor. 10:17
Pharaoh Builds a Tower, Gen. 11; Exod. 8:8, 19; 9:27–28; Esther 6:4
Pharaoh's Magicians Believe, Exod. 8:19
Pharaoh's Oppression of the Israelites, Exod. 1–2
Piety Reaches God, Hos. 6:6

Plagues, Exod. 7–12
Prayer, Ps. 51:6, 16–17; Hos. 6:6; Matt. 6:6; John 4:21–24
Prayer, Friday, John 4:23–24
Prayer, Purification, Matt. 15:16–20; John 2:6
Predestination, 2 Peter 3:9
Predestination or Free Choice, Matt. 5:45; Rom. 5–6
Prophets, Equality of, Matt. 4:17
Prophets, How to Judge, Deut. 18:21–22
Prophets, Murder of, Matt. 23:29–32
Purpose for Mankind, Isa. 14:12; Luke 4:35; Acts 16:17–18; James 2:19

Qualities of Believers, Rom. 12; Col. 3
Quarrels Between Believers, Matt. 18:15–17; Mark 3:24; 1 Cor. 6:1–6; 12
Qur'an, Consistent with Itself, Ps. 33; 56; 119:9–17, 105; Isa. 26:3
Qur'an, Purpose of the, Luke 24:13–35; Gal. 3; 2 Tim. 3:16
Qur'an, Only the Clean Can Touch the, John 15:3; Eph. 5:26
Qur'an, Superiority of the, Exod. 19:18–19; Num. 16; 2 Kings 4:32–35

Religion of Truth, John 19:30; Rev. 1:8; 21:6; 22:13, 18–19
Repentance, No Forgiveness for, Matt. 18:21–22
Repentance, Sincere, Gen. 3:21
Repentance Too Late, Gen. 25–27; Luke 16:19–31; Rev. 3:19–20
Revelation of the Qur'an, Exod. 4:10–12; John 8:34–36; 15:14–15; 1 Cor. 1:25–27;
    Eph. 1:7–10
Revelation, How God Speaks His, Luke 24:13–32; John 1:44–45; Acts 11–26;
    2 Tim. 3:15–17
Righteousness, Rom. 1:17; 3:19–24; 4:9–15

Sabbath, Mark 2:27–28; John 4
Samson and His Riddles, Judg. 14
Satan, Tempted by God, Isa. 14:12–15; James 1:13–15
Satan's Fall, Isa. 14:12–15; Dan. 8:10–12; Mark 5:1–13
Satan's Power, John 8:33–59; 1 Cor. 15:55–58; Gal. 3:26; 1 John 5:1–4
Satan's Purpose, Isa. 14:12–15; Ezek. 28:11–19
Saul, 1 Sam. 8–10
Scales, Isa. 40:15; Matt. 5:22; 17:20; Luke 17:6
Scroll of Deeds, Ps. 139:16; Matt. 12:35–37; 25:14–30; Rev. 17:8; 20:11–15; 21:27
Seven Heavens, Ps. 19:1; 97:6
Sexual Conduct, Lev. 18; 1 Cor. 6:18–20
Shadow Stands Still, Josh. 10; 2 Kings 20; Isa. 38
Shirk, **Unforgivable Sin,** Matt. 12:32
Signs or Miracles, Ps. 19:1
Sin, Consequences of, Exod. 32

Sinful Nature of Man, John 3:19

Sins, Past, Luke 19

Sins Vary in Size, Matt. 5

Smoke, 2 Peter 3:10

Sodom and Gomorrah, Gen. 18–19

Solomon, Exod. 20:24–26; Deut. 27:5; 1 Kings 11:4; 2 Cor. 11:14; Eph. 6:10–18

Solomon and Demons, Luke 10:17–20; 1 Cor. 10:18–22; 1 Tim. 4:1–5

Solomon's Bronze, 1 Kings 4:29–34; 5:13–18; 7:13–14, 47; 1 Chron. 22:14; 2 Chron. 1:11–12; 4:18; Ps. 18:34

Solomon's Horses, Deut. 17:16; 1 Kings 4:26; 10:26–28; 2 Chron. 1:14–16; 9:25; Isa. 31:1

Solomon Talks to Animals and Commands Jinn, 1 Kings 4:33; Prov. 6:6–8

Solomon's Wisdom, 1 Kings 3:7–15, 16–28

Son of God, Luke 3:38

Spider, Matt. 7:24–27

Stars, Gen. 1:16–17; Ps. 147:4–5; Luke 10:18; Rom. 8:19–23

Stars to Guide Us, Gen. 1:14–18

Straight Path, Mal. 3:1; Mark 1:2; John 14:6

Sun and Moon, Gen. 1:14

Sweet and Salt Waters, James 3:9–12

Temptations, James 1:13–14

Testimony of the Angels and Dead, Luke 16

The Good Shall Inherit the Earth, Ps. 37:29; Matt. 6:19–20; 19:29; Mark 8:34–37; Luke 12:16–21

Thunder, Ps. 19; 29:7–11; 97; 144:3–10; 148:7–14; Isa. 1:18

Treatment of Non-Muslims, Deut. 24:17–18; Matt. 5:43–48; Luke 6:27–31; Rom. 12:20–21; Heb. 13:2

Tree of Eternity, Gen. 3:10, 15

Trinity, John 17

Trust God, Eccl. 12:13–14

Two-Horned Person *(Zul-qarnain)*, Rev. 20

Unforgiving Spirit, 2 Cor. 5:16–21

Unworthy Mosque, John 4:1–26

Using Religion for Financial Gain, 1 Tim. 6:3–10

Usury/Borrowing with Interest, Deut. 23:19, 20

Value of Man, Jer. 31:3; John 3:16; Heb. 2:5–9

War, Facing Death in, Matt. 26:52–53

War, Fighting over Spoils of, Josh. 7; 10; Judg. 7

War, Mutilation of Enemies in, 1 Sam. 17; 2 Sam. 4; Matt. 5:43–44

War, Preparation for, Matt. 5:25–26, 39–45; John 16:33
War, Spoils of, Matt. 8:20; Mark 8:34–38
Way (Cause) of God, Rom. 12:19
Weak in Faith, 2 Cor. 3:6; James 1:5–8
Winds, Matt. 8:23–27
Works, Isa. 64:6; John 6:29; Rom. 11:6
Worldly Gain Versus Faith, Luke 9:25

Glossary

Abu Bakr. First caliph.
ain al-qatr. Spring of brass.
Aisha. Favorite wife of Muhammad. He married her when she was very young.
an'am. Cattle, blessings, the grazing money. (Na'am is the plural.)
Asia. The wife of Pharaoh.
'asr. Late afternoon.

Badr. Important battle in Islam. Muslims won a great victory.
bismillah. In the name of God. It marks the beginning of most suras.
Buhayira. Christian priest Muhammad knew.
buraq. Animal bigger than a mule with two wings in its thighs. It was thought
    that Muhammad rode this animal in an overnight journey to Jerusalem.
butun. Stomach.

Eid al-Adha. Feast of Sacrifice.

fajr. Dawn.
fajur. Debauchery.
Fatima. Muhammad's daughter.
furqan. Criterion. That which divides between the redeemed and lost. Another
    name for the Qur'an, the measure or canon.
fussilat. Patterned or explained.

Gahalia. Pre-Islamic times. Time of ignorance.

Hadith. The sayings of the Prophet Muhammad. Volumes of extra-qur'anic material that help explain the Qur'an.
hajj. Pilgrimage.
halal. Allowed by God, permissible.
Harat. Mountain in Saudi Arabia.
Hefza. Wife of Muhammad.
hezballah. Party of God.
hijab. Veil or covering.
hijra. The migration or flight, when Muhammad fled from Mecca to Medina. It marks the beginning of the Muslim calendar (AD 622).
horiya. Chaste women in paradise.
Hud. Prophet to the 'Ad people.

ibn. Son. Could be used in the spiritual sense or also could mean "from."
ihram. Preparation for the pilgrimage.
Injil. The Gospels.
in sha Allah. God willing.
isha. Full darkness or nighttime.

jihad. Holy war. Struggle in the cause of God.
jinn. Demonic spirits that help people.
jizya. A ransom required of non-Muslims if they did not want to convert or die.

Ka'ba. Center of Islamic worship located in Mecca, Saudi Arabia. Muslims believe the site was built by Abraham and Ishmael. Known to be where a meteorite fell and a center of pagan worship in pre-Islamic times.
kafara. To cover or pay wages of sin.
Khadija. First wife of Muhammad.

Lat, 'Uzza, Manat. Three gods who were at the Ka'ba.

magrib. Sunset.
Mecca. Birthplace of the Prophet Muhammad. It is located in Saudi Arabia and is the holiest city in Islam.
Medina. City in Saudi Arabia to which Muhammad fled. Second holiest city in Islam.
muhassanat. Protected women.
mutawafik. "I will let you die," or "I am coming to you."

Nassara. Christians.
nutfa. Clot of blood.

ommi. Illiterate or Gentile.

qawwamun. Of more value.

Qibla. The point in a mosque toward which Muslims bow in prayer. It shows the worshipers the direction of Mecca. Formerly it directed them toward Jerusalem.

Quraish. Tribe in Mecca. Custodians of the Ka'ba.

Qur'an. The holy book of Islam.

rahma. Mercy.

Rajab, Zul-qa'd, Zul-hajj, Muharram. Four sacred months in Islam.

Ramadan. Month of fasting in Islam.

sajda. Prostrate.

salaam alekum. "Peace be upon you." The Muslim greeting.

Salih. Prophet to the Thamud people.

saqr. Stone. Satanic figure on Solomon's throne.

sharia. Islamic law.

shehada. The word of witness/testimony. The declaration that makes a person Muslim.

Shi'ite. A branch of Islam. Followers of Imam Ali.

shirk. To put any partners with the God of Islam, the unforgivable sin in Islam.

Sunni. A branch of Islam. Followers of the Caliph Abu Bakr. Orthodox Muslims.

sura. Chapter of the Qur'an.

talbiya. What is recited during the hajj.

tawaf. Circumambulation of the Ka'ba.

tawhid. Oneness. The theology of Islam.

Tawrat. The books of Moses or the first five books of the Old Testament.

Thamud. A people group who did not obey God and killed the female camel. They were destroyed.

Tur. Mount Sinai.

Uhud. Important battle in Islam in which the Muslims were defeated.

umma. Holy Muslim nation. Brotherhood of Islam.

walid. Physical son.

Waraqa, Ibn Nofel. Cousin of Khadija, who was a Christian monk.

wuquf. Standing.

zabbeeba. "Raisin." Callus or scar that develops on the forehead as a result of long-term prostration in prayer. It is a sign of piety in Islam.

Zabur. Psalms.

zakiyan. Pure.
Zaqqum. Cursed tree that grows in hell.
zihar. Pre-Islamic method of divorce.
zikr. Qur'an or the Bible. God's Word.
zuhr. When the sun starts to go down.
zul-qarnain. Two-horned person.

Bibliography

English Language Texts

Ali, Yusuf, ed. *The Holy Qur'an*. Beltsville, MD: Amana Corp., 1983.

Craig, Andrew. "Scientists Uncover Sodom's Fiery End." BBC News. August 15, 2001. Http://news.bbc.co.uk/2/hi/middle_east/1497476.stm.

Elass, Mateen. *Understanding the Koran*. Grand Rapids: Zondervan, 2004.

Esack, Farid. *The Qur'an: A User's Guide*. Oxford, England: Oneworld Publications, 2005.

Esposito, John L. *What Everyone Needs to Know About Islam*. New York: Oxford University Press, 2002.

Fortescue, Adrian. "The Seven Sleepers of Ephesus." *The Catholic Encyclopedia*. Vol. 5. New York: Robert Appleton Company, 1909. http://www.newadvent.org/cathen/05496a.htm.

Fregosi, Paul. Jihad *in the West: Muslim Conquests from the 7th to the 21st Centuries*. New York: Prometheus Books, 1998.

Gabriel, Mark A. *Jesus and Muhammad*. Lake Mary, FL: Charisma House, 2004.

Geisler, Norman L., and Abdul Saleeb. *Answering Islam: The Crescent in the Light of the Cross*. Grand Rapids: Baker, 2002.

Gilchrist, John. *The Qur'an: The Scripture of Islam*. Mondeon, South Africa: Muslim Evangelical Resource Center, 1995.

Ginzberg, Louis. *The Legends of the Jews*. Vol. 1. Translated by Henrietta Szold. http://classiclit.about.com/library/bl-etexts/lginzberg/bl-lginzberg-legends-1–3c.htm.

Greeson, Kevin. *CAMEL Training Method.* Bangalore, India: WIGTake Resources, 2004.

"Hajj: Pilgrimage to Mecca." 2004. http://www.religionfacts.com/islam/practices/hajj-pilgrimage.htm.

Hilali, Muhammad Taqi-ud-Din al-, and Muhammad Muhsin Kan. *Interpretation of the Meanings of the Noble Qur'an in the English Language.* Riyadh, Saudi Arabia: Maktaba Dar-us-Salam, 1993.

Irwin, Robert, ed. *Night and Horses and the Desert: An Anthology of Classic Arabic Literature.* New York: Anchor, 2002.

"Is the Qur'an Miraculous?" http://www.answering-islam.org/Quran/Miracle/mirac1.html.

"Meteorites in History and Religion." http://www.meteorite.ch/en/basics/history.htm.

"Mu'allaqat." Http://inthenameofallah.org/Mu'allaqat.html.

Safa, Reza F. *Inside Islam: Exposing and Reaching the World of Islam.* Lake Mary, FL: Charisma House, 1996.

Salamah, Ahmad Abdullah. *Shia and Sunni Perspective on Islam.* Saudi Arabia: Abul-Qasim Publishing House, 1991.

Stanton, H. U. W. *The Teaching of the Qur'an: With an Account of Its Growth and a Subject Index.* London: Society for the Promotion of Christian Knowledge, 1919.

———. *The World of Islam: Resources for Understanding.* CD-ROM. Global Mapping International, 2000.

Strobel, Lee. *The Case for Christ: A Journalist's Personal Investigation of the Evidence for Jesus.* Grand Rapids: Zondervan, 1998.

Thomas, G. "Muhammad, the Qur'an, and Christian Sources." http://answering-islam.org/Quran/Sources/cradle.html.

Wagner, William. *How Islam Plans to Change the World.* Grand Rapids: Kregel, 2004.

Wood, Bryant. "Is there any evidence for the biblical story of Sodom and Gomorrah's destruction by fire and brimstone (sulfur)?" Associates for Biblical Research, 1995, 2001. http://www.christiananswers.net/q-abr/abr-a007.html.

World Book Encyclopedia. 22 vols. Chicago: World Book, 2004.

Arabic Language Texts

Abd-el Karim, Khaalil. *Al-Jabour al-Tariqiya lil-Sharia al-Islamia* [The Historic Roots of Islamic Law]. Cairo, Egypt: Sina Publications, 1990.

Committee of the Qur'an and Sunna (Traditions). *Al-Muntakhab* [The Selectives]. Qur'anic Commentary. 20th ed. Cairo, Egypt: The High Council of Muslim Affairs, Egyptian Ministry of Religion, 2002.

Ibn Hisham. *Al-Sira al-Nabawiya* [The Tale of the Prophecy]. 4 vols. Beirut: Dar al-Kutab al-Almiya, 2000.

Ibn Kathir. *Al Bedaya wa Nahiya* [The Beginning and the End]. 14 vols. Cairo, Egypt: Dar al-Hadith, 2002. (Original work written about AD 1380.)

———. *Tafseer al-Qur'an al-Azeem* [Explaining the Great Qur'an]. 4 vols. Beirut: Sherika Abna Sherif al-Ansari, 1993. (Originally written in 1300s.)

Khalil, Morcos Aziz. *Istehala Tahreef al-Kitab al-Muqadas* [The Impossibility of Abrogating the Holy Bible]. 20th ed. Cairo, Egypt: Church of Holy Mary, 2005.

Mahali, Jalal al-Deen al-, and Jalal al-Deen al-Seyouti. *Tafseer al-Galileen* [Al-Galileen Qur'anic Commentary]. 2nd ed. Beirut: Dar al-Jil, 1995.

Nisabouri, Abi-Al-Hasin Ali al-. *Asbab al-Najoul* [Reasons for Revelation]. Beirut: Dar al-Jil, n.d. (Original writings about AD 1100.)

Shafaey, Hussein Muhammad Fahmy al-. *Al-Daleel al-Mufahres li-Afaz al-Qur'an al-Kareem* [Concordance of the Pronounced Words of the Honorable Qur'an]. 2nd ed. Cairo, Egypt: Dar al-Salaam, 2002.

Index of Biblical References

Index of Subjects

About the Authors

Dr. Raouf Ghattas, from his earliest days as a schoolboy in Egypt, was taught and memorized great portions of the Qur'an. Though from an evangelical Christian background, he was impacted by both Islam and the teaching of the Qur'an. As a native Arabic speaker, he is able to draw from primary resources in *A Christian Guide to the Qur'an*. Dr. Ghattas has served more than twenty-five years among Muslims in both the United States and the Islamic world. He earned his doctorate in Muslim evangelism from Southwestern Baptist Theological Seminary.

Raouf's wife, Carol, also has a great understanding of the Muslim world. Following short-term service in West Africa, she returned to the United States to earn a Master's of Divinity degree from Southwestern Baptist Theological Seminary. She has served alongside her husband for over eighteen years, living in five different Muslim countries within the North Africa and Middle East regions. She has read widely in the area of Muslim women and also has pseudonymously authored books that present the realities Muslims face in coming to Christ.